Design Patterns with Java

Olaf Musch

Design Patterns with Java

An Introduction

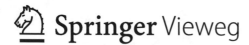 Springer Vieweg

Olaf Musch
Braunschweig, Germany

ISBN 978-3-658-39828-6   ISBN 978-3-658-39829-3   (eBook)
https://doi.org/10.1007/978-3-658-39829-3

With approved content from the 1st edition of "Florian Siebler-Guth, Design Patterns with Java".

This Springer Vieweg imprint is published by the registered company Springer Fachmedien Wiesbaden GmbH, part of Springer Nature.
The registered company address is: Abraham-Lincoln-Str. 46, 65189 Wiesbaden, Germany

The original version of the book has been revised. A correction to this book can be found at https://doi.org/10.1007/978-3-658-39829-3_27

A Warm Welcome to You!

I'll start with a confession: this book isn't actually mine.

It is the updated version of the book *Design Patterns mit Java – Eine Einführung in Entwurfsmuster* (*Design Patterns with Java – An Introduction to Design Patterns*) by Florian Siebler, which was published by Hanser-Verlag in 2014. He felt that an update was necessary due to the many new Java versions that have appeared in the meantime. However, due to time constraints, he could not tackle the revision himself. Therefore, he asked me if I would like to take over his book in my own name and bring it up to date.

@Florian: Thank you very much for the trust.

The introductory chapter on the term "design patterns" was written by him as a guest post, and I was very happy to include it.

And because it also corresponds to my personal style of speaking, in this book I also step into the first-person perspective of the author, from which I speak to you. With this book, I would like to give you a description of the "original" design patterns adapted to the Java version currently valid at that time, as they are also mentioned in the book *Design Patterns – Elements of Reusable Object-Oriented Software* by the authors Erich Gamma, Richard Helm, Ralph Johnson, and John Vlissides (also called "Gang of Four", GoF for short), originally published in 1994 (Gamma, Erich (2011): *Design patterns. Elements of reusable object-oriented software*. 39th printing. Boston: Addison-Wesley. ISBN 978-0201633610 (Addison-Wesley professional computing series)). In the meantime, many more patterns have been compiled and published, and antipatterns have been dealt with as well: The things that should not be done this way and by which typical structures you can recognize them. However, I will limit myself here to the 23 patterns of the above-mentioned work.

However, after a clarification of terms and a small chapter on basics, I do not want to present you with a dry theory of structures, but rather discuss the possible approaches to certain tasks on the basis of concrete examples and derive the pattern/pattern suitable for this purpose in each case, so that you also understand the why of a pattern.

A few programming tricks from Java practice will also be mentioned, but I would like to assume a basic knowledge of the Java programming language and object-oriented programming (OOP). At the time of writing, I created the examples with NetBeans 12.6 and Java 16 on a PC with Windows 10, and there they work as described.

As for the English translation of this book, AI is terribly bad in translating names of classes, methods, or variables within source code. So it took some amount of manual work to adjust these and the comments in all the examples. If you happen to come across some odd-sounding remains of German names and abbreviations, it's purely my fault. If you like, drop me a note on this. In the closing chapter, you'll find my email contact.

To conclude this preface, I would like to thank the most important people who have contributed directly and indirectly to the creation of this book:

Florian Siebler-Guth, whose book first gave me the idea to get back into Java programming after a long time, and then also gave me the opportunity to incorporate my comments into a follow-up edition myself.

Benjamin Sigg, who assisted me as a technical reviewer with his vast Java experience.

At Springer-Verlag Sybille Thelen, who actively supported us in the rededication of the authorship, and David Imgrund, who then as an editor always advised me in a very open and friendly manner.

To my wife Christine and our daughter Jessica, who had to (or were allowed to – a matter of perspective) put up with my reclusiveness during writing times.

Braunschweig, Germany   Olaf Musch

Contents

The Term "Design Pattern"

1

In this chapter I give an overview of what design patterns are. I show you the historical background, that is, where patterns find their origin. I also draw your attention to the advantages and disadvantages of patterns. Furthermore, you will learn how to categorize patterns. And finally, I introduce the template by which patterns are described in Gamma et al.

1.1   What Are Design Patterns?

In this section, I describe what design patterns are and how you can benefit from them.

1.1.1   Historical and Intellectual Background

In 1977, architect Christopher Wolfgang Alexander describes in his book "A Pattern Language: Towns, Buildings, Construction" (Alexander, Christopher; Ishikawa, Sara; Silverstein, Murray; Jacobson, Max (1977): A pattern language. Towns, buildings, construction. 41st ed. New York, NY: Oxford Univ. Press. ISBN 978-0195019193 (Center for Environmental Structure series, 2)) various patterns for house construction and urban development. For example, one of his patterns deals with the question of how far above the floor a window sill should be planned. Windows have the job of connecting people in the house to the outside world. The connection is best accomplished when you stand about 3 feet from the window and can see both the sky and the street. If the windowsill is too high, you may not be able to see out. If the windowsill is too low, there is a risk of mistaking the window for a door, which is a potential safety hazard. Alexander therefore suggests that the windowsill be provided between 12 and 14 inches above the floor. On higher floors, the windowsill should be about 20 inches above the floor for safety reasons.

O. Musch, *Design Patterns with Java*, https://doi.org/10.1007/978-3-658-39829-3_1

From this example, you can see different characteristics of patterns:

- Patterns are described by a set of information. The **context** says something about when the pattern applies: *You want to have a window in a wall*. The **problem** names a conflict of goals: *the window sill must not be too high and not too low*. The **solution** shows at an abstract level how the problem has been solved successfully in the past: *the window sill is at a height between 12 and 20 inches*.
- A pattern is not a dogma that must necessarily be followed. Rather, there may be reasons to deliberately violate the 12–20 inch rule. For example, only skylights are often installed in certain spaces: prisons or swimming pool shower rooms. Conversely, decorated storefronts are not in danger of being mistaken for doors; thus, their sills may be lower than 12 inches.
- Patterns do not give specific recommendations for action. In the example, Alexander suggests planning the window sill at 12–14 inches or at about 20 inches. Thus, when designing a building plan, an architect finds a wide range to consider depending on the context. Consequently, patterns are not algorithms or concrete implementations, but abstract proposed solutions that must be adapted to the problem at hand.

Ten years later, in 1987, Kent Beck and Ward Cunningham develop five patterns for GUI development in a similar fashion and present them at OOPSLA 1987 (http://c2.com/doc/oopsla87.html). **Important to note**: The characteristics of patterns just mentioned apply to software development patterns in the same way.

In 1994 Erich Gamma, Richard Helm, Ralph Johnson and John Vlissides formulated a total of 23 patterns for software development in their book "Design Patterns – Elements of Reusable Object-Oriented Software". In this book the hype about patterns finds its beginning. In addition to the pattern catalog by Gamma et al. there are meanwhile numerous other pattern catalogs for different programming languages and different application areas. Gamma et al. are aware of this. They write that their collection is not complete and fixed, rather it is a snapshot of their thoughts. In their view, the collection contains only part of what experts might know; in particular, it lacks patterns for concurrency, distributed programming, or real-time programming.

> To avoid a Babylonian confusion of language, please note: When the following text refers to "design patterns", "patterns", "patterns" or "design patterns", it means design patterns of software development.

1.1.2   Advantages and Disadvantages of Patterns

Patterns, as I just wrote, do not describe concrete solutions, algorithms, and certainly not prêt-à-porter implementations that you could simply copy-and-paste into your applications. Why should you bother with patterns anyway? What benefit do you get from working your way through the catalog of patterns described in this book? I'd like to provide the answer in this section.

1.1.2.1 Patterns Transport and Preserve Knowledge

The patterns in this pattern catalog were not invented by researchers in white lab coats or wise gurus with long beards. Rather, the patterns were found. Much like the number pi – no one has ever defined pi. You will find this number if you examine numerous circles for the ratio of their diameter to their circumference. Accordingly, Gamma et al. examine many software systems and found similarities. If a particular solution occurs in three or more systems, it is considered a pattern (called the Rule of Three). Gamma et al. give this design a catchy name and described their observations as follows: *"None of the design patterns [...] describes novel designs. We considered only those designs that have been applied many times and have proven themselves in different systems."* So when you look at patterns, you learn how other developers have solved certain problems. You can look at what approaches they have taken, and what solutions have proven successful.

1.1.2.2 Patterns Create a Common Vocabulary

Imagine further that you and your team are working on a large software system. Your task is to develop a specific subsystem. There are many dependencies in this subsystem. Your colleague, who is working on another part of the system, wants to use your subsystem. However, he has difficulty resolving the dependencies and asks you to provide a **facade** (one of the patterns I will introduce later) for it. Since you've been dealing with patterns, you know that your colleague wants simplified access to your subsystem, where the dependencies behind them are already resolved. So patterns define a vocabulary that allows you and your colleague to communicate at a higher level of abstraction. Table 1.1 gives you an impression of the scope of the vocabulary.

1.1.2.3 Patterns Help to Understand a Programming Language Better

Patterns describe language-independent abstract solution approaches. This means that each generation of developers is challenged to develop their own implementations. Gamma et al. wrote their exemplary implementations in Smalltalk, among other languages. Implementations in Java may look quite different. Many patterns are already anchored in Java's class library. It is decidedly exciting to look for and identify the patterns there. By studying design patterns in Java, you will learn a lot about Java along the way.

At this point I would like to address a blur. The question of whether or not you are dealing with a design pattern depends on your point of view. For a procedurally minded programmer, concepts like inheritance, encapsulation, or polymorphism would be design patterns. However, if you are native to object-oriented programming languages, you will consider the aforementioned concepts as fixed language components.

Table 1.1 Categories of design patterns according to Gamma et al

	Class-based	Object-based
Creational patterns (Generation patterns)	Factory method	Abstract factory
		Builder
		Prototype
		Singleton
Structural patterns (Structural pattern)	Adapter	Adapter
		Bridge
		Composite
		Decorator
		Facade
		Flyweight
		Proxy
Behavioral patterns (Behavior pattern)	Interpreter	Chain of responsibility
	Template method	Command
		Iterator
		Mediator
		Memento
		Observer
		State
		Strategy
		Visitor

1.1.2.4   Patterns May Lead to Inappropriate Designs

Patterns can inspire and motivate a developer. He might try to implement as many patterns as possible in his programs. However, this can lead to difficulties. Many patterns require the developer to introduce an additional layer of abstraction. This can cause a design to become unnecessarily complicated or performance to suffer. *"A design pattern should only be applied when the flexibility provided is really needed,"* read Gang of Four on this. Just because you can use patterns doesn't mean they always have to. They are tools to be used judiciously. Years ago I once heard a British colleague say *"A fool with a tool is still a fool"*, which should be heeded here too. Not everywhere where you could use a tool (in this case Design Patterns) it makes sense to do so. I will go into this again in the final chapter on combining patterns.

1.1.3   A Pattern Is Not a Code Is Not a Pattern

Before you start implementing a pattern, let's discuss the question of what a pattern is in the first place. If you search the Internet for singleton, for example, you will find an implementation for every programming language. Even for Java, there is an implementation that is perhaps something of a "standard". But this implementation is not the Singleton Pattern itself. A pattern itself only describes what the goal is, what to look for when implementing the pattern, and what the advantages and disadvantages are. GoF presents a code example for each pattern in its book. Nevertheless, it is up to you alone how to realize the pattern. This is the only way to transfer patterns to all languages with their respective peculiarities. Compare this with the construction plan of a house, which describes where the walls are, but not how the walls are to be built.

Most books on design patterns show concrete implementations that have proven practical; I also present these "standards" to you. Nevertheless, in the spirit of the pattern, it is allowed to find a different solution.

1.1.4   So What Are "Design Patterns"?

So what are design patterns in software development? Design patterns describe solutions for recurring problems on an abstract level. They bring together the knowledge of the developers. This makes it easier to pass on experience and to fall back on proven solutions, i.e. to reuse them. In addition, they expand the vocabulary of the developers.

Among other things, you will get to know the State Pattern and the Strategy Pattern. In a direct comparison of these two patterns, you will see that a pattern always moves in a certain context, or always solves a clearly defined problem.

1.1.5   Patterns in Practice

Once you have worked through this book, how do you put the patterns into practice? When you have read this book, you will not have every pattern with all its details in your head. You should not develop this ambition at all. But you have heard that there is a pattern that describes what to do in situations when an event source is supposed to inform its observers about state changes. You pick up my book in the concrete situation of your everyday life and read the structure, the advantages and disadvantages again. Does the pattern fit your specific situation? Is the application of the pattern appropriate? Based on these questions you will solve your concrete problem. The more patterns you know and have applied in the past, the more your wealth of experience will increase and the more flexibly and unerringly you will be able to use and evaluate patterns. Programmers are like wine – the older they get, the better they become.

> **Tip**
> But please use patterns wisely. Knowledge of design patterns should not tempt you
> to lard your software with patterns. Most patterns require you to develop additional
> classes. If you try to implement as many patterns as possible in a manageable appli-
> cation, the result will be a poorly maintainable, unnecessarily bloated system. Have
> the courage to forgo a pattern or even remove a pattern! Patterns are not an end in
> themselves. Your goal as a programmer should be to create clear and unspectacular
> program code.
>
> Let me mention one more point in this context: Extensions. A constant of applica-
> tion development is that requirements – and thus the source code – grow. On the one
> hand, it makes sense to design programs in such a way that they can be extended in
> the future. But on the other hand, targeting future requirements should be done very
> cautiously. Keep in mind that you are writing programs to be used in the "here
> and now".
>
> On the website stackoverflow.com, a large developer community that has been
> around since 2008, I found the following phrase that I really liked: *"Design Pattern
> is meant to be a solution to a problem, not a solution looking for a problem."*[1]

1.2   Categorize and Describe Design Patterns

Design patterns are grouped into categories and described according to a specific template.
I show these formalities in this section.

1.2.1   Different Categories of Patterns

The Gamma et al. pattern catalogue contains 23 patterns. These are divided into three
categories. Within these categories, a further distinction is made as to whether a pattern is
more object-based or more class-based. Here I present the three categories:
Creational Patterns: They hide the creation process and help make a system independent of
how its objects are specifically created, composed, and represented. A class-based creational
pattern uses inheritance to vary the class of the object being created, while an object-based
creational pattern delegates creation to another object. There are two recurring leitmotifs in
these patterns. First, they all encapsulate knowledge of the concrete classes used by the system. Second, they hide how instances of these classes are created and assembled. Everything
the application knows about the objects is determined by the defined interfaces.

---

[1] https://stackoverflow.com/questions/11079605/adapter-any-real-example-of-adapter-pattern#com
ment14506747_11079605

Structural Patterns: They deal with the composition of classes and objects to form larger structures. Class-based structural patterns use inheritance to merge interfaces and implementations. Object-based structural patterns, on the other hand, describe ways to merge objects to gain new functionality.

Behavioral Patterns: they deal with algorithms and the assignment of responsibilities to objects. They describe not only patterns of objects or classes, but also the patterns of interaction between them. Class-based behavior patterns use inheritance to distribute behavior among classes. Object-based behavior patterns use composition instead of inheritance. Patterns in this category describe complex flows of control that are difficult to trace at runtime. This shifts the focus away from control flow to how objects interact with each other. Table 1.1 shows an overview of the categories and the patterns. It is noticeable that there are more object-based patterns than class-based ones. The "Adapter" pattern is both class-based and object-based. You may not be familiar with all of the patterns. That doesn't matter-the purpose of this book is to introduce you to all the patterns in detail.

> **Other Categorization Schemes**
>
> Buschmann et al. [Buschmann, Frank; Löckenhoff, Christiane (2000): Pattern-oriented software architecture. A pattern system. 1st, corr. Nachdr. Munich: Addison-Wesley] criticize that *"a distinction between structure-oriented and behavior-oriented patterns is too inaccurate"* because they do not name *"the specific problem areas a developer faces when designing software."* They introduce architectural patterns and idioms in addition to design patterns, and develop other categories. To give you an idea of their categorization, I have excerpted Buschmann et al.'s scheme in Table 1.2. You will also find more patterns there than in Table 1.1.
>
> Architecture patterns are used at the beginning of the design *"when the basic structure of the application is defined"* (page 360). Design patterns are used by Buschmann et al. when the basic structure is *"refined and extended"* (page 360). Idioms are *"used during the implementation phase"* (page 361).
>
> In this book, I refer exclusively to the patterns of Gamma et al. and their categorization scheme. However, I want to give you an idea that you will encounter other patterns and other pattern categories in literature and practice. The distinction between architectural pattern, design pattern, and idiom is not relevant in this book.

1.2.2 Defining a Sample Template

Documentation is often structured according to the same template – think, for example, of the arc42 documentation template for software architectures, which you can find at www.arc42.com. If the reader knows the template, he immediately knows where to find which information. Patterns are also documented according to a uniform scheme. From a bird's eye view, each pattern must have at least one **name**, as well as one section each about the

Table 1.2 Categories of design patterns according to Buschmann et al., pages 376 f

	Architectural Patterns	Design Pattern	Idiom
From chaos to structure	Layers	Interpreter	
	Pipes-and-filters		
Generation		Abstract factory	Singleton
		Prototype	Factory method
		Builder	
Structural decomposition		Composite	
Organization of work		Master-slave	
		Chain of responsibility	
		Command	
		Mediator	
Access control		Proxy	
		Facade	
		Iterator	
Variation of services		Bridge	Template method
		Strategy	
		State	
Service extension		Decorator	
		Visitor	
Management		Memento	
Adaptation		Adapter	
Communication		Publisher subscriber (observer)	
Resource management		Flyweight	

problem to be solved, the concrete **solution** itself, and about possible **consequences** when applying the pattern.

In order to describe this minimum set of information in a uniform way, Gamma et al. use the following template:

Pattern name: The name of the pattern is a keyword that uses one or two words to name the problem, solution, and implications. The name is part of the vocabulary and allows us to communicate and document at a higher level of abstraction.

Category: The category is based on the classification described in Sect. 1.2.1.

Purpose: This section briefly describes the purpose and aim of the design.

Also known as: Where there are other names for the design, they are referred to in this section.

Motivation: A concrete scenario is used to demonstrate a problem and explain how the pattern solves this problem. The scenario promotes the understanding of the abstract relationships behind the pattern.

Applicability: This section describes in which situations the pattern can be applied. So here the context is mentioned.

Structure: The classes and objects involved in the pattern are represented in diagrams. Gamma et al. use OMT, a precursor of UML, for this purpose.

Participants: The classes and objects involved are described. You will also learn there which tasks they have.

Interactions: In this section, you will read how the participants work together.

Consequences: Each pattern has advantages and disadvantages; these are mentioned here. You will get hints for implementation, especially traps and helpful tips.

Implementation: code snippets demonstrate the realization of the pattern as well as different implementation variants.

Known uses: You will learn where the pattern is used. This is useful to get examples of the use of a pattern.

Related patterns: Often patterns look very similar; you will learn where the differences are, but also how two patterns work together.

I will not list these sections in the book as formally as Gamma et al. It is important to me to present the relevant information to you in a way that is easy to understand – and to do this I am deliberately breaking with the formal structure. However, just like Gamma et al., I will describe one pattern in each chapter. At a second point, I deviate from Gamma et al.'s scheme: I cite the purpose description only at the end of a chapter. The reason for this is that I myself have had the experience that when I read the purpose description, I do not initially understand what is meant by it. On the other hand, if I have dealt with the pattern beforehand, it is catchy. In short, if I understand the purpose description, I understand the chapter as a whole. And that's exactly the kind of learning check I want to give you.

In the next chapter I will introduce object-oriented design principles. After that, starting in Chap. 3, I will describe the patterns. The examples use the current (at the time of writing this book) language features of Java 16 – including some preview features. As far as these help to understand the meaning of a pattern or to keep the source code simple, I go into more detail. At the very least, I then mention the names of APIs or numbers of pertinent "specification requests" that you can use as reference points for your own research on these features. However, I essentially assume that you know the language features of Java 16 at least roughly. The goal of this book is to explain the patterns. Sometimes the newer language features of Java help with this, but sometimes they make things more "complicated" or the code longer than necessary. In this case, I don't use them. In the book I print only the most necessary aspects of the examples. In this form the programs would not be executable, and I did not mark the cuts everywhere. I have also removed source code comments here for printing, but they are there. The link to the additional material of a chapter can be found at the beginning of each chapter in the footer.

You will find in the zip file you download the source codes as NetBeans projects, which you can open directly in NetBeans. The development environment I personally prefer, NetBeans itself, can be found at https://netbeans.apache.org/. Of course you can use any other development environment you like. Even with a simple text editor and a command line you can develop Java applications.

The Java Development Kit (JDK) 16 I used can be found at https://jdk.java.net/archive/ (when this book is available in stores, it should no longer be the very latest JDK). However, the examples should at least run under Java 17 as well.

If I mention an example project in a chapter, you will also find it in the subfolder of the respective chapter. The same applies to special documents or files that are relevant in the respective context.

1.3   Summary

Go through the chapter again in key words:

- Design patterns are proven solutions to an indefinite number of problems that recur in this or a similar form.
- Design patterns create a vocabulary that is part of general education for programmers.
- Design patterns cannot be invented, only discovered – just like the number Pi.
- The GoF – Gang of Four – has been instrumental in introducing design patterns into software development.
- The GoF book includes 23 patterns, but there are many more.
- The GoF has divided its patterns into three categories:

  - Creation patterns describe how objects can be created efficiently,
  - Structural patterns describe how classes can be combined to form meaningful larger units,
  - Behavior patterns describe the interaction of individual objects.

- A sample description is composed of the following essential elements:
  - A catchy and concise name,
  - A problem section that shows when the pattern is applied,
  - A solution section that describes the units involved and their interrelationships,
  - A section on consequences, which discusses the advantages and disadvantages of the pattern.

Object-Oriented Programming and Design Principles

2

Good software systems are not only implemented correctly, but are also characterized by being extensible and understandable, among other things. In this chapter, I describe object-oriented programming and some object-oriented design principles that promote correctness, extensibility, and understandability.

2.1 Object-Oriented Programming

You hear very often that you don't need patterns if you master and apply the rules of object-oriented programming. Is that true? How are patterns and object-oriented programming related?

If you program in an object-oriented way, you will certainly work with inheritance – you have something general and derive something specific from it. In most Java introductions, inheritance is presented as the ultimate. Yet inheritance has drawbacks, and I'd like to address those now. You have a class and you create a subclass that inherits the behavior defined in the superclass. You can now inherit further, but the further down the inheritance hierarchy a class is, the lower the possibility of reusability. Also, any changes you make to the superclass will affect all of the subclasses; this weakens the encapsulation, which usually indicates an inappropriate design. But probably the biggest disadvantage of inheritance is that the inheritance hierarchy grows very rapidly in both breadth and depth. An example will illustrate this.

Let's think about a software that is needed to manage the animals of a zoo. At the top of the inheritance hierarchy of animals is certainly the class `LivingBeing`. In this class, you want to store the number of legs. Wait – what if you want to include fish in the hierarchy? They'd have to carry the `numberLegs` attribute as well, even though there are no fish with legs. Fine, let's agree on the compromise that fish are not included in the inheritance hierarchy. So, the superclass stores the number of legs. Let's start with birds – birds

© The Author(s), under exclusive license to Springer Fachmedien Wiesbaden
GmbH, part of Springer Nature 2023
O. Musch, *Design Patterns with Java*, https://doi.org/10.1007/978-3-658-39829-3_2

can fly, so you need to develop a subclass `Bird` that stores statements about flight behavior, such as how fast a bird can fly. It occurs to me that penguins are also counted as birds, even though they can't fly. Now you have the choice of not including penguins in the inheritance hierarchy either, or of creating two different subclasses: `FlyingBird` and `NonFlyingBird`. But that should be the least of your problems for now. An animal has legs to be able to walk. In the superclass `LivingBeing`, you now include the information about walking behavior. This enables you to represent not only birds, but also dogs, cats, camels, monkeys and lions. But wait – some birds can't run at all, only hop. Again, you have to worry about constraints in the inheritance hierarchy. Do you want subclasses to inherit attributes and methods they don't need? Or do you want to exclude hopping birds from the inheritance hierarchy? If not, you must consequently create the following subclasses from the subclass `Bird` in addition to the subclasses `FlyingBird` and `NonFlyingBird`: `RunningBird` and `HoppingBird`. However, most birds can both run and fly. How could I deal with this situation? Actually, you would need to develop classes that allow both running (alternatively hopping) and flying. So, you need a class `FlyingRunningBird`, a class `HoppingFlyingBird`, etc.

To take things up a notch, you could start looking at the feeding habits of animals. A lion is certainly a carnivore, and since it's outside the complicated inheritance hierarchy of birds, the requirement doesn't sound particularly difficult. So, include the attribute `quantityMeatPerDay` in the superclass `LivingBeing` - this information is certainly important for the zoo! But wait. Since there are also pigeons in the inheritance hierarchy of birds, they inherit the attribute as well. However, pigeons are not suspected of feeding on meat, so they really shouldn't carry this attribute around. So, the information about how much meat per day an animal eats should not be stored in the class living beings. What is the solution? Introduce a class `CarnivorousNonBird` below the class `LivingBeing`. The lion can be an instance of this class. Cows, like pigeons, do not eat meat. So below the class Living beings, develop the class `VegetarianNonBird`. This class will certainly hold the information of how much meatless food the zoo needs to provide per day. You already notice that another problem is beginning to mature. Among the birds there are also carnivores like eagles and vegetarians like the pigeons. So you can start again on the inheritance line of birds and distinguish between carnivores and vegetarians. Eagles will then be instances of the class `CarnivorousFlyingRunningBird`.

Figure 2.1 shows how the class diagram for such a project could look like.

The example is certainly correct from the point of view of object orientation; nevertheless, the solution is not particularly practical. It contains too many compromises or restrictions and is also too inflexible. Design patterns suggest alternatives that help you create flexible and extensible software using the methods of object-oriented programming.

> I have deliberately exaggerated the example because I want to convince you that inheritance can lead you into a very rigid system in which there is a hierarchy that cannot be surveyed in breadth or depth. The classes are so special that they cannot be reused in any other place.

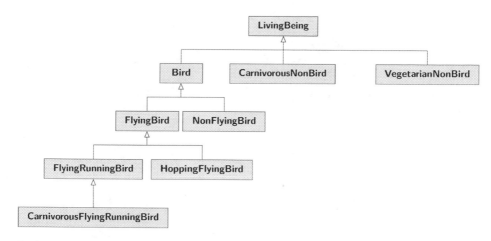

Fig. 2.1 Example of clumsy design

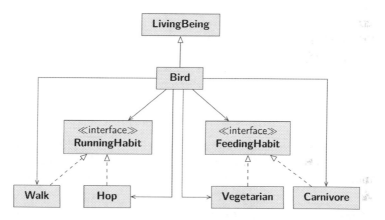

Fig. 2.2 Example of better design

The example would certainly have been much better developed with *composition*. Specifically, this means that you develop an interface `FeedingHabit`, from which the classes `Carnivore` and `Vegetarian` are derived. These classes store how much meat or how much grass is intended per day. The cow, just like the pigeon, must have the attribute `feedinghabit = new Vegetarian()`. And consequently, both the lion and the eagle will get the attribute `feedinghabit = new Carnivore()`. So, the relevant behavior is not inherited, but defined in a separate class. The class diagram Fig. 2.2 shows the interaction.

What is gained by this? Your inheritance hierarchy becomes much clearer. In addition, you can define new behavior **very easily.** You can subsume everything that makes good software under the term "easy": For example, places where changes need to be made can be identified quickly; moreover, existing code does not need to be tested again. A change is not only easier to maintain, but also less prone to errors. The following extension illustrates this statement. If you define snails and worms as meat, ducks must consequently be carnivores; but they also eat grass, so you have a hybrid here. This is not a problem – you let the `Omnivore` class inherit from the interface `FeedingHabit`, and you can provide a new behavior without breaking existing code. The duck gets the attribute `feedinghabit = new Omnivore()`. In a corresponding way, the running habit could be represented.

> Design patterns use the tools of object-oriented programming to develop flexible, extensible, and maintainable solutions. Even if you can apply the rules of object-oriented programming perfectly, you should definitely look into design patterns. You will find further on – at the Builder Pattern – another example of how the toolbox of OOP does not provide you with a satisfactory solution when it comes to object creation.

2.2   Programming Against Interfaces

In the chapter on the Observer Pattern, I will point out the need to program against interfaces. What is gained by this? What exactly is meant by interface? The question about the term interface is necessary, because I think it is important to distinguish it clearly from the term interface.

Object orientation requires that you encapsulate the attributes of an object, the state of an object. Access from the outside should not be possible. The attributes may only be accessed indirectly via methods. Each method has an identifier, a parameter list and a return value – this is the signature of a method. All public methods together form the interface of an object. The type is the name for this interface.

Methods do not necessarily have to be defined; it is sufficient that they only declare the signature; they are then abstract. It is the task of derived classes to override these methods and implement them concretely. Derived classes are the subtype of the abstract class, which is the supertype in an inheritance hierarchy. Classes with abstract methods are themselves abstract. However, abstract classes can define non-abstract methods as well as abstract methods. They can even define all methods, so that an abstract class declares no abstract methods at all. If a class declares only abstract methods, you as a Java programmer can create it as an interface. Since Java does not allow direct multiple inheritance, the introduction of interfaces is an important language element. You can implement as many interfaces as you like, so that one object can correspond to – or "take on" – many interfaces. Even though we Java programmers usually mean interfaces when we talk about interfaces for this reason, in the Patterns environment you must always keep in mind that interfaces can be either interfaces or abstract classes.

Background Information

Since Java 8, static and non-static methods can be defined in interfaces. It is there-fore possible to "inherit" behavior from an interface. The difference between abstract class and interface is becoming blurrier – against this background, it is also impor-tant to interpret the term interface broadly in the context of design patterns.

The difference between abstract classes and interfaces is that interfaces define roles, while abstract classes have the task of establishing an inheritance hierarchy. Interfaces, unlike abstract classes, are stateless, and when you define a method in an interface, you give the implementing class a default behavior. This is useful if you want to extend an interface, but do not want to or cannot adapt all the implementing classes.

It is always very laborious in programming when an interface is extended; all classes implementing this interface have to be adapted. With the default methods it has become much easier.

In the Observer Pattern and also in the Mediator Pattern, you will have any number of objects that are related to each other. Look at the wine trading simulation there. You can exchange the consumers there just as you can the producers. All that matters to the media-tor there is that he is dealing with objects of type `ConsumerIF` or `ProducerIF`. It does not matter which concrete class is behind it, whether it is a private customer or a corner shop. The objects are loosely coupled, and loose coupling, like high cohesion, is a sign of good design.

In the Observer pattern, you will put both students and employees in the "Observer" role. For the Event Sources, it will only be important that they communicate with objects that match the expected `JobObserver` interface and define the `update()` method. Both the number and the type of specific implementation of the participants may vary in both projects. Can I convince you that by programming against an interface, your imple-mentation will gain substantially in independence and flexibility?

If not, I would like to refer to the chapter on the iterator as a final example. You will deal with lists there. There are a variety of lists: `ArrayList`, `LinkedList`, and many more from the class library, as well as, of course, the lists you program yourself. All of these lists implement the List interface. Now, when a method returns a list – generally speaking, an object of type List – you don't have to worry about the implementation behind it. The `getList()` method in the example below returns some list whose class you don't know. The `testList()` method calls the `getList()` method and has a list returned to it.

Then the `size()` method is called on the returned object, which is prescribed in the List interface. At no point within the test method is it relevant whether you are returning the size of an `ArrayList`, a `LinkedList`, or some other list.

```
List list;
void testList() {
    list = getList();
    System.out.println("Number  of  elements:"  +  list.size()
);
  }
  List getList() {
      // ... returns any object of the type "List"
  }
```

> You develop good *code* if you stick to the principle that the GoF has formulated:
> "Program towards an interface, not an implementation".

2.3   Single Responsibility Principle (SRP)

A principle of object-oriented programming says that a class should be responsible for only one thing – no more, but also no less. This principle is called the Single Responsibility Principle. This principle goes back to Robert Cecil Martin ("Uncle Bob"), who put it this way: *"A class should have only one reason to change"*. If you go to the cleancoder.com website and click on the link to the "Old Articles", you will get an overview of many old (and worth reading) articles by Bob Martin, including almost at the end of the list the link to his article on the Single Responsibility Principle, which is freely available on Google Docs:

https://docs.google.com/open?id=0ByOwmqah_nuGNHEtcU5OekdDMkk

There you will find the above quote on page 2. You will learn about the Single Responsibility Principle in practice in the chapter on the Singleton Pattern. This pattern is considered by some programmers to be an antipattern. One of the reasons for this is that the Singleton violates this very principle: There's a class that's responsible both for creating its single instance and for its actual business logic.

The chain of responsibility, which we will get to know in Chap. 6, also violates this principle. In the example there, it is the task of a trader to buy and sell products. His job is not to inform the next retailer of a purchase request. But why will you be able to accept so easily in these examples that the principle has been violated?

On the one hand, you will appreciate the SRP because it prevents a god class from developing in a system. This is generally understood to mean classes with a large number of functions and responsibilities, which therefore appear overpowering – and are therefore very difficult to keep track of. On the other hand, if responsibilities are separated, maintenance and testing are made easier. On the other hand, no one is saying that Single Responsibility is a sacred cow that should never be slaughtered. The Singleton and Chain would have been impossible to implement without a lot of effort if you didn't violate the principle. Also, regardless of the discussion about patterns, it is hardly feasible in practice to really assign a single responsibility to a class. If you know you're violating the principle and have good reason to do so, feel free to violate it. Strive to achieve Single Responsibility, but have in mind that the principle is not an end in itself. It is meant to help you increase cohesion and loosen coupling. But it should in no way force you to choose a cumbersome design.

2.4   Inheritance May Be Evil

You might want to skim this section when reading the book for the first time. I mention many patterns here that you will only get to know in the following chapters. But be sure to look here again at the end.

Code usually has components that never or rarely change. However, most of the time there are also components that change or can change. **Identify the variable code parts and encapsulate them.** Look at the Strategy Pattern. You will have a variety of different strategies to choose from there to sort an array. In the very first version, you'll use a variety of if statements or a switch statement to determine the appropriate strategy for the specific situation. This approach is unsatisfactory for several reasons: you're lugging around code in a class that, in doubt, you'll never need. If you want to implement a new strategy, you have to change existing code that has already been tested. If a strategy needs to be changed, that change would affect all the code. Bugs are guaranteed to creep in if you have to change code in multiple places.

With the State Pattern you get the same problem. As a consequence, you define variable code parts in your own classes in both cases. Also consider the Template Method Pattern. Here you have to define parts of the algorithm in subclasses. Or think of the Command Pattern – you encapsulate commands in their own Command classes. Want more examples? Take a look at the Iterator. You can't write a "universal iterator" because you'll never know all objects of type List. So, you put the responsibility where it belongs, in the appropriate subclass. Put another way, you encapsulate access to an aggregate. What happens. You identify variable pieces of code and encapsulate them. In most cases, Strategy and State for example, you define the code parts in question in new classes. In another case – the Template Method pattern – you move the variable code part to a subclass.

In general, it makes sense to use inheritance very cautiously. In the introduction, I used the example of zoo software to show you that inheritance can lead you into an unmanageable system under certain circumstances. As an alternative, I suggested composition. The approach is exactly the same as what you will see with the Strategy Pattern and the State Pattern. And in fact, most patterns resort to composition instead of inheritance. The GoF has established the principle: *"Prefer object composition to class inheritance."* Their reasoning is that *"your classes and your class hierarchies [stay] small and [...] are less likely to [grow] into uncontrollable monsters."*

In the context of inheritance, another principle needs to be addressed: the *Liskov Substitution Principle (LSP)*. It states that subtypes must behave like their base types: The base type must be replaceable by the subtype. This principle sounds trivial at first, but its importance should not be underestimated. Consider the case where a method of the base type does not throw an exception, but the overridden method in the subclass does. When can this situation become a problem? A client has been programmed to use the base type; it does not expect that an exception might be thrown. Consequently, it may not be able to process the subclass exception in any meaningful way. Or – another example: A point in a three-dimensional space describes its coordinates differently than a point in a two-dimensional space. It is therefore not permissible to form an inheritance hierarchy here. The LSP forces us to think carefully about each inheritance hierarchy and to check each subclass to see if it is indeed a subtype of the base class: a programmer **IS a** human. But: a rectangle **IS NOT a** square. The LSP therefore also reminds us again that we need to be cautious about inheritance.

2.5   Open/Closed Principle (OCP)

The open-closed principle goes back to Bertrand Meyer (Meyer, Bertrand (2009): Object-oriented software construction 2nd ed., 15th ed. Upper Saddle River, NJ: Prentice Hall PTR. ISBN 978-0136291558.), who requires that modules be both open and closed. Open they must be in order to extend functionality. Closed they must be in the sense that code may not be changed to implement new functionality. Meyer described this principle almost 30 years ago and developed several approaches to it. In his book, he sketches out some possible solutions, discards them, and finally offers inheritance as a solution. From today's perspective, however, inheritance will never be considered the solution par excellence. Today, when you develop systems that need to be both open and closed, you resort to composition and design patterns: you program against interfaces and prefer composition to inheritance. Above all, you deal with design patterns because their most sacred task is to show you ways to make your systems conform to the OCP.

Let me give you two examples of how patterns help you develop systems that are both open and closed. In the Template Method Pattern, you define an algorithm that is so sensitive that it can't be changed. Your product manager would get a stomachache if you tried to touch the code again. The class may even have already been tested and shipped to customers. In short, never ever, under any circumstances, will you want to change the code again. It is closed to change. On the other hand, you need to allow your client to redefine parts of the algorithm. To extend the existing system, he will write a class that inherits from your class.

However, inheritance is only one way to keep systems "open and closed". With the Strategy Pattern, you create the system so that each strategy is encapsulated in a class. If the system needs to be extended with a new sorting algorithm, it is sufficient to define another class that executes the desired algorithm. The user can use the algorithm without changing existing code.

2.6   **Principle of the Right Sense of Proportion**

In the first chapter, I already recommended using patterns with caution, because they almost always require you to define additional classes or interfaces. But it should be the goal of programmers to produce unspectacular, uncluttered code. You will regularly have to decide whether or not to use a pattern. You will need to rely on your experience when making this decision. It is always a good idea to look critically at your own code and the code of other programmers and think about it. The use of patterns is usually motivated by the fact that you want to account for future changes. Change is the constant of software development. That your code will grow is virtually a law of nature. Therefore, in the literature you will often find the advice that you should always build your systems with patterns and keep them open to all sides in order to be prepared for any eventualities that may arise in the future. I don't support this approach in such absolutes. If I want to prepare my software for all changes, the first release is certainly far from relying on easily maintainable unspectacular code. Write good programs that can be used here and now. This is also, in the vast majority of professional situations, exactly what a client/customer will be willing to pay for. Therefore, produce lean code that can be quickly reviewed and changed when needed. The KISS principle applies here: *Keep It Simple, Stupid*, roughly: *As simple as possible, as complex as necessary.*

Agile software development does not contradict the use of design patterns – where it makes sense. The problem on the other hand is that with too simple code you might get a higher rework effort in case of later changes. With today's possibilities of refactoring (rebuilding), which practically every modern development environment usually supports well, this is usually kept within limits or is at least "manageable" to a large extent. But then let such tools help you. Use modern development environments. With dozens of classes, a simple text editor quickly reaches its limits, even if it is technically possible and legitimate to use it.

But enough of the preface, in the following chapters we will deal with the individual Design Patterns, and at the end I will show you in a final step how you can combine several patterns, for example.

Tip

Try it:

You could, if you want to invest a little time, review the patterns in the following chapters to see if you can find the design principles again.

Do some research on the internet for more design principles – there are many more than the ones I've presented. Have a look at the page.

http://www.clean-code-developer.de.

In the Facade Pattern chapter, you will learn about another design principle.

Singleton

3

If you've worked with patterns in the past, you're probably familiar with the Singleton Pattern; it's probably the most well-known pattern. Therefore, we will simply start with this pattern in order to find an "easy" introduction.

3.1   The Task of the Singleton Pattern

Imagine that you have a class that defines something that is so unique that there can only be one instance of it. This one instance should be accessible via a global access point. Take the metaclass of a class as an example. For each class that is loaded into the Java Virtual Machine (JVM), an instance of a class is created that stores descriptive meta-information. This object is so unique that it must exist only once in the JVM. You can query it with `String.class`, but also with `(new String()). getClass()`. You can prove that the return value is one and the same object by comparing the references. Enter the following line in a Java shell:

```
System.out.println(String.class ==
                        (new String(). getClass()));
```

On the console, `true` is output, so the references are the same and thus object equality is proven. This is in line with your expectations – it would be bad if there were two meta classes of one class.

Supplementary Information The online version contains supplementary material available at https://doi.org/10.1007/978-3-658-39829-3_3.

O. Musch, *Design Patterns with Java*, https://doi.org/10.1007/978-3-658-39829-3_3

The singleton pattern comes into play in another place: Your application's runtime environment is so unique that it must exist only once. Consider the API documentation of the Runtime class:

> Every Java application has a single instance of class Runtime that allows the application to interface with the environment in which the application is running. The current runtime can be obtained from the getRuntime method. An application cannot create its own instance of this class.

You will resort to a singleton yourself if you manage your application's user rights, for example, or perhaps program a cache. A typical application can also be a thread pool. Also, resources like icons or images that you use in your program only need to be loaded once and can be stored in a singleton. Let's look at a few examples of how you can implement the Singleton Pattern.

3.2   A First Version of the Singleton

So how can the singleton pattern be implemented? You should first ensure that there is only one copy of the class. In Java, to prevent users from creating instances of a class, you must first set the constructor to private.

```
public class MySingleton {
    private MySingleton() {
    }
}
```

Now, access to the constructor is only possible from within the class or through other instances of this class. Since there is no (other) instance of the class, however, you must ensure that the one instance is created within the class. So define a method that creates an instance if there is no instance already; the instance of the class is returned to the caller of the method. This method must be public, of course. Keep a reference to this instance in a static variable:

```
public class MySingleton {
    private static MySingleton instance;
        private MySingleton() {
    }

    public static MySingleton getInstance() {
        if (instance == null)
            instance = new MySingleton();
        return instance;
    }
}
```

That's it! This is a simple way to implement the singleton pattern! The instance of the class is created at the latest possible time, namely when it is needed for the first time. Therefore, this procedure is called *lazy instantiation*, i.e. *delayed loading*.

You can find the code for this in the sample project Singleton_1.

In the application, you then get the reference to the one instance with `MySingleton single = MySingleton.getInstance()` and then call the actual function of the singleton with `single.doSomething()`:

```
public static void main(String[] args) {
    var singleton1 = MySingleton.getInstance();
    singleton1.doSomething();
    var singleton2 = MySingleton.getInstance();
    singleton2.doSomething();
}
```

And here I use a feature added in Java 10 for local(!) variables: The so called "Local-Variable Type Inference".

Instead of.

```
MySingleton singleton1 = MySingleton.getInstance();
```

Since version 10 with the JDK Enhancement Proposal (JEP) 286, Java is able to determine the type for local variables independently and without further specification by the programmer out of the context. This happens at translation time, so it does not compromise Java's type safety. In the example here, it is already obvious to the reader from the context that we want to have an instance of a MySingleton. The additional prefix MySingleton has thus become superfluous. It is sufficient to use a.

```
var singleton1 = MySingleton.getInstance();
```

to recognize the variable singleton1 as MySingleton and generate corresponding code.

NetBeans also suggests the switch to var. declaration in a hint if you stand with the cursor in a declaration line where this is possible. This feature facilitates the readability of the code in many cases, if one thinks of the sometimes very long class names in Java:

```
BufferedInputStream inputStream =
                        new BufferedInputStream(...);
```

then becomes simply.

```
var inputStream = new BufferedInputStream(...);
```

I will use this feature frequently in the sample code below, without going into further detail. It is quite catchy and only allowed if the type of the local variable can really be determined unambiguously. Therefore it should not cause you any problems in the further course.

3.3   Synchronize Access

The class described above runs beautifully as long as you don't use concurrency. What can happen? Assume the following case: You have two threads, both accessing the getInstance() method. The first thread gets to line 9 and finds that there is no instance yet. Then the Virtual Machine takes away its compute time and lets Thread 2 access the method. Thread 2 is allowed to work until the end of the method and creates an instance of the class, which is returned. Then Thread 1 gets allocated compute time again. The last thing he remembers is that the reference is zero. It will enter the block and create an instance as well. And now comes exactly what you wanted to avoid – you have two instances of the class.

Whenever you want to prevent code from being executed by two threads at the same time, lock the affected code:

```
public class MySingleton {
    // … abridged
    public static synchronized MySingleton getInstance() {
        if (instance == null)
            instance = new MySingleton();
        return instance;
    }
}
```

This code can be found in the sample project Singleton_2. The method can only be entered by a thread when no other thread is working with it (anymore). This solves the problem. However, synchronization is costly, so this approach is an unnecessary brake. Imagine – every time you want to get the one instance of the class, a lock is set on the method. So there must be an alternative.

3.4   Double Checked Locking

Do not lock the entire method, but only the critical part! First query whether an instance has already been created. If the method is called for the second time, the result of the comparison is false. Therefore, a lock is only required on the first call, when the comparison instance == null returns a true. So inside the if statement, you create a block that is synchronized. In this block, you query – this time in a thread-safe manner – whether there is an instance of the class. If not, create one. Finally, return the instance. Take a look at the example project Singleton_3.

```
public class MySingleton {
    private static volatile MySingleton instance;

    // ... abridged

    public static MySingleton getInstance() {
        if (instance == null) {
            synchronized (MySingleton.class) {
                if (instance == null)
                    instance = new MySingleton();
            }
        }
        return instance;
    }
}
```

By the way, in NetBeans you get a hint for line 6 ("synchronized (MySingleton. class)"). NetBeans detects double checked locking and still suggests the use of a local variable to improve performance. If you're using NetBeans, take a look at that too. It makes the code a bit longer, so I'll leave it out of the example here. This approach to Double Checked Locking is correct in theory. However, in some circumstances you run into a problem. Imagine the following scenario: You have two threads; thread 1 calls the getInstance() method. At line 5, it detects that no instance of the class has been created yet, and gets the lock on the following block. In line 7, it checks again – in a thread-safe manner – whether an instance of the singleton class has really not yet been created. If not, it creates an instance with the new operator (line 8). Depending on the runtime environment, the following happens during instantiation: First, memory is requested, then the memory is passed to the variable instance, which is now nonzero. Only in the next step is the constructor of the class called. And now our problem begins to mature: thread 2 enters the getInstance() method before the constructor call by thread 1. It determines that instance! = null, gets the instance returned, and works with it. Only later does Thread 1 execute the constructor, which puts the instance into a valid state.

You can prevent this by declaring the variable instance as volatile.

```
public class MySingleton {
    private static volatile MySingleton instance;
    // ... abridged
}
```

The problems around double-checked locking should almost justify a whole dissertation. I would just like to point out here that this solution can lead to runtime errors. There is no guarantee that the volatile keyword is implemented correctly in every virtual machine. For example, a JVM in a version below 1.5 may not implement this approach correctly at all. In such cases, you should strongly consider switching to more recent JVM versions. However, I hope that in 2021, when we are at Java 16, I won't have to convince anyone to migrate at least to Java 8 (2014), better 11 (2018). Java 11 is the most current "Long Term Support" version until Java 17 comes out (scheduled for fall 2021).

3.5   Early Instantiation – Early Loading

To avoid all problems in concurrent systems, you can resort to early loading. As usual, you create a static variable that holds the reference to the single instance. You initialize it as soon as you load it. A static method returns that instance. The code is really very simple. You can find it in the sample project Singleton_4:

```
public class MySingleton {
    private static final MySingleton INSTANCE =
                                    new MySingleton();

    private MySingleton() { }

    public static MySingleton getInstance() {
        return INSTANCE;
    }

    public void doSomething() {
        // Behavior of the object
        // … abridged
    }
}
```

Since no second instance of the class is to be created and cannot be created at all, the following solution (in the Singleton_5 example project) is also conceivable: Make the instance public, and you then additionally save the getInstance method:

```
public class MySingleton {
    public static final MySingleton INSTANCE =
                                    new MySingleton();

    private MySingleton() { }

    public void doSomething() {
```

```
        // Behavior of the object
        // ... abridged
    }
}
```

You avoid all problems resulting from concurrency with this approach. But you have to trust that the virtual machine will first create the instance before allowing other threads to access it – and that is exactly what you can rely on according to the specification.

Nevertheless, there are three things to keep in mind here as well:

1. The instance is created when the class is loaded. Assuming you have an extensive initialization routine, this will be run through in any case, even if you do not need the singleton afterwards.
2. You have no chance to pass arguments to the constructor at runtime.
3. The singleton pattern ensures that the class is instantiated only once per class loader. In the case of a web server, it may be that the class is loaded in more than one class loader within a virtual machine; then you have more than one instance of the singleton class again. Without going into detail, such situations are nowadays dealt with using Dependency Injection.

3.6   Singleton – The UML Diagram

In Fig. 3.1 you can see the (quite simple) UML diagram for the Singleton from the sample project Singleton_4, i.e. with the getInstance method.

3.7   Antipattern

You now know the Singleton Pattern and how to implement it. You know the advantages and disadvantages of the different implementations. But there are fundamental objections against the Singleton Pattern. I mean objections to the pattern as a definition and not to the realization shown. Search for the term "evil singleton" in your trusted search engine. I get over 2,000,000 hits.

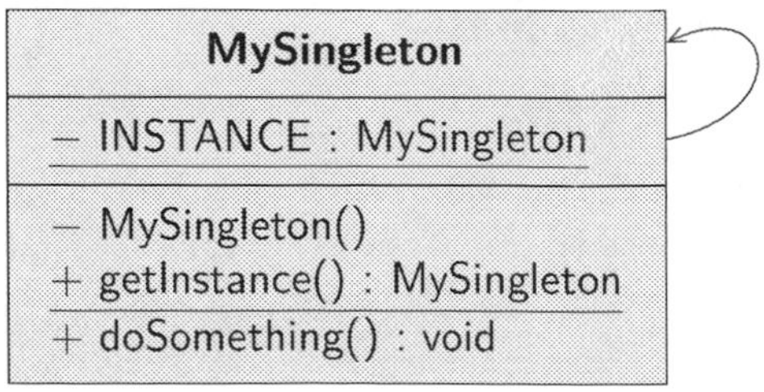

Fig. 3.1 UML diagram of the Singleton Pattern (example project Singleton_4)

MySingleton
− INSTANCE : MySingleton
− MySingleton() + getInstance() : MySingleton + doSomething() : void

3.7.1   Criticism of the Singleton

I would like to present a few of the criticisms.

- Each class should focus on exactly one task: Single Responsibility Principle. Singleton violates this principle in that the class must take care of both the business logic and its own object creation.
- Just as with global variables, the dependency is not immediately obvious. Whether a class makes use of a singleton class cannot be seen from the interface, but only from the code.
- The coupling is increased.
- Too extensive use of singleton tempts the programmer to program procedurally.
- If the instance has its own attributes, these are available in the complete application. It is questionable whether there is data that is actually needed "everywhere": in the view, in the controller, in the model and in the persistence layer.
- You restrict yourself when using singletons: You cannot create subclasses of singleton classes. If 1 day you do need a second instance, you have to rewrite the code again.
- Singletons create something like a global state. This makes the test procedure more difficult for you.

Considering these points, many programmers consider the singleton pattern to be an antipattern.

3.7.2   Is Singleton an Antipattern?

Antipatterns describe unsuitable procedures, negative examples, so to speak. Each antipattern can be described just as formally as a design pattern. They identify why it is not good to proceed in a certain way. Antipatterns help to learn from the mistakes of others.

The arguments against the use of the Singleton are certainly understandable. However, there are tasks that would be difficult to solve without a Singleton. I do not want to agree to a blanket evaluation – you will have to decide on a case-by-case basis and consider for each Singleton class whether it is really necessary.

3.8   Summary

Go through the chapter again in key words:

- A singleton is used when you have a class of which there may be only one instance.
- There must be a global access point for this one instance.
- Lazy instantiation creates the instance when it is needed.

- Simultaneous access – concurrency – to the singleton leads to runtime errors, especially during generation, and must be protected accordingly.
- Early instantiation avoids the problems of concurrency, but has other disadvantages.
- Antipatterns describe negative examples, i.e. unsuitable procedures.

3.9   Description of Purpose

The Gang of Four describes the purpose of the pattern "Singleton" as follows:

Ensure that a class has exactly one copy, and provide a global access point to it.

The pattern "Template Method" belongs to the behavior patterns and is quite catchy. It helps you when you need to implement an algorithm differently in subclasses, but on the other hand must not change it.

4.1 How Template Method Works

Take the classic order of input, processing, and output as an example. You want to input a string, convert it optionally to upper or lower case, and then output it to the console.

4.1.1 A First Approach

At first glance, the task seems to be solved quickly if you define two classes: Uppercase and Lowercase. I print the source code of Uppercase below. The rest can be found in the sample project Template_1. The method run() defines the algorithm: input, convert, output. The source code of the Lowercase class is identical. Only the bold part differs.

```
public class Uppercase {
    public final void run() {
        final var input = textEnter();
        final var converted = convert(input);
        print(converted);
    }
```

Supplementary Information The online version contains supplementary material available at https://doi.org/10.1007/978-3-658-39829-3_4.

```
    private String textEnter() {
        final var message = "Please enter the text:";
        return JOptionPane.showInputDialog(message);
    }

    private String convert(String input) {
        return input.toUpperCase();
    }

    private void print(String text) {
        System.out.println(text);
    }

    public static void main(String[] args) {
        new Uppercase().run();
    }
}
```

When a project has source code that is copy-and-pasted, it is usually an indication of poor design. It makes sense to move duplicate code to a common superclass-and that's exactly what you do in the following section.

4.1.2   The Second Approach

Now we build an abstract superclass that defines the algorithm on the one hand, and the methods that are identical in both classes on the other. Since the definition of the algorithm should be binding for all subclasses, it makes sense to declare the method run() final. You can find this code in the sample project Template_2.

```
public abstract class Input {
    public final void run() {
        var input = textEnter();
        var converted = convert(input);
        print(converted);
    }

    private final String textEnter() {
        return JOptionPane.showInputDialog("Please enter the text:");
    }

    protected abstract String convert(String input);

    private final void print(String text) {
        System.out.println(text);
    }
}
```

The subclasses `UppercaseConverter` and `LowercaseConverter` only override the abstract method `convert()`. As an example, I show the class `LowercaseConverter` here.

```
public class LowercaseConverter extends Input {
    @Override
    protected String convert(String input) {
        return input.toLowerCase();
    }
}
```

In the next section we will put this project into operation.

4.1.3   The Hollywood Principle

The client can now easily select the desired converter by instantiating it from the appropriate subclass:

```
public class Client {
    public static void main(String[] args) {
        Input input = new LowercaseConverter();
        input.run();
        Input newInput = new UppercaseConverter();
        newInput.run();
    }
}
```

The call is always made from the superclass. The algorithm is defined in the superclass and the superclass calls the corresponding actual functionality in the subclass. This procedure is what GoF calls the Hollywood principle: "Don't call us – we'll call you!"

Also note that at this point (highlighted in bold above), the declaration of the variable `input` does NOT work with a `var`. We want to have a local variable of the superclass type here, so that we can then assign instances of the various subclasses as we wish.

If you use var. at this point, the compiler recognizes the type LowerCaseConverter and assigns it to the variable. Until then everything is ok. But if you later want to build an UppercaseConverter with the same variable, you run into an error. Fortunately, however, already at compile time.

4.1.4   Introducing Hook Methods

You can extend the project with hook methods. A hook method is a method that can optionally be overridden. A default behavior – or no behavior at all – is defined in the superclass. The subclasses can – but do not have to – adopt this behavior. In the Template_3 sample project, there is such a hook method. The `save()` method returns whether the entered text should be saved to disk. In this case the method `saveToDisk()` is called. By default `false` is returned.

```
public abstract class Input {
    public final void run() {
        var input = textEnter();
        var converted = convert(input);
        print(converted);
        if (save())
            saveToDisk();
    }

    // … abridged

    protected boolean save() {
        return false;
    }

    private void saveToDisk() {
        System.out.println("Input saved");
    }
}
```

If the subclasses feel that the default behavior doesn't fit this way, they are free to override it. For example, the `UppercaseConverter` wants the text to always be saved – so it returns `true`:

```
public class UppercaseConverter extends Input {
    // … abridged

    @Override
    protected boolean save() {
        return true;
    }
}
```

The LowercaseConverter wants to let the user decide whether to save the text:

```
public class LowercaseConverter extends Input {
    // … abridged

    @Override
    protected boolean save() {
        var question = "Should the text be saved?";
        var answer =
            JOptionPane.showConfirmDialog(null, question);
        return answer == JOptionPane.YES_OPTION;
    }
}
```

Hook methods are also called insertion methods. They offer the possibility to influence the flow of the algorithm.

That's it – now you know the Template Method Pattern. Despite – or perhaps because of – its seemingly trivial formulation, the Template Method Pattern is extremely important for the development of frameworks such as the Java class library. You develop a basic framework, the algorithm, and build your extensions on it.

4.2   The "ListModel" Interface

You will be able to identify the Template Method Pattern wherever you encounter abstract classes. At this point, I'd like to briefly discuss the algorithm that the ListModel interface specifies; it describes what must happen and what data must be present for a JList to display data. A JList accepts any object as a data model that is of type ListModel. The ListModel interface prescribes four methods that are required to display data. A JList must be able to register and deregister with the model as an observer, a ListDataListener; to do this, the addListDataListener() and removeListDataListener() methods must be implemented. The JList must also be able to ask the database how many items to display; this is answered by the getSize() method. And finally, the JList must be able to query the element at a specific location; for this, there is the getElementAt() method, which you pass the index of the element you are looking for.

In the directory of this chapter, you will find the sample project ListModel_Example. This project demonstrates the procedure with a very simple example. If you analyze its source code, you will see that the methods for registering and deregistering listeners are so general that they can probably be used in all situations.

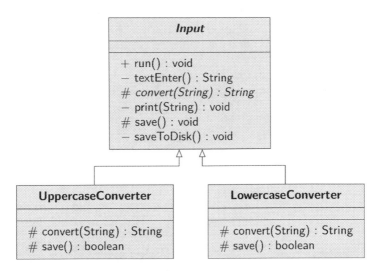

Fig. 4.1 UML diagram of the Template Method Pattern (example project Template_3)

In the class library there is the `AbstractListModel` class in which these two methods are implemented. If you need a different implementation than the default, you are free
to override these methods. Methods that describe the database, that is, `getSize()` and
`getElementAt()`, escape a standard implementation. You must always define these by
yourself. Please have a look at the AbstractListModel_Example project again.

4.3   Template Method – The UML Diagram

The UML diagram of the Template Method Pattern for the example project Template_3
can be found in Fig. 4.1.

4.4   Summary

Go through the chapter again in key words:

- You define a specific algorithm,
- Parts of the algorithm can be executed by the class itself; other parts are prescribed to
  the subclasses that implement the non-abstract parts,
- You describe the algorithm in a final method of the abstract superclass,
- The subclass or subclasses override the abstract methods of the superclass,
- Optionally, hook methods – insertion methods – can be overwritten,
- Hook methods allow you to partially vary the algorithm.

4.5   Description of Purpose

The Gang of Four describes the purpose of the Template Method pattern as follows:

> Define the skeleton of an algorithm in an operation and delegate individual steps to sub-classes. Using a template method allows subclasses to override specific steps of an algorithm without changing its structure.

You will now learn a pattern that is similarly easy and intuitive to understand as, for example, the Singleton or the Template Method pattern: the Observer pattern. The idea is that you have an object whose state changes (event source); any number of other objects (observers or listeners) want to be informed about these state changes.

5.1 Introduction

How is information distributed in a targeted and addressee-appropriate manner? Think of a newsletter distribution list. There is a newsletter for every topic that might be of interest. If someone is looking for a new apartment, he signs up for distribution list A; if someone is looking for a new job, he signs up for distribution list B. Everyone gets only the information that interests them, exactly when it is published. This principle, also called `pub-lish/subscribe`, is described by the Observer Pattern.

5.2 A First Realization

The sample project Observer_01 demonstrates a first realization of the pattern. You have someone who wants to announce news, an event source, in the example a job market. This class is able to register objects of the type `JobObserver` as interested parties, or observers; this type is defined by the interface `JobObserver`, which prescribes the method `newOffer()`.

```
public interface JobObserver {
    void newOffer(String job);
}
```

Supplementary Information The online version contains supplementary material available at https://doi.org/10.1007/978-3-658-39829-3_5.

The event source, i.e., the job market, defines three main methods: one to register observers and one to deregister them. Also, a method to save a new job and inform all observers about it. Saving jobs is not actually required in the sample implementation. But if you want to add evaluations about the reported jobs in the job market, for example, you will of course need it.

```
public class JobMarket {
    private final List<JobObserver> observerList =
                                    new ArrayList<>();
    private final List<String> jobList =
                                    new ArrayList<>();

    public void addJob(String job) {
        jobList.add(job);
        observerList.forEach(tempJobObserver -> {
            tempJobObserver.newOffer(job);
        });
    }

    public void addObserver(JobObserver jobObserver) {
        observerList.add(jobObserver);
    }

    public void removeObserver(JobObserver jobObserver) {
        observerList.remove(jobObserver);
    }
}
```

You can see in the code above that the information to all observers runs through the forEach method. And for each tempJobObserver from this list, the newOffer() method assigned via the lambda expression is then called. You can of course also use a common for loop at this point:

```
for(JobObserver temJobObserver : observerList)
    tempJobObserver.updateJob(job);
```

It provides the same functionality. The difference is that the for loop is an external iterator (which you write), while the forEach method is an internal iterator (which you only call because it's already built in). forEach also works with sets, queues, and maps, by the way.

The observers define what happens when the method newOffer() is called. The parameter of this method is the new job. In the example, the method randomly decides whether the observer applies for the job or not. Below you can see the abbreviated listing for the Student class. In addition, you will also find the class Employee in the project;

this is to model employees who are looking for a part-time job. They, too, must implement the JobObserver interface and thus their own version of the newOffer() method. In the example, I only made a small difference: students apply for a new job with 80% probability, employees only with 50% probability. After all, they already have a job.

```
public class Student implements JobObserver {
    @Override
    public void newOffer(String job) {
        var randomnumber = (int) (Math.random() * 10);
        var answer = "Student " + name;
        if (randomnumber <= 8)
            answer = answer + " applies for the job";
        else
            answer = answer + "does not apply";
        System.out.println(answer);
    }
}
```

The test program, which you will find in the project, creates two JobObservers and tests which of the two is informed about a new job under which circumstances. The expected console outputs can be found in the comments of the main method of the test driver.

5.3   Extending the Approach

Three things are certain in the life of a programmer: death, taxes, and changes in the requirements of one's software. In this project, too, the requirements will grow.

> **Tip**
> To maintain the greatest possible flexibility, always program against interfaces, never against implementations. Please note: In the language of design patterns, the term "interface" is not to be equated exclusively with an interface, and certainly not with interfaces in the sense of data transfer or function calls between systems. When we talk about an interface, we can also mean an abstract class. Consequently, you can "extend" or "implement" an interface, which describes the same process in the patterns language.
>
> This expression has become customary. It would certainly be more appropriate to speak of "assuming a role" instead of "implementing an interface" – the Student class could then assume the role of a JobObserver.

You have already seen in the previous project Observer_01 the advantage that the job market has no idea what kind of objects it registers. For them it is sufficient that the objects are of the type `JobObserver` – these can be students or employees.

What change could there be? It could be that students should not only be able to register with the job exchange of the university, but also with a job exchange of the employment agency. In the sample project Observer_02 you will find the interface `JobProvider`, which is implemented by the event sources. For the client, in our case the main method of the test class, it can be useful under certain circumstances not to be bound to a concrete implementation (job exchange or employment agency), but to be bound in general to objects of the type `JobProvider`. It can now exchange the concrete implementations and, for example, post a job with both providers at the same time:

```
var jobMarket = new JobMarket();
var employmentAgency = new EmploymentAgency();
var providers = new JobProvider[] {
    jobMarket, employmentAgency
};

// … abridged

var job = "temp in theater";
System.out.println("\nNew job: " + job);
for (var tempProvider : providers)
    tempProvider.addJob(job);
```

Again, I use the type inference with "var". No matter if it says "`JobMarket job-Market = new JobMarket();`" or "`JobProvider jobMarket = new JobMarket();`" or "`var jobMarket = new JobMarket();`", it will always create an object of type JobMarket. You can easily check this with a "`System.out.println(jobMarket.getClass());`" interspersed in between your code. As you can see, type inference also works with fields. The field with the two job providers is also created correctly.

A variation of this example is still conceivable: In the previous two examples, you passed a job as a string and passed it to the observers. This procedure is called push method. It is also possible that the event source only informs the observers that new information is available, without passing it immediately. It is then up to the observer to request the complete information from the event source. This procedure is called pull method.

In the example project Observer_03, the students and employees are not looking for jobs, but for apartments. Apartment offers are very extensive objects with their exposés and floor plans, which are only sent on request. The observers first decide randomly whether to request the information at all. Then they decide randomly whether they are interested in the apartment. Please analyze the project on your own.

5.4   Observer in the Java Class Library

In the Java class library, there is the interface `Observer`. This interface defines the role of an observer and prescribes the `update()` method. An object of type `Observable` and an object of general type `Object` are expected as parameters. A link to the event source is passed to the method to enable the observer to request further information from the event source. In addition, the event source can be queried for its data type (method `getClass()`). The parameter of type `Object` contains, for example, a job or an apartment.

The event source is therefore of the type `Observable`. Usually the suffix `-able` indicates an interface, but not here. `Observable` is a class that can be extended. As you are used to from your own implementation, there are methods in the `Observable` class to register and deregister Observers. Unlike your implementation, before you inform Observer, the `setChanged()` method must be called, which sets an internal flag. Only when this flag is set does the `notifyObservers()` method actually communicate the changes to the observers. This procedure can be useful if many changes are made to the database, but the observers are not to be informed until all changes have been completed.

However, the interface `Observer` and the class `Observable` are marked as "deprecated" and should no longer be used if possible. It is not type-safe and also not thread-safe.

For special Observer variants, the class library contains the package `java. util.Flow`, which is designed for thread-safe parallel processing of data and in which you will find the interfaces `Publisher` and `Subscriber`. Together with an `executor` and a `CompletableFuture`, the processing of many individual data packets from a source can be divided among parallel threads, which can then request their respective workload themselves. The code for this is very complex and beyond the scope of this book. However, you will find plenty of comprehensible examples on the Internet.

On the other hand, in the programming of user interfaces, events are triggered by the user to which the application must react: Pressing buttons, clicking with the mouse on buttons or menu items, or even inserting data into lists, which then have to trigger an update of the user interface again. Especially for the latter, there are also special observable interfaces for maps, sets, arrays or lists in the JavaFX library since version 2.0, e.g. javafx.collections.ObservableList.

We'll look at thread-safe observers in the next section, and we'll look at user interfaces after that as well.

5.5   Concurrent Access

The solution you saw in the Observer_03 project works flawlessly. But if you want to work with it on a concurrent system, you run into problems. Imagine that a thread is handing over a new flat and all observers are informed about it. At the same time, another thread is trying to unsubscribe an observer. There are then two threads that want to access the list of observers at the same time. Open the sample project Observer_04. I have reduced it to the most necessary classes so that you have, for example, only workers and no students. Start the main method of the class ObserverSim. This version starts two threads (ApartmentThread and DeRegisterThread) shortly after each other, both of which can work with the list of observers. The described situation, that two threads want to access the database at the same time, is provoked here deliberately. A concurrentModificationException is thrown after a short time. You may have to start the main method several times.

Another problematic situation can arise when observers are informed about a change and decide to unsubscribe as observers. This situation can be found in the example project Observer_05. In the update method, a random decision is made whether the observer still wants to be informed:

```
@Override
public void updateFlat(ApartmentMarket provider) {
    var random number = (int) (Math.random() * 10);
    if (random number <= 6) {
        var apartment = provider.getDetail();
        if (random number < 5) {
            // … abridged
            provider.removeObserver(this);
        }
    }

    // … abridged
}
```

Also in this case, a `ConcurrentModificationException` is thrown at some point, as Fig. 5.1 shows. The problem here is that the notification comes from the iterator that goes through the list of all observers. If an observer tries to delete itself in the

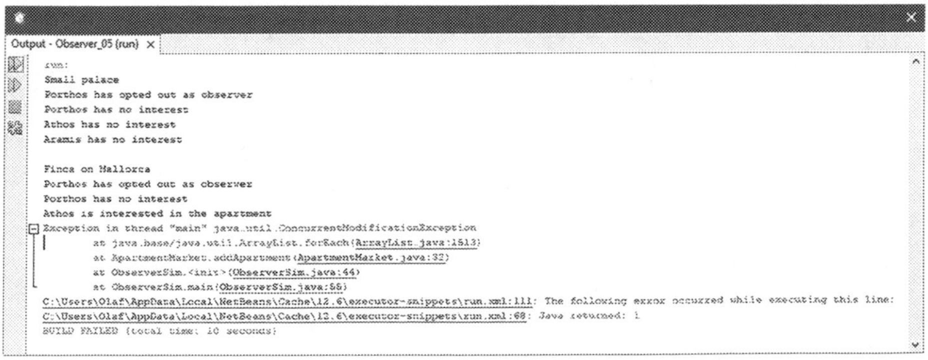

Fig. 5.1 Concurrent access can throw an exception. (Screenshot from NetBeans)

meantime, it causes the method `removeObserver` to manipulate the list, which is being used by the iterator, which may have to notify other observers. And that's where the exception hits.

In the upcoming sections, I will show you how to avoid difficulties from concurrency.

5.5.1   Synchronize Accesses

The example project Observer_06 offers an obvious solution, namely to synchronize accesses to the database.

```
public class ApartmentMarket {
    private final List<ApartmentObserver> observerList =
                                   new ArrayList< >();

    // … abridged

    public synchronized void
                    addApartment(Apartment apartment) {
        // … abridged
    }
    public synchronized void
            addObserver(ApartmentObserver observer) {
        // … abridged
    }

    public synchronized void
            removeObserver(ApartmentObserver observer) {
        // … abridged
    }
}
```

Does that solve all the problems? No! Observers cannot log in or log out as long as information is transmitted to observers. This solves the problem from project Observer_04. Project Observer_05 would still throw an exception. You also need to imagine the following situation: You are in the process of informing all your customers about an important new feature. Since the information is very extensive, it takes probably half an hour until the list of all observers is processed; it would be unpleasant if no new customers could register in this time. So, there must be another solution. By the way, the Observable class I introduced in Sect. 5.4 synchronizes the list of observers in exactly this way.

5.5.2   Copying the Database

The sample project Observer_07 shows you a different solution: The list of observers is
copied before the notification.

```
public void addApartment(apartment apartment) {
    this.apartment = apartment;
    List<ApartmentObserver> tempList;
    synchronized (this) {
        tempList = List.copyOf(observerList);
    }
    for (var tempObserver : tempList) {
        tempObserver.updateFlat(this);
        try {
            Thread.sleep(2000);
        } catch (InterruptedException ex) {
            // do nothing
        }
    }
}
```

This blocks the list only for a short moment. When you send the notifications, the copied list is always informed; if an observer logs in or out of the original list at the same time,
there is no conflict in access. The disadvantage of this solution is, of course, that the
observer list has to be copied more or less effortfully with every update.

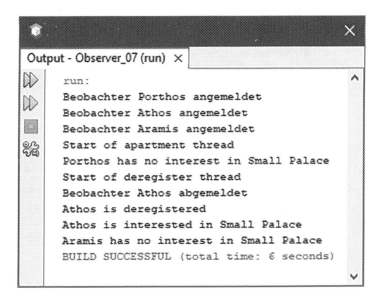

Fig. 5.2   Observer logs off and is still informed again

At this point, by the way, I use a function that was added in Java 10, along with a few others: List.copyOf(). This is the easiest and fastest way to copy a list. The syntax is very simple, and the same functions exist for the Set and Map classes: Set.copyOf() and Map.copyOf().

If you test the project, you will also notice that an observer who has just logged off will still be informed again – to do this, run the main method a few times (see Fig. 5.2).

5.5.3 Use of a Thread-Safe List

If you do not want to copy by yourself, you can also use a thread-safe CopyOnWriteArrayList. The sample project Observer_08 demonstrates the use of this class.

```
public class ApartmentMarket {
    private final List<ApartmentObserver> observerList =
                          new CopyOnWriteArrayList<>();
    // … abridged
}
```

However, working with a CopyOnWriteArrayList is comparatively expensive, because whenever a new element is to be inserted or an existing one deleted, the complete database is copied. In this respect, the same criticism applies as in the Observer_07 project. However, there is no trivial solution to this problem, and at least the implementation in the library java.util.concurrent is very efficient; you don't have to worry about the exact implementation yourself. In common practice, the best solution is probably to resort to a CopyOnWriteArrayList.

5.6 Observer as Listener

You take a different approach when you wrap the event in another class; it's like putting a letter in an envelope and mailing it. The serializable class EventObject from the package java.util expects a reference to the object that sends the event as a parameter in the constructor. The getSource() method returns this source. The toString method from the Object class is meaningfully overridden. The interface EventListener from the same package does not prescribe any methods, but only defines a role.

In the ListenerDemo sample project, there is a JobEvent class that extends EventObject. It expects the source and a string object that describes the new job as parameters. Of course, you could also provide a flat here instead of the string. The source is passed on to the Super class, the job is stored in its own data field.

```
public final class JobEvent extends EventObject {
    private final String job;

    JobEvent(Object jobProvider, String job) {
        super(jobProvider);
        this.job = job;
    }

    @Override
    public String toString() {
        return job;
    }
}
```

The interface `JobListener` extends the interface `EventListener` and prescribes the method `updateJob()`, which must be passed an object of the type `JobEvent`. Two classes – the students and workers you are familiar with – implement this interface in their own individual ways.

```
public interface JobListener extends EventListener {
    void updateJob(JobEvent jobEvent);
}
```

The `JobAgency` class maintains a list of JobListeners. When a new job is posted, the class generates an event of the type `JobEvent` and transmits it to all JobListeners.

```
public class Employment Office {
    private final List<JobListener> listener =
                            new CopyOnWriteArrayList<>();

    public void addJob(String newJob) {
        JobEvent jobEvent = new JobEvent(this, newJob);
        listener.forEach((tempListener) -> {
            tempListener.updateJob(jobEvent);
        });
    }

    // … abridged
}
```

Let's look at how this variant can be used practically in the next section.

5.7   Listener in GUI Programming

If you look at the EventObject class in the API documentation, you will see that many event classes that are needed in GUI programming are derived from it: ListDataEvent, ListSelectionEvent, AWTEvent, and quite a few more. One event, the TableModelEvent, I would like to introduce now. In the last chapter I briefly showed how a Jlist queries its data from the database. The interaction of a Jtable and its database is similar: You have a database that you need to describe to the Jtable so that it is able to display the data. The bridge between the two is the TableModel interface. The Jtable expects an object of type TableModel, which you pass to it using the setModel() method. With this object, the Jtable registers itself as a listener, which is why you must implement the methods addTableModelListener() and removeTableModel-Listener(). You use getColumnCount() to return how many columns to display. The getColumnName() method returns the heading of a column. Since you can return any data type, getColumnClass() tells you what class an object in a particular column is based on. The getRowCount() method is equivalent to the ListModel's get-Size() method; it returns the number of rows in a column. A cell in a table can always be edited; if you want to prevent this, the isCellEditable() method must return a false value. The methods getValueAt() and setValueAt() describe on the one hand which value is contained in a certain cell, on the other hand how the database should react when a cell has been edited. Each cell is uniquely defined by its column and row. In the MVC_1 sample project, the set jobs are displayed in a table (Fig. 5.3).

To generate this display, there are two classes, a display and a database. The database describes the data and the column header in a way that is understandable for the Jtable class. In addition, there are two methods that define what happens when a new job is posted. The addJob() method is passed a string containing the new job; it adds the job to the job list and calls the private fireStateChanged() method. This method generates a TableModelEvent and passes it to the listeners, which then update their display.

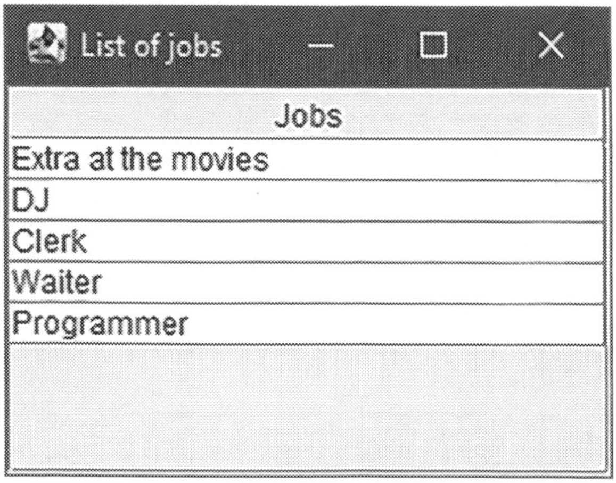

Fig. 5.3 Display of jobs in a table – Project MVC_1

```
public class Database implements TableModel {
    private final List<TableModelListener> listener =
                                new ArrayList<>();

    private final List<String> jobList =
                                new ArrayList<>();

    private final String[] headers =
                                new String[] {"Jobs"};

    public void addJob(String job) {
        jobList.add(job);
        this.fireStateChanged();
    }

    private void fireStateChanged() {
        TableModelEvent event =
                            new TableModelEvent(this);
        listener.forEach((tempListener) -> {
            tempListener.tableChanged(event);
        });
    }

    // … abridged
}
```

How is the data displayed? The display class builds a JFrame and passes an instance of the DataBase class to the JTable as a table model. Furthermore, it provides the method addJob(), which receives a job and passes it to the database.

```
public class Display {
    private final JFrame mainFrame =
                            new JFrame("Joblist");

    private final database jobModel = new database();

    Display() {
        var pnlDisplay = new JPanel();
        pnlDisplay.setLayout(new BorderLayout());
        var tblJobs = new JTable();
        tblJobs.setModel(jobModel);
        pnlDisplay.add(new JScrollPane(tblJobs),
                                BorderLayout.CENTER);
        mainFrame.getContentPane().add(pnlDisplay);
        mainFrame.setSize(500, 500);
```

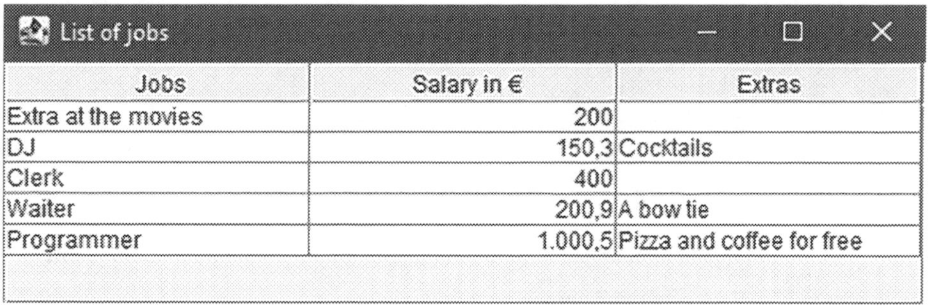

Jobs	Salary in €	Extras
Extra at the movies	200	
DJ	150,3	Cocktails
Clerk	400	
Waiter	200,9	A bow tie
Programmer	1.000,5	Pizza and coffee for free

Fig. 5.4   Screenshot "JTable_Demo"

```
        mainFrame.setLocationRelativeTo(null);
  mainFrame.setDefaultCloseOperation(JFrame.EXIT_ON_CLOSE);
        mainFrame.setVisible(true);
    }


    void addJob(String job) {
        jobModel.addJob(job);
    }
}
```

The `main` method of the `Display` class adds a new job to the display instance every second. I refrain from printing, please analyze the sample code for yourself.

Excursus: Working with Table Models

A table is only really a table if it also contains multiple columns. A table with one column is a list and you have seen that in the last chapter. In the sample project JTable_Demo, the salary offered is displayed next to the job. Since good employees are not so easy to find anymore, employers in certain industries still have to come up with an extra bonus to find applicants. The figure Fig. 5.4 shows the program in action. Two things have changed: First, there are two more columns: the salary and the extra bonus. Furthermore, the salary is displayed right-justified, the other two columns left-justified.

The most important change in the project is that a job is now no longer just a string, but a separate data type `Job`. The description of the job, the salary and an extra bonus are stored in it. I have overloaded the `Job` constructor. Jobs that are in demand don't need an extra bonus.

```
  public class Job {
      final String description;
      final double salary;
      final String extra;

      // ... abridged
```

```
    Job(String description, double salary, String extra) {
        this.description = description;
        . this.salary = salary;
        this.extra = extra;
    }
}
```

The `main` method of the start class again creates some jobs and passes them to the database:

```
public static void main(String[] args) {
    Job[] jobs = new Job[] {
        new Job("Extra at the movies", 200),
        new Job("DJ", 150.30, "Cocktails"),
        new Job("Clerk", 400),
        new Job("Waiter", 200.90, "A bow tie"),
        new Job("Programmer", 1000.50, "Pizza and coffee for free")
    };
    // … abridged
}
```

The last change concerns the data model. The array with the column headers has become larger. If you want to output the value of a specific cell, first have the job in this row returned. Then query the relevant value depending on the column.

```
public class Database implements TableModel {
    private final List<TableModelListener> listener =
                                    new LinkedList<>();
    private final List<Job> jobList = new ArrayList<>();
    private final String[] headers = new String[] {
        "Jobs", "Salary in €", "Extra"
    };

    @Override
    public Object getValueAt(int rowIndex,
                                    int columnIndex) {
        Job job = jobList.get(rowIndex);
        return switch (columnIndex) {
            case 0 -> job.description;
            case 1 -> job.salary;
            case 2 -> job.extra == null ? "" : job.extra;
            default -> job.description;
        }
    }

    // … abridged
}
```

Another important change relates to the specification of the data type of a column. The second column (index = 1) is of type `double`. All other columns are strings. By default, a `double value` is displayed by `JTable` right-justified, strings left-justified.

```
@Override
public Class<?> getColumnClass(int columnIndex) {
    return switch (columnIndex) {
        case 1 -> Double.class;
        default -> String.class;
    };
}
```

As you can see, the effort to describe the database increases with the number of columns. However, it is not difficult to implement a `TableModel`.

In the two program excerpts above you can see another Java novelty compared to Java 8: Switch Expressions. They have been available as a preview feature since Java 12, were supplemented by the `yield` keyword in Java 13 (which I will show you in a later chapter), and have been included in the Java standard since Java 14.

Take another close look at the two examples in bold. Several things stand out at first glance:

1. `Switch` is now available as an expression, in both cases now in the `return statement of` a method. But they can just as well be on the right side of an assignment or a comparison.
2. The colon in the switch statement is now replaced by an arrow (as in lambda expressions). Behind it in the two examples above is then exactly what would also be on the right side of an assignment or in a comparison.
3. There is no `break` (and also no `return`). Unlike the switch statement, the processing in the switch expression ends at the end of the respective expression for the selected case. The processing does not "fall through".
4. The default case – in the first code snippet – is identical to one of the normal cases, but must still be in its own case distinction.

The switch statement still exists. But with the newly added switch expressions, suitable code can be formulated much more elegantly and readably. It is also possible to process several statements in one case, which are then combined with curly brackets. To define the return value of the expression in this case, the `yield command` (instead of a `return` or a `break`) is used.

For the case distinction of `enum values` the compiler checks whether all values are either checked or alternatively a default case is available. Conversely, this means that the default case can be omitted when explicitly checking all cases. For all other types in the case distinction, however, a default case must be specified.

The `AbstractTableModel` class overrides the methods that are amenable to standard handling: registering and unregistering listeners, for example. By default, it also provides that cells may not be edited. You can (but don't have to) override these methods. This is the same principle as the Template Method pattern, where the `AbstractListModel` class did some of the work for you. In the directory for this chapter, you'll also find the AbstractTableModel_Demo sample project; here, the database is derived from an `AbstractTableModel`. There is no need to discuss the code – in this version, the database only needs the methods required to describe the data to be displayed. All other methods are inherited from the superclass.

Why have I described the `TableModel` here? In very few Java introductions I find explanations of the interface `TableModel`. Most of them describe the class `DefaultTableModel`. Maybe that's the reason why the `TableModel` leads a rather shadowy existence in practice. In practice, you will much more often find table models that rely on the `DefaultTableModel`. It is better documented and – at least at first glance – easier to use. In fact, however, the class is not without its problems. To name just one criticism, it uses vectors for the internal representation of the data – and that costs performance unnecessarily. I am therefore promoting the idea of developing your own table models on the basis of `TableModel,` and hope to be able to interest you a little in this.

5.8   The Model-View-Controller Pattern

The MVC_1 project leads to a discussion about the MVC pattern. MVC stands for model, view, and controller. Each of these entities has clearly defined tasks: The Model contains the data, the View is responsible for displaying it on the screen, and the Controller mediates between the two. The user – in the example the `main method` - always accesses the controller. If the data basis changes, it informs the logged-on listeners, the view units, of the change. The view then queries the data from the data basis and thus brings itself back into a consistent state. All components, for example `JList` and `JTree,` work according to this principle.

What is gained with this solution? You can register any number of observers – views – with the data model. Both data model and view are independent of each other and can be exchanged.

Where can the MVC model be verified in the MVC_1 project? The database, i.e. the model, is the `TableModelObject` with its job list. The `Display` class uses an instance of the `JTable` class to display the data on the screen. One might now be tempted to define the class `JTable` as a view. However, this assumption is wrong. But why?

The database expects an object of the type `TableModelListener` as listener. If the class `JTable` were the view, it would have to implement the interface `TableModelListener`. However, you can see from the API documentation that `JTable` does not implement this interface at all. So where is the listener? When you pass a table model to a `JTable object` with `setModel()`, it connects the database to an instance of the inner class `AccessibleJTable`. This inner class implements the `TableModelListener` interface and defines the `tableChanged()` method that you called in the database. The `tableChanged()` method queries the `TableModelEvent` for the scope of the change and tells the `JTable` superclass to redraw itself. So, the View in terms of MVC is this inner class `AccessibleJTable`; whereas the class `JTable` is the controller. Since the view accesses data and methods of the `JTable` class that encloses it, the boundaries of controller and view become blurred; you combine them into the delegate. In practice, Java programmers also tend to speak of model-delegate instead of model-view-controller. In Java introductions, the classes `JTable`, `JButton`, and so on, like to be represented as views. This is fine to explain the principle behind it. However, when looked at closely, this view is not correct.

Background Information

In the directory of this chapter, you will also find the sample project MVC_2. Here, the classes `Student` and `Employee` reappear, which you still know from further above. Both implement the `JobListener` interface, which extends the `TableModelListener` interface. So Student and Worker take on the role of the View and must override the `tableChanged()` method. I won't go into any more detail about the code; it's not difficult to understand.

Most books on design patterns – including the GoF – describe a statistic (the model) in the Observer Pattern, which is displayed once as a pie chart and then as a bar chart (view). In my example, the database is the job board, which is displayed by two different views. However, the principle is the same.

5.9   Observer – The UML Diagram

In Fig. 5.5 I show you an example of the UML diagram for the sample project Observer_08.

5.10   Summary

Go through the chapter again in key words:

- The Observer Pattern is always used when the status of an object changes and any number of other objects are to be informed of this.

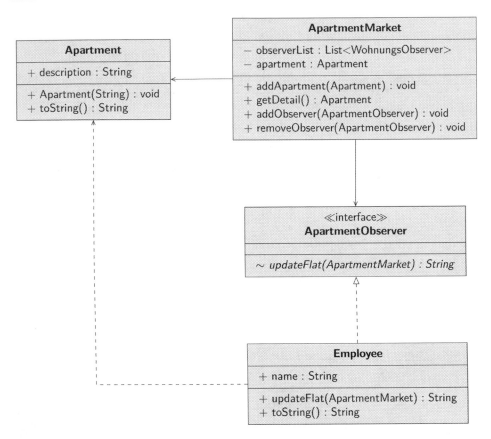

Fig. 5.5 UML diagram of the Observer Pattern. (Sample project Observer_08)

- There is an event source and observers.
- Observers must be interchangeable.
- Two threads cannot access the list of observers at the same time.
- It is useful to copy the list or use a `CopyOnWriteArrayList` before informing the observers.
- The class library of Java (still) contains the class `Observable` and the interface `Observer`, whose use is not unproblematic.
- The GUI programming is based on the MVC pattern.
- MVC separates the responsibilities into model, view and controller.
- The model contains the database.
- The view displays the data.
- The controller mediates between the model and the view.
- In Java, the boundaries between view and controller are fluid, which is why we speak of a delegate.

5.11   Description of Purpose

The Gang of Four describes the purpose of the "Observer" pattern as follows:

Define a 1-to-n dependency between objects so that changing the state of one object causes all dependent objects to be notified and automatically updated.

Chain of Responsibility

6

The Chain of Responsibility is a behavior pattern. Again, it involves sending a message to a large number of objects. Remember – with the Observer pattern, you sent a message to all objects that are registered as listeners. Using the chain of responsibility, a message is passed down a chain of objects; the first object that can process that message gets the responsibility. It is also possible for a message to be processed by several objects in succession, as well as for the message to be modified on its way through the chain.

6.1 A Real World Example

Imagine you want to apply for a driver's license. So you go to the first room in the corridor at the citizen center. There you ask whether you can apply for a driving license. The official in the first room does not process driving licenses, but hunting licenses, so he is not responsible; therefore he sends you to the second room. There, too, you ask and either get help or are sent one room over. At some point you will meet an officer who is responsible for driving licenses and he will help you.

This already makes one feature of the pattern clear: you have a system of objects that could **all** potentially process the message.

6.2 First Code Example: Grocery Shopping

Your vision of the future is taking shape: You have a refrigerator with an RFID receiver. The fill level of your beer bottles is checked regularly. Even if the number of slices of sausage and cheese drops, it will be registered. And if eggs and bread are running low, the

Supplementary Information The online version contains supplementary material available at https://doi.org/10.1007/978-3-658-39829-3_6.

O. Musch, *Design Patterns with Java*, https://doi.org/10.1007/978-3-658-39829-3_6

fridge will know that too. Of course, since you're a motivated programmer, you don't have time to go to the supermarket to shop yourself. Fortunately, stores in the area have banded together to form an electronic supply chain. When refrigerators report that a customer is running low on a product, each of the retailers checks to see if he can bring the customer new food. If not, they pass the order on to the next possible retailer.

6.2.1   The Foodstuffs Required

In the first step, you define which foods are to be supplied by the electronic supply chain. In the example project CoR_1 this should be bread, cheese, sausage, eggs and beer. You define these goods in an enumeration.

```
public enum Ware {
    CHEESE("Cheese"), SAUSAGES("Sausages"),
    EGGS("Eggs"), BEER("Beer"), BREAD("Bread");

    private final String description;

    private Ware(String description) {
        this.description = description;
    }
    @Override
    public String toString() {
        return description;
    }
}
```

In this project, the job, the "problem", is passed through a variable from the enumeration. Do you remember the Observer pattern? There you used a listener and an event object. This principle also fits with the Chain of Responsibility: you create an event object and pass it to the first link in the chain. This link decides whether it can process the event; if not, the event is forwarded. I will show you below that the Java class library does exactly this.

In the next section you will get to know the sellers of the goods.

6.2.2   The Sellers

As traders I define the beverages store, the bakery and the farm shop of Old McDonald, where you can get fresh cheese, sausages and eggs. All merchants must have identical methods in addition to their actual tasks (purchasing, manufacturing, etc.): sell and pass on the order if it cannot be served. So you define an abstract superclass that holds a reference to the next merchant in the chain. You call the `setNext()` method when you want to add another merchant to the chain. Each dealer first checks whether it itself already references a following dealer. If so, it will not store the new merchant, but pass it to the next merchant, which will now check if it is the last one in the chain. If so, it will save the new merchant as the following merchant. In addition, each trader must also provide a `sell()` method – you declare this in the superclass, but don't define it yet.

```java
public abstract class AbstractMerchant {
    private AbstractMerchant next;

    public abstract void sell(Groceries article);

    public void setNext(AbstractMerchant merchant) {
        if (next == null)
            next = merchant;
        else
            next.setNext(merchant);
    }

    protected void forward(Groceries article) {
        if (next != null)
            next.sell(article);
    }
}
```

As an example of a specific merchant, I am only printing the bakery here. The other merchants can be found in the sample project. The `sell()` method is representative of an arbitrarily complex problem solution. However, the principle behind it is always the same: If I can solve the problem, I solve it, otherwise I pass it on.

```java
public class Bakery extends AbstractMerchant {
    // … abridged

    @Override
    public void sell(Groceries article) {
        if (article == Groceries.BREAD)
            System.out.println(name + " sells " + article);
        else
            forward(article);
    }
}
```

Food is defined, the dealers are ready. The test class is still missing.

6.2.3   The Client

The main method of the test class is the client that demonstrates how to handle the chain. First, you create any number of merchants and link them:

```
public class Testclass {
    public static void main(String[] args) {
        var farmshop = new FarmShop("Old McDonald's");
        var bakery = new Bakery("Ben's Bakery");
        var liquorstore =
                new LiquorStore("BeeBee's Beer & Wine");
        bakery.setNext(liquorstore);
        liquorstore.setNext(farmshop);
        bakery.sell(Groceries.CHEESE);
        farmshop.sell(Groceries.EGGS);
        bakery.sell(Groceries.SAUSAGES);
        bakery.sell(Groceries.BREAD);
        liquorstore.sell(Groceries.BEER);
    }
}
```

Now the client can pass a purchase order to the first link in the chain. The order is now passed on to a dealer until one recognizes his responsibility and delivers the desired goods.

6.2.3.1 Extension of the Project

If you look at the project critically, you will surely notice a weak point: If there is no supplier for eggs, for example, the request will not be processed at all. Comment out the line in which the farm shop is created and restart the project. You find that the request is simply ignored. So it makes sense to provide a default behavior. To do this, extend the `AbstractMerchant` class. You can find the code for this in the example project CoR_2.

```
public abstract class AbstractMerchant {
    // … abridged
    private void printMessage(Purchase purchase) {
        System.out.println("Unfortunately, no merchant is able to
sell " + purchase
    + "can deliver.");
    }
    protected void forward(Purchase purchase) {
        if (next != null)
            next.sell(purchase);
        else
            printMessage(purchase);
    }
}
```

6.2.3.2 Variations of the Pattern
Would it have made a difference if you had created a list – ArrayList or LinkedList – and stored the merchants in it? You could have iterated over the list with a loop and stopped the loop from the moment one of the traders sells the goods. But the Chain offers a lot more possibilities than an aggregate.

Designing Hierarchies and Selecting any Entry Point
In the trader example, there are many traders, but they are not in any hierarchy among themselves. Let us think through a completely different example. In a company, the number of hierarchical levels increases in proportion to the size of the company. In a company with ten employees, the line to the boss is likely to still be very direct – flat hierarchies are indeed flat. If a company has 100 employees, you need at least one level of department head and below that perhaps a level for unit heads. Companies with 500 employees have, in probably this order: the board of directors, the department heads, the sub-department heads, the unit heads, the group heads, and finally the team heads. Such a company needs strict rules to justify this hierarchy. An example could be: When someone goes on a business trip, the group leader must approve the trip if it does not exceed 1 day and is within the company's local area. If a trip is longer than a day, the unit manager must sign off on the trip. If a long distance trip is coming up that is longer than a day, the department head must be involved. If you are an ordinary employee, you will always give your travel request to your team leader, who is the first in the chain. The team leader will check their responsibility and either approve your travel request or, if they are not responsible, pass it on. However, if you yourself are a sub-department head and want to travel for two days, you will probably not hand in your travel request to one of your subordinate unit heads, but to your next superior, the department head.

For the chain of responsibility, this means that each client can choose a different entry point for its message.

Links in the Chain Modify the Request
However, I would like to elaborate on two more special features of the pattern and take up the example with the traders again. You can define the sell method as you like. In the following example, it should be possible for you to pass an object of type Purchasing. The Purchasing class is an auxiliary class. It has two attributes: the goods themselves, as you already know from project CoR_1, and the quantity. When a merchant sells the goods, he calls the method `sell()`; the method `stillDemanding()` returns whether the customer wants to buy more of the same article.

```
public class Purchasing {
    protected final ware;
    private int quantity;
    Purchase(Groceries article, int quantity) {
        this.article = article;
        this.quantity = quantity;
    }
```

```
    public void sellGood() {
        quantity--;
    }
    public boolean stillDemanding() {
        return quantity > 0;
    }
    @Override
        public String toString() {
        return article.toString();

    }

}
```

A trader now sells the desired goods until either he himself can no longer offer any or the quantity demanded is zero. The question of whether he has any goods at all is decided by a random generator. Using the example of the bakery, let's look at the changes.

```
public class Bakery extends AbstractMerchant {
    // … abridged
    @Override
    public void sell(purchase purchase) {
        if (purchase.article == Groceries.BREAD)
            while (isAvailable() &&
                    purchase.stillDemanding()) {
                System.out.println(name + " sells " +
                    purchase.article);
                purchase.sellGood();
            }
            if (purchase.stillDemanding())
                forward(purchase);
    }

    private boolean isAvailable() {
        double number = Math.random() * 10;
        return number >= 5;
    }
}
```

So each link in the chain can now modify the request – in this case: the purchase.

6.3   An Example from the Class Library

Where can this pattern be demonstrated in Java? Take a look at the example project CoR_3. The main method builds a new window. An instance of the class JFrame contains an instance of the class JPanel and this in turn contains an instance of the class JLabel.

Furthermore, there is an EventListener that, when a component is clicked with the mouse, outputs on the console which component was clicked.

```
private final MouseAdapter adapter = new MouseAdapter() {
    @Override
    public void mouseClicked(MouseEvent e) {
        var source = e.getSource();
        System.out.println(source.getClass());
    }
};
```

This EventListener is assigned to all three components:

```
myLabel.addMouseListener(adapter);
myFrame.addMouseListener(adapter);
myPanel.addMouseListener(adapter);
```

Run the program and observe which source is output each time you click the window, panel, or label. If you click the label, the label is named as the event source. If you click on the panel, the panel is and in the other cases, the window.

Comment out the first line so that no event handler is assigned to the label. If you now click on it at runtime, the panel is output as the event source. Each component checks its responsibility and passes the event on to the surrounding container if necessary – until the window can no longer hand over its responsibility. A second characteristic of the pattern can be seen here: Processing goes **from the specific to the general**, from the leaves to the root. You will get to know the composite pattern further on, where the processing goes from the root to the leaves, i.e. vice versa.

The example project CoR_4 goes one step further. The GlassPane of the window is activated and gets the EventListener assigned.

```
Component glass = myFrame.getGlassPane();
glass.setVisible(true);
glass.addMouseListener(adapter);
```

Now it doesn't matter where you click – it's always the GlassPane that processes the MouseEvent. In practice, you can intercept user input and mouse clicks this way, for example, when your program is performing a large calculation. You effectively cover the user interface with the GlassPane to protect it from unwanted access. Once you set the "visibility" of the pane back to `false`, the covered interface is accessible again. The GlassPane is an object of type JPanel, so on the console this type is always named as the event source. Now this example doesn't really add anything new to the theme of the pattern, but it's a handy tip that I like to put here.

6.4   Chain of Responsibility – The UML Diagram

Figure 6.1 shows the UML diagram for the example project CoR_2.

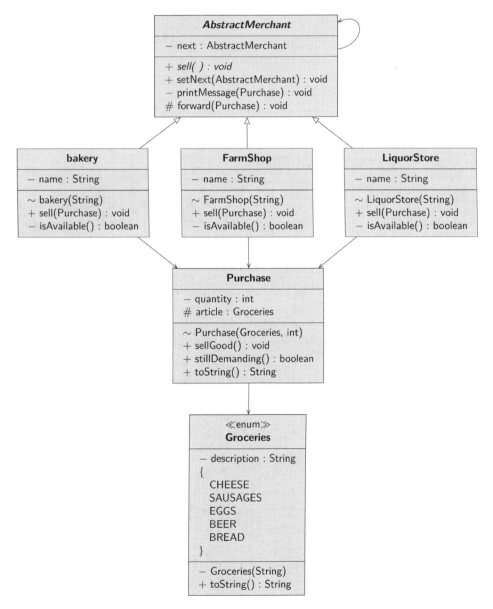

Fig. 6.1   UML diagram of the Chain of Responsibility Pattern (example project CoR_2)

6.5   Summary

Go through the chapter again in key words:

- Any number of objects can potentially solve a problem.
- These objects are concatenated in a chain or organized in a tree.
- A request is only passed to one link in the chain.
- If the object cannot solve the problem, it passes the request on.
- An object can modify a request.
- Every other object checks its jurisdiction; either it responds to the request or it forwards it.
- There is a risk that a request will go completely unanswered; therefore, a default behavior should always be implemented.

6.6   Description of Purpose

The Gang of Four describes the purpose of the Chain of Responsibility pattern as follows:

> Avoid coupling the trigger of a request to its receiver by allowing more than one object to complete the request. Chain the receiving objects and route the request along the chain until one object completes it.

7

The mediator pattern enables the flexible interaction of several objects/classes that may not know each other. The mediation function can be varied very flexibly, but can also lead to very extensive implementations. In contrast to the Observer or the Chain of Responsibility, the Mediator also has its own tasks to perform. This gives him a central role. However, there is also the danger that it becomes very extensive and even confusing.

7.1 Distinction from the Observer Pattern

To start with, I would like to contrast Mediator and Observer. The purpose of Observer is to relate an event source to any number of observers. The relationship was uni- or bidirectional: The event source knows the interface of the observers and maybe vice versa. However, it becomes problematic when each observer also wants to be an event source for every other observer. This might be the case, for example, if you are programming a chat. There are an unspecified number of participants, all of whom are interested in the events – messages – of the others. If you were to program a chat room using the Observer Pattern, each participant would have to keep a list of all the other participants. New participants – in the Mediator Pattern, we talk about colleagues – would have to register with all existing participants and in turn reference all existing participants. Extrapolate how many relationships you have with – say – 33 participants, i.e. colleagues. You need a different approach for that.

Supplementary Information The online version contains supplementary material available at https://doi.org/10.1007/978-3-658-39829-3_7.

O. Musch, *Design Patterns with Java*, https://doi.org/10.1007/978-3-658-39829-3_7

7.2   Task of the Mediator Pattern

If 33 colleagues all knew each other, you would have an inefficient spider web of over 1000 relationships. The mediator now has the task of decoupling event sources and observers. He mediates between the participants.

The mediator is scalable. I would like to create the following scenario as an illustration:

You can have a class in your program that manages the orders of an online shop; but instead of, or even in addition to, this class, the "Orders" unit can also be a whole department of employees who enter additional orders in the telephone service. The "Orders" unit reports a new order for processing to the mediator – which can again be either a single class or a department of employees.

The mediator asks customer management – which again can be a class or a whole department – whether the customer is already registered. If not, the mediator asks customer management to create a new record; if the customer is already on file, the mediator asks accounting (you know: class or department) whether the customer has reliably paid his bills. Depending on the accounting department's answer, the mediator instructs the shipping unit to ship the goods either by invoice or by cash on delivery. Now, if 1 day there is a need to add another unit to the system, only the mediator needs to be adjusted. Let the case arise that the head department wants to be informed of all purchases above a certain sales value. All you have to do is create a message in the mediator; the other units would not know anything about it.

7.3   Mediator in Action – An Example

The following simulation shows you the mediator in action. You have one unit that produces wine; this unit is a simplified producer, in reality winemakers, cooper and the glycol industry are behind this unit. Another unit represents costumers or retailers, the consumers. Consumers buy wine at the respective low price. Since there are x consumers and y producers, the dependencies are reduced to the middleman, the mediator. The mediator receives the consumer's requests and forwards them to the producers. Finally, the producers tell the mediator what price they want; the mediator forwards this information to the consumers. In addition to a method for negotiating the price, the mediator needs other methods for registering and unregistering consumers and producers. The sample code can be found in the WineSim project.

7.3.1   Definition of a Consumer

A consumer must have a method with which it can register with the mediator; I will dispense with the possibility of de-registering so as not to inflate the example unnecessarily.

In any case, the consumer must have a method to request wine. This method is given the quantity of units – for example bottles:

```
public interface ConsumerIF {
    double requestPrice(int quantity);

    void register(MediatorIF mediator);
}
```

A consumer registers with the mediator and submits its request to the mediator.

```
public class PrivateCustomer implements ConsumerIF {
    private final String name;

    private mediatorIF mediator;


    public PrivateCustomer(String name) {
        this.name = name;
    }

    // … abridged


    @Override
    public double requestPrice(int quantity) {
        System.out.
        println(name + " requests " + Quantity
            + " bottles of wine.");
        double totalPrice = mediator.getQuote(units);
        return totalPrice;
    }
}
```

In the next section, let's take a look at the producers of the wine.

7.3.2   Definition of a Producer

Producers must provide two methods – one for registering with the mediator and one for the mediator to address his requests to.

```
public interface ProducerIF {
    double getQuote(int quantity);
```

```
        void register(MediatorIF mediator);
    }
```

A producer calculates the price for a unit on the basis of a random number and depending on the requested number of units and communicates this price to the mediator.

```
public class ProducerImpl implements ProducerIF {
    private mediatorIF mediator;
    private final String name;

    public ProducerImpl(String name) {
        this.name = name;
    }

    @Override
    public double getQuote(int quantity) {
        double discountFactor = 1.0;
        if (quantity > 100)
            discountFactor = 0.7;
        else if (units > 50)
            discountFactor = 0.8;
        else
            discountFactor = 0.9;
        double price = Math.random() * 9 + 1;
        price *= discountFactor;
        String strPrice =
        NumberFormat.getCurrencyInstance().format(price);
        System.out.
            println("Producer " + name + " asks "
                + strPrice + " per bottle.");
        return price * units;
    }
}
```

Note that here, although the producer quotes the price per bottle (outputs it to the console) when submitting an offer, he then returns the total price to his caller. Of course, the mediator has to take this into account in his calculation. We'll deal with that in the next section.

7.3.3 Mediator Interface

The methods of the mediator are declared in the interface MediatorIF.

```
public interface MediatorIF {
    double offerDetermine(int units);
    void addProducer(ProducerIF producer);
    void removeProcuder(ProducerIF producer);
    void addConsumer(ConsumerIF consumer);
    void removeConsumer(ConsumerIF consumer);
}
```

A specific mediator, for example a wholesaler, must implement these methods.

```
public class Wholesale implements MediatorIF {
    private final List<ProducerIF> producers =
                                    new ArrayList<>();
    private final List<ConsumerIF> consumers =
                                    new ArrayList<>();

    // ... abridged
    @Override
    public double getQuote(int quantity) {
        List<Double> quotes = new ArrayList<>();

        for (ProducerIF tempProducer : producers) {
          Double quote = tempProducer.getQuote(quantity);
            quotes.add(quote);
        }
        var price = Collections.min(offers);
        var strPrice =
            NumberFormat.getCurrencyInstance().
                format(price);
        System.out.println("The best offer for "
                + quantity
                + " bottles is: " + strPrice);
        return price;
    }
}
```

In the example, the list of consumers is not currently used by the mediator. But you can think about what you need to add if a producer wants to use the mediator to request the addresses of customers to send an advertisement (assuming the customers have given their consent). Now we can test the project.

7.3.4   Testing the Mediator Pattern

How can you test the interaction of the classes? You create any number of consumers and any number of producers and register them all with the mediator. Then you let the consumers request the price for a certain number of bottles. The mediator asks all the producers for quotes, determines the cheapest one, and forwards it to the consumers.

```java
public class Test class {
    public static void main(String[] args) {
        // create a mediator
        MediatorIF wholesale = new wholesale();

        // create two customers
    ConsumerIF jim = new PrivateCustomer("Jim Collins");
    ConsumerIF jack = new PrivateCustomer("Jack Meyers");

        // create three suppliers
        ProducerIF vineyard_1 =
                        new ProducerImpl("Vineyard 1");
        ProducerIF vineyard_2 =
                        new ProducerImpl("Vineyard 2");
        ProducerIF vineyard_3 =
                        new ProducerImpl("Vineyard 3");

        // register with the mediator
        jim.register(wholesale);
        jack.register(wholesale);
        vineyard_1.register(wholesale);
        vineyard_2.register(wholesale);
        vineyard_3.register(wholesale);

        // Generate enquiries and obtain quotations
        int quantity = 50;
        double price = jim.requestPrice(quantity);
        System.out.println("\n");


        unit = 10;
        price = jack.requestPrice(quantity);
    }
}
```

This leads to the following output (with random prices, of course):

```
Jim Collins requests 50 bottles of wine.
Producer Vineyard 1 asks 6,69 € per bottle.
Producer Vineyard 2 asks 4,52 € per bottle.
Producer Vineyard 3 asks 5,75 € per bottle.
The best offer for 50 bottles is: 225,76 €

Jack Meyers requests 10 bottles of wine.
Producer Vineyard 1 asks 7,65 € per bottle.
Producer Vineyard 2 asks 2,42 € per bottle.
Producer Vineyard 3 asks 1,73 € per bottle.
The best offer for 10 bottles is: 17,30 €
```

7.4   Mediator in Action – The Second Example

The mediator pattern is also very common in the implementation of user interfaces. In the model-view-controller model, the controller is precisely the mediator that mediates between the view/use and the abstract model of an application. Let's look at an example of this.

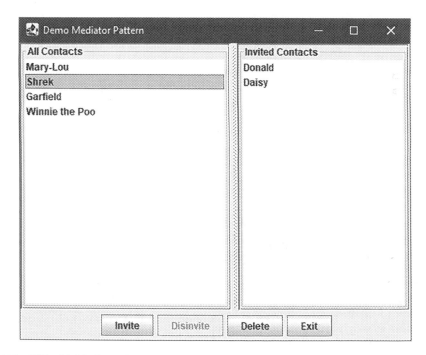

Fig. 7.1 GUI with Mediator from the SwingExample example

7.4.1   Mediator in GUI Programming

You have a GUI that shows two lists. The left list shows all contacts in your address book; the right lists all contacts who will be invited to the next party. For this example, we need four buttons. One button moves a contact to the list of invited contacts, another button moves a contact back to the general list of all contacts. A third button deletes a selected contact and the fourth button exits the program. The screenshot in Fig. 7.1 shows how the finished program should look like. The source code can be found in the project SwingExample.

Various dependencies are to be defined:

- The Exit button is always activated, regardless of the dependencies described below. If you click on it, the program is terminated.
- If a contact is marked on the right list, the button Do not invite is activated. Clicking this button moves the contact to the left list.
- If a contact is selected on the left list, the Invite button is activated.
- When the user clicks on this button, the selected contact is moved to the right list.
- Only one contact can be selected in both lists.
- The Delete button is activated when an entry is selected in one of the lists.
- If no contact is selected – neither in the right nor in the left list – no button – except Exit – is activated.
- When a contact has been moved or deleted, all markers are cleared and all buttons are disabled except for the Exit button.

7.4.2   Structure of the GUI

I print the source code of the project only in abbreviated form and limit myself to the essential key points. Please analyze the source code further on your own. The two lists are instances of the class JList. The four buttons are instances of the class JButton. All components register with an instance of the class Mediator, which is the core of the project. It stores references to all components involved. It also defines methods that are called when an event is fired. Let's look at the flow using the Invite button as an example. When the Invite button is activated, the Invite() method of the Mediator is called. Within this class, all the buttons – except for the exit button – are first disabled. Then the method gets the models of the two JList instances and moves the selected entry into the list of invited contacts.

```
class Mediator {
    private JButton btnInvite;
    private JButton btnDisinvite;
    private JButton btnDelete;
```

```
        private JList allContactsList;
        private JList invitedContactsList;

        // … abridged
        void invite() {
            btnInvite.setEnabled(false);
            btnDelete.setEnabled(false);
            btnDisinvite.setEnabled(false);

            var selectedItem =
                (String) allContactsList.getSelectedValue();

            var tempModel = allContactsList.getModel();
            var allContactsModel =
                (AllContactsModel) tempModel;

            tempModel = invitedContactsList.getModel();
            var invitedContactsModel =
                (InvitedContactsModel) tempModel;

            allContactsModel.removeData(selectedItem);
            invitedContactsModel.addData(selectedItem);

            allContactsList.clearSelection();
            invitedContactsList.clearSelection();
        }
    }
```

The Invite button is deactivated after it is created and is registered with the Mediator. The ActionListener passed to the button provides for the Invite () method of the Mediator to be called when the button is activated.

```
    public class GUI {
        private final JFrame frmMain = new JFrame();

        public GUI() throws Exception {
            // … abridged
            var btnInvite = new JButton("Invite");
            btnInvite.setEnabled(false);
            mediator.registerInviteButton(btnInvite);
            btnInvite.addActionListener((ActionEvent e) -> {
                mediator.invite();
            });
        }
    }
```

Note that I've used lambda notation here. This saves me from typing ...`new ActionListener` and `@Override public void actionPerformed` ... and makes the code much easier to read.

In this way, all components are created and positioned on the GUI. Each component registers with the Mediator and calls a specific method there.

7.5   Mediator – The UML Diagram

For the example project WeinSim you can see the UML diagram in Fig. 7.2.

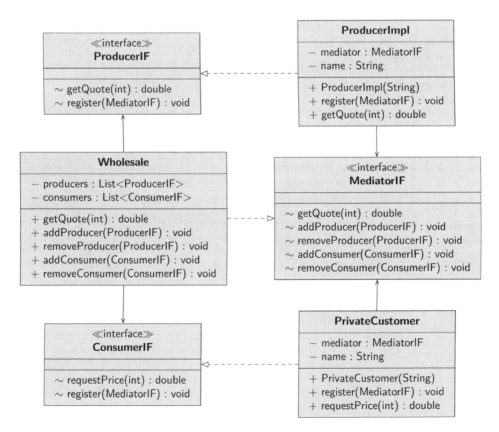

Fig. 7.2 UML diagram of the Mediator Pattern (example project WeinSim)

7.6   Criticism of Mediator

Let's take a critical look at the project SwingExample. What stands out? On the one hand, as with the wine trading simulation, you can see the advantage that the colleague classes involved don't know each other – and don't need to know each other. They are loosely coupled, which is always an indication of a good design. You can insert new colleagues at any time – the changes to the source code are limited to the mediator.

On the other hand, the disadvantage should not be concealed. If you analyze the Mediator class, you will find a relatively large class. And this is exactly the danger of the mediator: you risk developing a "god class"[1] that grows rapidly and becomes confusing as the number of components involved increases.

7.7   Summary

Go through the chapter again in key words:

- The Mediator Pattern loosens the binding between objects.
- Many participants – colleagues – depend on each other.
- Colleagues don't know each other.
- The mediator mediates between the colleagues.
- The mediator carries out its own tasks and can become very extensive.

7.8   Description of Purpose

The Gang of Four describes the purpose of the "Mediator" pattern as follows:

> Define an object that encapsulates the interaction of a set of objects within itself. Mediators promote loose coupling by preventing objects from explicitly referring to each other. They allow you to vary the interaction of objects independently of them.

---

[1] "God-class" is what it's called because only the good Lord still keeps track of the code.

The State Pattern encapsulates state expressions in objects. This can be useful when an object shows different behavior depending on its state. Think of a garage door. The door can be open, but it can also be closed. You can open a closed door; however, there is little point in trying to open an open door. But how can you prevent someone from trying to open an open gate or close a closed gate? The state pattern solves this problem by representing each state by its own object; as a result, everyone can only do what is supposed to be allowed in the current state.

8.1 Excursus: The Enum Pattern

Let's first digress and look at the Enum Pattern before we tackle the State Pattern.

8.1.1 Representing a State by Numerical Values

If you want to represent two state expressions, you quickly get the idea of representing these state expressions by numerical values and passing these values to final variables. Within a switch statement you query the values and react to them:

```
public class GateManager_1 {
    static final int OPEN = 0;
    static final int CLOSED = 1;
    private int state = OPEN;

    void printState() {
```

Supplementary Information The online version contains supplementary material available at https://doi.org/10.1007/978-3-658-39829-3_8.

O. Musch, *Design Patterns with Java*, https://doi.org/10.1007/978-3-658-39829-3_8

```
        switch (state) {
            case OPEN ->
                System.out.println("Gate is open");
            case CLOSED ->
                System.out.println("Gate is closed");
            default ->
                System.out.println("*** Error ***");
        }
    }

    void setState(int state) {
        this.state = state;
    }

    // ... abridged
}
```

In this code section, pay attention to the Switch Statement(!), where I use the arrow syntax after the respective case, which was inserted with Switch Expressions (compare my first explanations of Switch Expressions in Sect. 5.7). Switch statements also benefit from this syntax innovation, because I save the break commands here.

When you create an object of this class, you can either pass one of the defined constants to the setState() method, or you can pass an arbitrary int number by error. Depending on the state, a different text is output to the console in each case. In the example project GateManager you will find the classes GateManager_1 to GateManager_5 described above or in the following. For the sake of simplicity, I have combined them into one NetBeans project. In GateManager_1 you will find a main method within the class that demonstrates the procedure described above.

8.1.2   Representing a State by Objects

An alternative approach is to represent the state characteristics by objects of their own data type. To do this, declare a class State. Within this class, two static final variables of this type are created. To prevent the user from creating further objects of the type state, the constructor is declared private – access is now only possible within the class. The technique is the same as you have already seen with the Singleton pattern. You can find said data type as a static inner class in the GateManager_2 class.

```
public class GateManager_2 {
    // ... abridged
    public static class State {
        public static final state OPEN =
                                new state("open");
```

```
        public static final state CLOSED =
                                new State("closed");

        private final String description;

        private state(string description) {
            this.description = description;
        }
    }

    // ... abridged
    private state state = state.OPEN;

    void setState(State state) {
        if (state != null)
            this.state = state;
    }
    // ... abridged
}
```

Now, only the state characteristics specified in the State class can be used. So this solution has become type safe. Since this approach was used very often, it was called Enum Pattern. One disadvantage is that you can no longer query the state expressions in a switch statement during processing.

8.1.3   Implementation in the Java Class Library

Programmers are often faced with the necessity of representing state expressions in a type-safe manner. This is what enumerations are for in Java. The compiler translates enums so that the bytecode corresponds exactly to the enum pattern shown above. Instead of class, you now write enum. Also, a bit of typing has been taken away from the programmer; the modifiers static final and the explicit object creation can be omitted; the various options are separated by commas. You can find this variant in the class GateManager_3.

```
enum state {
    OPEN("open"), CLOSED("closed");
    private final String description;

    private state(string description) {
        this.description = description;
    }
}
```

Enums again allow you to query state expressions in a switch statement:

```
void printState() {
    switch (state) {
        case OPEN ->
                System.out.println("Gate is open");
        case CLOSED ->
                System.out.println("Gate is closed");
    }
}
```

Are you missing the default case in this switch statement? Since the checked state is an enum datatype, we don't need that anymore as long as all the individual values are also covered in the cases. That is the case here, and thus the need for the default case is eliminated. Another handy Java customization introduced with Switch Expressions and also available for Switch Statements.

In the next section, you will change the states of an object.

8.2   Changing the State of an Object

In the previous paragraph, you saw how you can define state expressions in a type-safe way. It can now be interesting to see how you transfer one state to another and how the behavior of an object is changed as a result.

8.2.1   A First Approach

In the GateManager_4 class, the first step is to consider how to transition one state to another:

```
public class GateManager_4 {
    enum state {
        // … abridged
    }

    private state state = state.OPEN;

    private void open() {
        System.out.println("The gate is opened");
        this.state = state.OPEN;
    }
```

```
        private void close() {
            System.out.println("The gate is closed");
            this.state = state.CLOSED;
        }
    }
```

Actually, this solution is optimal, isn't it? When a gate is closed, you open it to transfer it to the other state. If it is open, you close it and then also have a different state. But with this coding, it is possible for the user to open a gate that is open or close one that is closed. And that's exactly what shouldn't happen. So query the state expressions beforehand!

8.2.2   A Second Approach

Include an if statement in each method that allows opening or closing only if it changes the object to a different state. If the user tries to open an open gate or close a closed one, alert them with an error message. You can find this code in the class GateManager_5.

```
public class GateManager_5 {
    enum state {
        // ... abridged
    }
    private state state = state.OPEN;

    private void open() {
        if (state == state.CLOSED) {
            System.out.println("The gate is opened");
            this.state = state.OPEN;
        }
        else
            System.out.println("Gate is already open");
    }

    private void close() {
        if (state == state.OPEN) {
            System.out.println("The gate is closed");
            this.state = state.CLOSED;
        }
        else
            System.out.println("Gate is already closed");
    }
}
```

Fig. 8.1 Three state characteristics and their transitions

This solution works flawlessly. But where could it show weaknesses? It is no longer useful when further state expressions are added and there are extensive dependencies between them.

I would like to extend the example by the fact that your client requests a new condition. The gate should not only be closed, but also be able to be locked with a lock. You now have the third state LOCKED. The state LOCKED may only be set if the gate is closed. Conversely, the LOCKED state can only be changed to the CLOSED state. Figure 8.1 shows the three states and their possible transitions.

You need to relate three state expressions and make the object's behavior dependent on them. When a fourth state is added, you can imagine the work that will come your way.

How the method open() could look like in this case is shown in the following listing, which is only commented out in the sample code:

```
private void open() {
    switch (state) {
        case OPEN ->
            System.out.println("Gate is already open");
        case CLOSED -> {
            System.out.println("The gate is opened");
            this.state = state.OPEN;
        }
        case LOCKED ->
            System.out.println("The gate is locked");
    };
}
```

Similarly, the other four methods would have to define the correct behavior for each state – even if the behavior is only to issue an appropriate error message. The scope of the methods increases with each new state. The class becomes unwieldy and difficult to maintain. Errors can creep in very quickly. In short: It's high time for the State Pattern.

8.3   The Principle of the State Pattern

The definition of the state characteristics by enumerations is no longer sufficient. Describe each state by its own class.

8.3.1   Defining the Role of All States

In order to be able to exchange the state expressions, they must have a common data type. You first create the abstract class State, in which all methods from the state diagram are provided. In addition, this class holds a reference to the goal, which is passed to it in the constructor. The following code can be found in the StatePattern_1 sample project.

```
public abstract class State {
    public final gate;
    State(Gate gate) {
        this.gate = gate;
    }
    abstract void open();
    abstract void close();
    abstract void lock();
    abstract void unlock();
}
```

Each state is represented by its own class and extends the abstract class. So, within the state, you define what should happen when a particular method, for example open(), is called. When you define a state, you need to think about what a method in that state should look like. Let's walk through the example using the Open state. If a gate is open and someone tries to open it again, print an error message. Similarly, an open gate cannot be unlocked or locked; therefore, print error messages in these methods as well. However, if the user wants to close an open gate, change the state to closed.

```
public class Open extends State {
    Open(Gate gate) {
        super(gate);
    }

    @Override
    public void open() {
        System.out.println("The gate is already open.");
    }

    @Override
    public void close() {
        System.out.println("The gate will be closed.");
        gate.setState(new Closed(tor));
    }

    @Override
    public void lock() {
```

```
        System.out.println("Close the gate first.");
    }

    @Override
    public void unlock() {
        System.out.println("The gate is not locked.");
    }
}
```

The other state classes are defined accordingly.

How does this change affect the gate? The Gate class defines a state field that references the current state. All the methods you know from the state diagram can be called on this state. So the gate itself can define an open() method that passes the call to the state field. Here I print the abbreviated source code of the Gate class.

```
public class Gate {
    private state state = new Open(this);

    public void setState(State state) {
        this.state = state;
    }

    public void open() {
        state.open();
    }

    // ... abridged
}
```

The gate calls the desired method on the current state. However, it has no idea which state is currently stored. If you call the same method twice on the same object, a different state may be active, the behavior of the object may be different, and you may have the impression that you are working with the instance of a different class.

8.3.2   The Project from the Client's Point of View

In the client class of the project, the Gate is put to use. Compare the source code, which I only print here in abbreviated form, with the console output:

```
public static void main(String[] args) {
    GATE.open();
    GATE.close();
    GATE.open();
```

```
Output - StatePattern_1 (run)  ×
    run:
    The gate is Open.
            The gate is already open an cannot be opened again.
    The gate is Open.
            The gate will be closed.
    The gate is Closed.
            The gate will be opened.
    The gate is Open.
            The gate is not locked, so it cannot be unlocked.
    The gate is Open.
            Please close the gate before locking it.
    The gate is Open.
            The gate will be closed.
    The gate is Closed.
            The gate will be locked.
    The gate is Locked.
            The gate is locked and cannot be opened.
    The gate is Locked.
            The gate will be unlocked.
    The gate is Closed.
            The gate will be opened.
    The gate is Open.
            BUILD SUCCESSFUL (total time: 0 seconds)
```

Fig. 8.2 Console output of the sample project StatePattern_1

```
GATE.unlock();
GATE.lock();
GATE.close();
GATE.lock();
GATE.open();
GATE.unlock();
GATE.open();
}
```

The resulting console output can be found in Fig. 8.2.

Notice how many times the open() method is called: four times in total. With each call, the context, i.e. the gate, reacts differently. For the client, this solution is very convenient – it does not know how the gate works internally, it especially does not have to deal with the different state classes.

Nevertheless, two disadvantages should not be concealed. First, you need a separate class for each state. Some state characteristics depend "somehow" on each other, others not at all. This creates the risk that the project becomes confusing. Without a clear state diagram, you may be at a loss.

A second point can become a problem. You create a new object with every state change. If you have frequent state changes or the state class is very costly to instantiate, this solution is not to be favored. Let's look at alternative implementations below.

8.3.3   Changes to the Project

I would like to present two options. The first alternative is to manage the state objects centrally in the context. The second alternative is to create the state objects in the super-class of all state classes and to pass the correct object to the caller with each method call.

8.3.3.1 Manage State Objects Centrally in Context

If you don't want to create a new object every time the state changes, you need an alterna-tive solution. Let the context define variables that represent each state. Also, for each state, the context defines a method that sets the State `currentState` field to the desired state. You can find the code for this in the StatePattern_2 sample project:

```
public class Gate {
    private final state openState = new Open(this);
    private final state closedState = new Closed(this);
    private final state lockedState = new Locked(this);

    private state currentState = openState;

    public void setOpenState() {
        currentState = openState;
    }

    public void open() {
        currentState.open();
    }

    // ... abridged
}
```

The state classes now no longer pass state objects to the context, but instruct the context to assume a certain state. How it does that is up to it. However, this binds the context very strongly to the state classes.

8.3.3.2 State Objects as Return Values of Method Calls

Another alternative implementation is that you basically return state objects as return val-ues. If the state does not change, it returns a reference to itself, that is, `this`. To do this, you define variables in the abstract superclass that represent the various state expressions. You can find this variant in the sample project StatePattern_3:

```
public abstract class State {
    protected static final state OPEN = new Open();
    protected static final state CLOSED = new Closed();
```

```
        protected static final state LOCKED = new Locked();

        abstract state open();

        // ... abridged
    }
```

The final variables are declared `protected` to allow the subclasses to access them.

```
public class Open extends State {
    @Override
    public State open() {
        System.out.println("The gate is already open.");
        return this;
    }

    @Override
    public State close() {
        System.out.println("The gate is closed.");
        return super.CLOSED;
    }
    // ... abridged
}
```

The context is now responsible for setting the received state object as the current state. This makes the project very flexible, new state classes can be inserted easily. Because the context no longer has to provide a set method, incorrect state values are not accidentally passed or set.

8.4   The State Pattern in Practice

You will find the state pattern quite often in practice. For example, network protocols often work with state expressions. As an example, I have chosen RFC 1939, which describes POP3. You can find the text of the RFC in the subfolder for the state pattern.

RFC 1939 recognizes three different state specifications: AUTHORIZATION, TRANSACTION, and UPDATE. These are actually referred to as states in the RFC. The POP3 server waits for requests. When a request arrives, a TCP connection is established. The session is initially in the AUTHORIZATION state, where the user's name and password are requested. If the name can be identified and the password is correct, the session enters the TRANSACTION state. In this state, commands can be sent to the server. For example, a list of stored e-mails can be requested. Furthermore, an e-mail can be marked for deletion. When the QUIT command is received, the session changes to the UPDATE state. In this state, the e-mails marked for deletion are actually deleted. Afterwards, the connection is terminated.

If the QUIT command is issued in the AUTHORIZATION state, the session is terminated without UPDATE. Calling QUIT therefore has two completely different effects
depending on the state. Commands that refer to the stored messages are only permitted in
the TRANSACTION state.

Take a look at the sample POP3 project, which demonstrates the transition of these
three state expressions. I have stored four state classes in the `states` package: Three for
the states defined in the protocol and one class for the START state, which is needed when
the server is waiting for requests. There is also a class `POP3_Session` in this package.
This class is the context that the clients access. The client only "sees" the context. It has
no information that a variety of state classes are needed in the background. From this point
of view, analyse the `main` method of the `ApplStart` class.

8.5   State – The UML Diagram

The UML-diagram for State-Pattern from the example project StatePattern_3 can be seen
in Fig. 8.3.

8.6   Summary

Go through the chapter again in key words:

The enum pattern allows you to define different state specifications in a type-
safe manner.

- Usually a private constructor is defined.
- Instances of the classes are declared static and final.
- The enum pattern is implemented by the enumeration since Java 5.

The most important points about the State Pattern:

- An object can have different state characteristics.
- Depending on the state, the object shows different behavior.
- The transition from one state to another should be specified in the state classes
  themselves.
- Enumeration is usually not sufficient for this.
- To the client, it looks like it's dealing with an instance of another class.
- The state instances can either be regenerated each time the state changes or kept in a
  central location. Which solution you choose depends on whether the state is likely to
  change frequently or whether the creation of an instance of a state class is cost-intensive.
  In this case, you create the state instances when you start the program and store them in
  a central location.

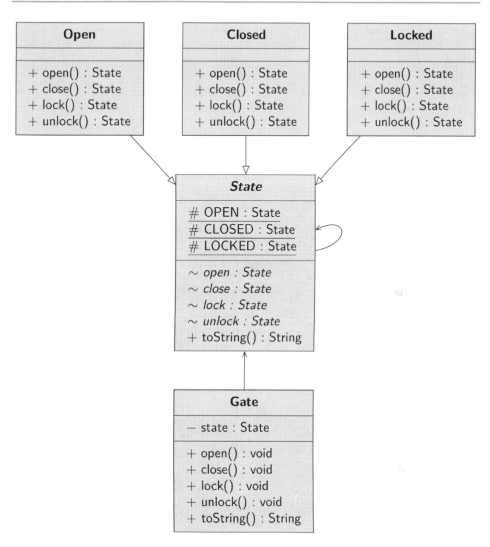

Fig. 8.3   UML diagram of the State Pattern (example project StatePattern_3)

8.7   Description of Purpose

The Gang of Four describes the purpose of the pattern "State" as follows:

> Allow an object to change its behavior when its internal state changes. It will look like the object has changed its class.

Command

9

In this chapter, I want to show you a behavior pattern that detaches a command call from command execution. What is meant by this? Imagine the head of your company saying in a department head meeting, "I need the latest statistics!" Malice is guaranteed to strike in the form of your own department head raising his finger and saying, "I'll take care of it!" Predictably, he will also assign you to do it, saying, "You do it, you can do it!" What happened there? The boss requests an action, you execute it, and in between there is an entity (your department head) that passes on the task. In other words, command invocation and execution are detached from each other and only loosely coupled via a command object – and that is exactly the goal of the Command Pattern.

9.1 Encapsulating Commands in Classes

But first, let's leave the scene in the office and think about how to book a vacation trip. You go to the travel agency and state your travel wishes. The person in the travel agency types on his computer for a while and you can go on holiday with peace of mind. But in fact, it's not the travel agent who runs the trip, it's a tour operator who takes care of the flight and, at the destination, the hotel. Let's take a closer look at this, but in addition we will also deal with the Date and Time API added in Java 8, which replaces the old java.util.Date.

9.1.1 Version 1 – Basic Version

In the first step, which has nothing to do with the Command Pattern, I will program a travel agency and a tour operator. The travel agency defines the method `bookTrip()`. It is passed the destination, departure day and return day as arguments. The data is packed into

Supplementary Information The online version contains supplementary material available at https://doi.org/10.1007/978-3-658-39829-3_9.

O. Musch, *Design Patterns with Java*, https://doi.org/10.1007/978-3-658-39829-3_9

an object of the class Trip and passed to the tour operator, which then carries out the trip
in real terms, i.e., executes the trip command. You can find the following example in the
sample project Travel_1.

```
public class Trip {
    final String destination;
    final String from;
    final String to;
    final DateTimeFormatter dtFormatter =
          DateTimeFormatter.ofPattern("MM/dd/yyyy");
    Trip(String destination, LocalDate from, LocalDate to) {
        this.target = target;
        this.from = from.format(dtFormatter);
        this.to = dtFormatter.format(to);
    }
    @Override
    public String toString() {
        return "Travel to " + destination + " from "
                                    + from + " to " + to;
    }
}
```

Note the use of the date functions: First, the constructor of the Trip class receives the
start and end dates of the trip as values of type `LocalDate`. For this, the Trip class must
use the `import java.time.LocalDate.`

This LocalDate belongs to the Date and Time API, which was implemented in Java 8
with the Java Specification Request JSR-310. The reason for replacing the `java.util.`
`Date` used until then were its weaknesses: Lack of type safety, lack of extensibility, unclear
responsibilities (Date with time specification built in but without time zone) and some others.

In contrast, the `java.time` package and its four subpackages `chrono`, `format`,
`temporal`, and `zone` provide largely unified commands for various date and time
types, consistent and clear command definitions, and thread-safe immutable objects.

Take another look at the sample code above:

The constructor is about converting a LocalDate into a string. This is done by means of
a DateTimeFormatter, which is provided with the pattern "`MM.dd.yyyy`" for the representation or conversion, which is common for the US. This conversion is not mandatory,
but without it the date would be output according to the ISO standard ISO-8601 in the
format yyyy-MM-dd. Decide for yourself what suits you better.

By the way, a variable of type LocalDate has no time parts at all. It contains the year,
month, and day, as well as all the necessary methods. The counterparts for processing
time information will be discussed separately in a later chapter.

The actual conversion into a string is then possible in two ways, both of which I've used to introduce you to them

- Either you use the `format` method of the LocalDate and specify the DateTimeFormatter as parameter
- Or you use the `format` method of the DateTimeFormatter and pass it the LocalDate as parameter

In both cases, however, the appropriately formatted text comes out. We will see how to create a LocalDate in a moment when we create the test class.

The tour operators negotiate contracts with hotels, airlines and local bus companies and run the tour. Each tour operator gets its own company.

```
public class Tour Operator {
    private final String company;
    Tour operator(String company) {
        this.company = company;
    }
    void execute(Trip trip) {
        System.out.println(company + " operates the
            following trip: " + trip);
    }
    @Override
    public String toString() {
        return company;
    }
}
```

An instance of the travel agency is created by passing an object of type TourOperator to its constructor. The method `execute()` is passed the data of the trip as parameters, which are stored as strings.

```
public class TravelAgency {
    private final TourOperator operator;
    TravelAgency(TourOperator operator) {
        this.operator = operator;
    }
    void bookTrip(String destination, LocalDate from, LocalDate to) {
        var trip = new Trip(destination, from, to);
        operator.execute(trip);
    }
}
```

In the main method of the test class, a travel agency and a tour operator are created. Then three trips are booked. Let's take a closer look at this because of the Date and Time API. I have highlighted the relevant code passages in bold.

```java
public class Testclass {
    public static void main(String[] args) {
        var operator = new TourOperator("ABC-Travel");
        var travelAgency = new TravelAgency(operator);
        LocalDate from, to;

        // book a trip
        of = LocalDate.of(2023, Month.NOVEMBER, 4);
        to = from.withDayOfMonth(15);
        travelAgency.bookTrip("Washington", from, to);

        // book another trip
        from = toDate("12/30/2023");
        to = from.with(nextOrSame(DayOfWeek.TUESDAY));
        travelAgency.bookTrip("Rome", from, to);

        // and book another trip
        from = toDate("02.10.2023");
        to = from.plusWeeks(2);
        travelAgency.bookTrip("Beijing", from, to);
    }
    private static LocalDate toDate(String date) {
        LocalDate tempDate;
        try {
            tempDate = LocalDate.parse(date,
            ofLocalizedDate(FormatStyle.MEDIUM));
        } catch (DateTimeParseException ex) {
            tempDate = LocalDate.now();
            ex.printStackTrace();
        }
        return tempDate;
    }
}
```

Note that you need to specify some imports to use the Date and Time API. For this example, these are.

```java
import java.time.DayOfWeek;
import java.time.LocalDate;
import java.time.Month;
import java.time.format.DateTimeFormatter;
import java.time.format.DateTimeParseException;
import static
    java.time.temporal.TemporalAdjusters.nextOrSame;
```

Let's go over the bolded lines in the test class again in detail.

I create the start date of the first trip using `from = LocalDate.of(...)`. Note that no new is used in this. The `of` method creates the object for me (more precisely, a private method `create` called by `of` does that) and returns it. We will learn more about this "factory" approach in the chapters on the Abstract Factory and the Factory Method. As parameters for the call, I use year, month, and day each separately. For the month I use the standard enumeration `Month` with the English month names, in this case `Month.NOVEMBER`. The first trip therefore starts on 11/4/2023.

However, the customer wants to be back on the 15th of the same month, so I simply calculate an appropriate end date using `from.withDayOfMonth(15)`. In doing so, the Date and Time API now creates a new LocalDate with the day changed to the 15th.

For the second and third journey I use the self-written method `toDate`, which determines a corresponding LocalDate from a text. For this I use the `parse` method of the LocalDate and give it – as already explained in the class `Trip` – also a DateTimeFormatter. This can be used in both directions – for parsing as well as for formatting. Since the parser can throw an exception if it can't do anything with the text, there must be a corresponding try-catch block here. For the case of the exception, I return `null`. You should not be tempted here to set the current date, for example. This may cause major problems down the line and is hard to reproduce.

The duration of the second trip is a tricky thing. The client wants to be back on "the following Tuesday". Instead of flipping through the calendar myself now, I can elegantly solve this with the command `with(nextOrSame(DayOfWeek.TUESDAY))`: Adjust the start date to "next or same day of week Tuesday" and return it to me as the new date. For the days of the week, there is also an enumeration that simply saves me from having to ask which day of the week started the index (was Monday now the 0 or the 1?).

The third trip should last exactly two weeks. This can also be easily solved using `plusWeeks`. This command category also includes plusDays, plusMonths and plusYears.

In the Travel class and in the Test class you will find commented out alternative lines of code for the DateTimeFormatter. Just have a look at the comments in the Travel class on your own.

After this excursion into the possibilities of the Date and Time API, now back to the actual topic: What you should note in the analysis is that the travel agency calls methods of the tour operator directly. But that's about to change!

9.1.2 Other Suppliers Appearing

The travel business is booming – the travel agency has yet to open a branch. I have combined both travel agency and branch under the interface provider. The interface prescribes the method `bookTrip()`, which you already know from the last version. The sample project Travel_2 simulates this situation.

Fig. 9.1 Class diagram of the
sample project Travel_2

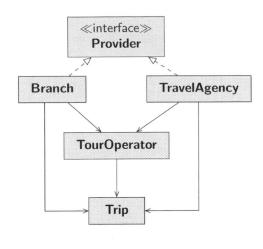

```
public interface Provider {
    void bookTrip(String destination, LocalDate from,
                                       LocalDate to);

}
```

Otherwise, the code of the classes has not changed. How are the classes used? In the example code of the test class, you will find the following procedure: You create a tour operator. You pass the instance to the constructor of a provider. To book a trip, you call the provider's method `bookTrip()` – nothing has changed since the previous version. Figure 9.1 shows the class diagram of this project version.

However, I used a few more date manipulation options when compiling the travel dates to show you more possibilities of the Date and Time API.

If you analyze the project Travel_2, you notice that the code of the classes `Branch` and `TravelAgency` is almost identical. Redundant code is always an indication of an inappropriate program design. Above all, redundant code is a source of errors that should not be underestimated. It is therefore necessary to eliminate duplicate code.

How would you proceed if you have many equal factors in mathematics, for example, $5 * 3 + 5 * 2 + 5 * 9$? You factor out the same factor in front of the bracket: $5 * (3 + 2 + 9)$. You do exactly the same with the redundant program code at the providers.

9.1.3   Encapsulating a Command

In the sample project Travel_3, you now pull the same program code in front of the parenthesis by introducing the class `TripCommand,` which lies between the suppliers and the tour operator. This class solely defines the command that is executed to book a trip. When it is created, an instance of a tour operator is passed to the constructor and its reference is stored in a data field. The `book()` method will be supplied with the same arguments that were passed to the `bookTrip()` method in the previous project.

```
public class TripCommand {
    private final TourOperator operator;
    public TripCommand(TourOperator operator) {
        this.operator = operator;
    }
    public void book(String destination, LocalDate from,
                                         LocalDate to) {
        Trip trip = new Trip(destination, from, to);
        organizer.conduct(travel);
    }
}
```

The providers – I'm only showing the travel agency here – have now become quite slim. An instance of the class `TripCommand` is passed to their constructor, whose reference is stored in a data field. The method `bookTrip()` now accesses the instance of the class `TripCommand` instead of a travel agent itself.

```
public class TravelAgency implements Provider {
    private final TripCommand tripCommand;
    TravelAgency(TripCommand tripCommand) {
        this.tripCommand = tripCommand;
    }
    @Override
    public void bookTrip(String destination,
                      LocalDate from, LocalDate to) {
        tripCommand.book(destination, from, to);
    }
}
```

The changes that have been added in this program version are shown in Fig. 9.2.

But what are the changes in the usage of the classes? In the main method of the test class, which you can find in the sample project Travel_3, the following procedure is provided: First, two objects of type `TourOperator` are created. These objects are passed to the constructors of two instances of the class `TripCommand`. Finally, the TripCommand instances are passed to the constructors of the providers as arguments. It is irrelevant to the provider which tour operator is working in the background. It only ever calls the `book()` method of its TripCommand instance.

What is gained by this approach? At first, it looks like this solution is quite cumbersome – after all, an additional class is needed. But in fact, several things happen: First, you have eliminated duplicate code as much as possible. This means you can easily add more travel providers. You can also pass the same command to different providers. In addition, the suppliers are now as decoupled from the travel providers as you are from the boss of your company with his statistics.

Swapping out a command into its own class is the core of the Command Pattern.

Fig. 9.2 Class diagram of the
sample project Travel_3

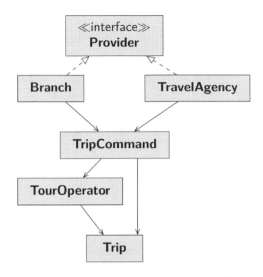

The Command Pattern recognizes several terms, which I will present more formally to conclude the introduction. There is the *caller* or *invoker*; this is the head of the company requesting a statistic, but this is also a provider selling a trip. The invoker makes use of a *command*; that's an instance of the class `TripCommand`, for example; but a command object is also your department head, who passes on the boss's requests to you. And finally, there are those who execute the command, these are the *receivers* – for example, the operators that actually carry out the trips.

9.2   Command in the Class Library

In this chapter I would like to give you two examples that show the use of the Command Pattern in the Java class library.

9.2.1   Example 1: Concurrency

If you want to implement concurrency in a program, create an object of type `Runnable`. The `Runnable` interface requires you to override the `run()` method. This method will contain the code that you want to execute concurrently. You can implement the execution of the command in two ways: Either the `Runnable` object executes the code itself, or it delegates the execution to another object. In our example, the travel agency object has delegated the command to execute a trip to the tour operator. However, it is not mandatory to have the recipient execute the command. It would also be conceivable to have the entire business logic, or at least a large part of it, executed by the command.

This would look like this, for example:

```
Runnable runnableDemo = new Runnable() {
    @Override
    public void run() {
        // ... concurrent code
    }
};
```

You then create an instance of the Thread class and pass an instance of that class to the constructor:

```
Thread threadDemo = new Thread(runnableDemo);
```

And finally, you call the `start()` method on the Thread instance, which results in the code of a Runnable type class being executed. As an Invoker, the Thread class is as loosely coupled to the Receiver as travel providers are to tour operators.

```
threadDemo.start();
```

> While it is obvious, please note that the `Runnable` does not define any behavior of the `Thread` class. The interface `Runnable` and the prescribed method `run()` are only created so that an object can execute a command of a different object, of whose definition it has no knowledge. If I may formulate the principle casually: The socket supplies power at a defined interface – whether a lamp, a computer or a washing machine is operated with it, it is quite indifferent. None of the devices mentioned defines any behavior of the socket.

9.2.2 Example 2: Event Handling

You are programming a GUI. On the GUI there should be a button that can be activated by the user. You pass an `ActionListener` to the button that contains the code to be executed when the button is activated. An object of type `ActionListener` must override the `actionPerformed()` method. When the button is activated, this method is called. To demonstrate the procedure, first create the button:

```
JButton btnExample = new Jbutton("Non-Sense");
```

Then follows an anonymous class for the code to be executed in the action:

```
ActionListener actionListener = new ActionListener() {
    @Override
    public void actionPerformed(ActionEvent e) {
        // ... something
    }
};
```

And finally, pass the Command object, the ActionListener, to this button:

```
btnExample.addActionListener(actionListener);
```

The whole thing also works much shorter and clearer with the lambda expressions added in Java 8, but does the same thing:

```
JButton btnExample = new JButton("Non-Sense");
btnExample.addActionListener((ActionEvent e) -> {
    // … something
}
```

Did you notice that this code is structurally quite similar to concurrency example from before? The logic is indeed the same: you need an object of a certain type to whose previously defined interface (run() in one case, actionPerformed() in the other) another object can send messages. Once the invoker has called the defined method of the command object, the work is done for it. The programmer has defined what should happen when the Invoker has become active. But the Invoker has no knowledge of how it happens – and that's exactly the knowledge it doesn't need to have, and shouldn't have.

9.3   Reusing Command Objects

The classes JButton and JMenuItem have the same superclass AbstractButton. So, you can reuse the ActionListener from the previous section and add it to the MenuItem in the main menu of your interface at the same time:

```
JMenuItem mtmExample = new JMenuItem("Non-Sense");
mtmExample.addActionListener(actionListener);
```

In the next paragraph, you take it a step further.

9.3.1   The "Action" Interface

The Action interface enhances the ActionListener interface. You can pass both Action and ActionListener to a caller as a command. The binding between the caller and the command object is much tighter for an object of type `Action`. Among other things, the `Action` interface provides the `setEnabled()` method, which determines whether the Action object is enabled or disabled. You can also use an action object to specify the text and icon of the caller.

> Remember what was said about the Template Method Pattern? In that context, I introduced you to the `AbstractListModel` class as a template-like implementation of the `ListModel`. The `AbstractListModel` class overrides all methods for which a default behavior can be reasonably implemented. The methods that are context-dependent, for example to describe the database, are delegated to subclasses. Exactly the same thing takes place here. The interface Action specifies the algorithm and the class `AbstractAction` partially implements it. The logic of how to change the state is already implemented; if you change the enabled state of the Action object, the state of the Invoker is also changed. This behavior should make sense in most cases; however, you can override it. In any case, the actionPerformed() method defies standard behavior, and you must override it.

9.3.2   Use of the "Action" Interface

I would like to demonstrate the reusability of commands with the following example. Take a look at the Action sample project. In it, two buttons and two menu items are created. The same action object – a command object – is passed to each button and menu item, i.e. to two different callers.

First, you create a button and a menu item:

```
var mnDisable = new JMenuItem();
var btnDisable = new JButton();
```

These are added to a GUI. A Command object, an object of type `Action`, is also created. The constructor of the class takes a string containing the display text of the caller. The only method that needs to be overridden is the `actionPerformed()` method. When triggered, it disables the object. The default implementation of the `AbstractAction` class is to disable the invokers as well.

```
AbstractAction actDisable = new AbstractAction("Disable") {
    @Override
    public void actionPerformed(ActionEvent evt) {
        this.setEnabled(false);
    }
};
```

Fig. 9.3 Same labels and
same actions

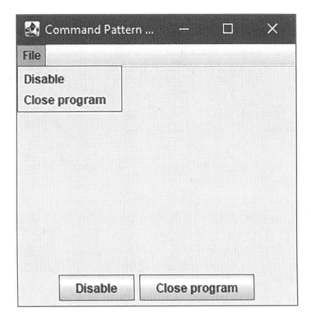

Both button and menu item are supplied with the same command object.

```
btnDisable.setAction(actDisable);
mnDisable.setAction(actDisable);
```

The text you passed to the constructor is used as the display text by both components.
If you click either the button or the menu item, both button and menu item are disabled.
Figure 9.3 shows you what the GUI looks like.

9.4   Undo and Redo of Commands

In this section I describe one last aspect of the Command Pattern. Commands can be
undone and redone. You will find two examples of this. The first example is fairly simple.
The second is a bit more extensive; I will only present the source code in broad strokes – I
want to give you something to tinker with for long winter evenings with this example.

9.4.1   A Simple Example

The example project RadioCommand shows how a radio (the older ones among us may
remember) can be operated with the Command Pattern. Besides the frequency adjustment,
which I'll leave out here, there are four very simple commands: turn on, turn off, turn up
and turn down. All commands implement the interface Command, which specifies two

methods. The `execute()` method executes the command, the `undo()` method returns a command that must be executed to undo its own execute method.

```
public interface Command {
    void execute();
    Command undo();
}
```

I will explain the command for switching on the radio here as a representative of all other commands. An object of the type radio is passed to the constructor of the command. The command is executed on this object. So if the `execute()` method is called, the command turns the radio on. If the `undo()` method is called, the radio is turned off, so the turn on command returns a turn off command.

```
public class OnCommand implements Command {
    private final Radio radio;
    public OnCommand(Radio radio) {
        this.radio = radio;
    }
    @Override
    public void execute() {
        System.out.println("The radio will turn on.");
        radio.turnOn();
    }
    @Override
    public Command undo() {
        return new OffCommand(radio);
    }
}
```

The radio must now provide the appropriate methods so that the commands can be executed.

```
public class Radio {
    private int volume = 0;
    public void turnOn() {
        volume = 1;
        System.out.println(">Radio: I'm on now.");
    }
    public void turnOff() {
        volume = 0;
        System.out.println(">Radio: I'm off now.");
    }
    public void decreaseVolume() {
        if (volume >= 1) {
            volume--;
```

```
                    System.out.println(">Radio: I'm playing" +
                                        "softer: " + volume);

        }
    }
    public void increaseVolume() {
        volume++;
        System.out.println(">Radio: I'm playing louder: "
                                        + volume);

    }
}
```

The radio, in Command Pattern terminology, is the receiver that executes the commands. Invoker is a class Logbook to which the context sends the command call and the undo. The Invoker logs all command invocations. This allows the context to undo the last command in each case.

```
public class Logbook {
    private final List<Command> history =
                                new ArrayList<>();
    public void execute(Command command) {
        history.add(command);
        command.execute();
    }
    public void undo() {
        int size = history.size();
        if (size > 0) {
            Command command = history.remove(size - 1);
            Command undoCommand = command.undo();
            System.out.println("\tundo: " + undoCommand);
            undoCommand.execute();
        }

    }
}
```

The test class creates an object of the type Radio. In addition, the commands are created and parameterized with the radio. The commands are then passed to the logbook and executed.

```
Radio radio = new Radio();
var onCommand = new onCommand(radio);
var offCommand = new offCommand(radio);
var softerCommand = new SofterCommand(radio);
var louderCommand = new LouderCommand(radio);
var logbook = new Logbook();
logbook.execute(onCommand);
// … abridged
log.undo();
```

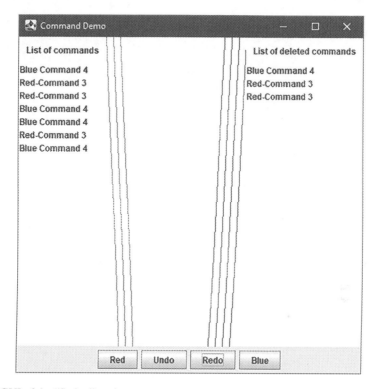

Fig. 9.4   GUI of the "Swing" project

Let's tackle a bigger swing example in the next section!

9.4.2   A More Extensive Example

The Swing sample project demonstrates the undo and redo functionality. On the GUI of the application you will find four buttons. One button is labeled Red and one is labeled Blue. When you click one of these buttons, red or blue lines are painted on the canvas. The last command executed is appended to the end of the list on the left side. If you click the undo button, the last executed command is undone – deleted, that is. However, it is not actually deleted, but written to the list of commands to be restored on the right. If you click redo, the command is restored, which is equivalent to calling it again. If you select a command in the list on the left and click undo, the selected command is deleted. Likewise, if you highlight a command from the right-hand list and click redo, that exact command is restored. In Fig. 9.4, you can see what the GUI will look like. I have drawn a few lines and deleted them again.

The idea for this project goes back to James W. Cooper (Cooper, James William (2000): Java design patterns. A tutorial. Reading, Mass.: Addison-Wesley. ISBN 0201485397.).

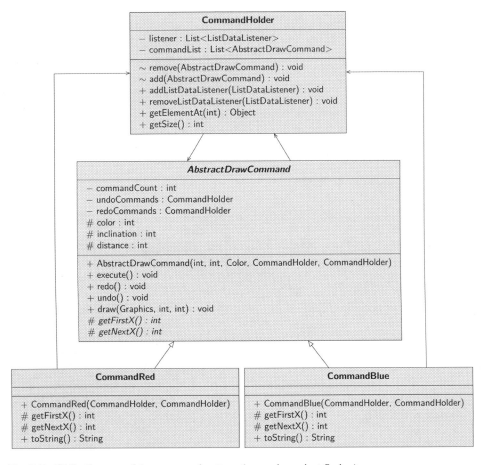

Fig. 9.5 UML diagram of the command pattern (example project Swing)

9.4.3   Discussion of the Source Code

I would like to leave the source text essentially to you for your own research. I will therefore only present the essential key points to you. The class diagram of the project can then
be found in Fig. 9.5.

9.4.3.1 The Classes Involved

There are two commands, the CommandBlue and the CommandRed. The Commands
have partially the same code, which is outsourced to an abstract superclass
AbstractDrawCommand. And finally, you will find the CommandHolder class,
where the commands are stored in the order they are processed. The invoker is the GUI.

9.4.3.2 Task of the GUI

The GUI class creates the components: a JPanel as a canvas on which the lines are painted, two JList instances that display the executed and the deleted commands. And finally, on the GUI you will find four buttons, instances of the JButton class. The CommandHolder implements the ListModel interface, so it can be used as a model for the lists. The GUI class creates two CommandHolder instances, one for the undo list and one for the redo list, and passes both to the constructors of the CommandRed and CommandBlue commands.

```
private final CommandHolder undoCommands =
                                new CommandHolder();
private final CommandHolder redoCommands =
                                new CommandHolder();
private AbstractDrawCommand cmdRed =
        new CommandRed(undoCommands, redoCommands);
private AbstractDrawCommand cmdBlue =
        new CommandBlue(undoCommands, redoCommands);
```

When the btnRed button is activated, the execute() method of the CommandRed class instance is called. This draws a red line on the canvas – the canvas object – and causes it to redraw itself.

```
btnRed.addActionListener((ActionEvent evt) -> {
    cmdRed.execute();
    canvas.repaint();
});
```

The listener for the btnBlue button looks likewise. Before I go into the listeners for undo and redo, I would like to take a closer look at the command classes.

9.4.3.3 Operation of the Command Classes

The CommandRed and CommandBlue classes define two different commands: One command draws a red line that slopes toward one direction, and the other command draws a blue line that slopes toward the other direction. In doing so, each command must perform two tasks: It must first set the parameters for the lines, and it must also be able to draw its lines on the canvas as many times as it is called. The parameters of the line, i.e. color, distance and slope, are stored in the subclasses. The superclass holds in a non-static data field the information about how many times the command has been called.

If the execute method is now called, the counter is first incremented. Then a reference to the command is passed to the CommandHolder, which stores all commands in the order they are called. When the lines are to be drawn, the canvas passes a reference to its Graphics instance, the pen, to the command and causes it to draw as many lines as it has been called.

9.4.3.4 Undo and Redo

To the right and left of the canvas you see two lists in which the commands are stored one after the other. You can select any command object and call the undo command on it. The logic of undo is defined in the command itself. The command decrements its counter, clears itself from the undo list, and writes itself to the redo list – admittedly, unlike the tasks of real projects, this logic is very simple. When you initiate a redo, the command is deleted from the redo list and then executed again, i.e. the execute method is called.

9.4.4   Undo and Redo Considered in Principle

In both examples, you have perfect undo and redo functionality. The undo reverses the execution and the redo corresponds exactly to the original execute command. In reality, you will also encounter situations where an exact reversal is not possible at all. For example, if you bought chocolate in a supermarket and then ate it, you would certainly not be able to return it. However, it is also conceivable to encounter situations in which an order can only be partially reversed. Perhaps you bought a book. The retailer takes the book back, but does not refund your money, but gives you a voucher for it. This only partially restores the condition as it existed before. You are rid of the book, but you do not have your money back.

9.5   Command – The UML Diagram

The UML diagram for the command pattern comes from the Swing sample project. You can find it in Fig. 9.5.

9.6   Summary

Before I summarize the key points of the pattern, I want to draw your attention to one thing: its similarity to the Chain of Responsibility pattern. Both patterns decouple command invocation and command execution. In the Chain of Responsibility, the caller sends its command to a chain of possible recipients; however, it has no way of knowing whether or how the command will be processed. In the Command Pattern, there is a clearly defined command executor, the Receiver. It is loosely coupled with the invoker.

Go through the chapter again in key words:

- Commands are outsourced to their own classes: mnemonic: "factor out" the command in front of the brackets.
- The command pattern decouples invoker and receiver.
- A command class can execute the call itself or delegate it to an executing unit.

- Each command class can be parameterized with a different executing unit: for example, different tour operators.
- The Invoker sends messages to the Command object only; it does not need to know the Receiver.
- Invoker and command object exchange their messages via defined interfaces.
- A command object can be replaced at runtime.
- A command can be undone.
- An undone command can be restored.
- The Command Pattern allows you to keep a history.

9.7   Description of Purpose

The Gang of Four describes the purpose of the "Command" pattern as follows:

> Encapsulate a command as an object. This allows you to parameterize clients with different requests, queue objects, keep a log, and undo operations.

Strategy

10

The Strategy Pattern is a behavioral pattern. You will always fall back on it when you can solve a task with different strategies; the term strategy in this context is a synonym for "algorithm" or for "behavior". For example, you have a vacation photo and you want to save it in either jpg format or bmp format. You want to decide at runtime in which format to save the image. The Strategy Pattern solves the problem for you that you can implement one and the same task with different algorithms – to save a picture in different formats. You can easily add new algorithms – strategies.

10.1   A First Approach

To get into the subject, you will sort an array. There are very many sorting algorithms that have their advantages in different areas. In this chapter, I will introduce three algorithms: the SelectionSort, the MergeSort, and the QuickSort. Let's start with a very naive approach. You have a class in which all the algorithms are defined in different methods. You specify at runtime which algorithm you want to call. Depending on the input, the relevant method is called. You can find the source code in the example project BadApproach. I didn't implement the sorting algorithms themselves; what matters here is the structure of the application, not the implementation of sorting algorithms.

```
public class BadApproach {
    // … abridged
    BadApproach() {
        this.choose();
    }
}
```

Supplementary Information The online version contains supplementary material available at https://doi.org/10.1007/978-3-658-39829-3_10.

```
void choose() {
    var question = "How should the data be sorted?";
    Object return = JOptionPane.showInputDialog(null,
                        question, "selection sort");
    var response = (String) return;
    switch (response) {
        case "selection sort" ->
                            sortWithSelectionSort();
        case "merge sort" -> sortWithMergeSort();
        case "quick sort" -> sortWithQuickSort();
        default ->
            System.out.println("Unknown selection");
    }
}


private void sortWithSelectionSort() {
    // ... the Selection Sort Algorithm
}
private void sortWithMergeSort() {
    // ... the Merge Sort Algorithm
}
private void sortWithQuickSort() {
    // ... the Quick Sort Algorithm
}
}
```

Note that in the switch statement of the choose() method, I use the "arrow syntax" from the switch expressions we learned about in Sect. 5.7. This eliminates the need for a break in the switch statement. The code becomes shorter and easier to read. You can modify this approach by using an if statement instead of the switch statement. However, you still can't avoid making case distinctions. So, it's very messy to implement new algorithms. Also, you have all the algorithms defined in one class. Therefore, the already large class contains a lot of code that you may never use. You realize that the class source code is very inflexible; it is every maintenance programmer's nightmare. So, let's look at the Strategy Pattern, which fixes these drawbacks.

10.2   Strategy in Action – Sorting Algorithms

The principle of the Strategy Pattern is that you can encapsulate algorithms and make them interchangeable. How could this be done? Define three classes that define the three sorting algorithms. If these three classes are of the same data type, the context can interchange them as desired. Figure 10.1 shows the class diagram of the Sort sample project we will discuss in this section.

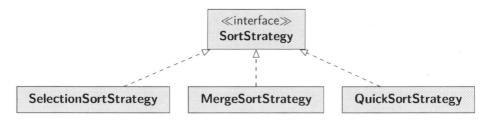

Fig. 10.1 Class diagram of the Sort sample project

10.2.1 The Common Interface

I have provided you with three classes with the sorting algorithms mentioned in the Sort sample project. They all implement the interface `SortStrategy`. The interface pre-scribes the method `sort()`. The int array to be sorted is passed to this method.

```
public interface SortStrategy {
    void sort(int[] numbers);
}
```

Let us now take a brief look at the logic of the sorting algorithms.

10.2.2 The Selection Sort

The Selection Sort searches an array element by element and finds the smallest value. This is written to the beginning of the still unsorted rest array and then this is sorted.

As an example, consider the sequence of numbers below:

In the first step, the zeroth position, i.e., the value 17, is assumed to be the smallest element. This zeroth position is compared with every other following position. In doing so, you notice that there is another position that contains the smallest value in the array, namely the 3 at the fourth position. The two positions swap their value. So, in the second step, you have the following array:

The smallest of all values is now at position zero. You continue at position 1. The value 45 is compared with all the following values, and you notice that the 17 at the fourth position is the smallest value. So, you swap positions 1 and 4. Now the array looks like this:

Now compare the second position, the value 21, with all the following positions and swap the 20 for the 21 and so on. You continue until the array is sorted altogether.

The code of the `SelectionSortStrategy` class encapsulates this algorithm:

```
public class SelectionSortStrategy
                        implements SortStrategy {
    @Override
```

```
public void sort(int[] numbers) {
    for (var i = 0; i < numbers.length - 1; i++)
        for (var j = i + 1; j < numbers.length; j++)
            if (numbers[i] > numbers[j]) {
                var temp = numbers[i];
                numbers[i] = numbers[j];
                numbers[j] = temp;
            }
}
```

Note that this example implementation always brings every smaller number to the front, not just the smallest. So, there are significantly more swap operations due than really necessary. There is certainly something that can be optimized. When searching for the smallest number, you can also first go through the entire field before actually swapping. This makes it possible to speed up this procedure by more than a factor of 3. I have already included the necessary adjustments (commented out) in the context. You will see that it is really only three lines: Re-cloning the number field, assigning the strategy, and executing it. You are now left with implementing the `Selection2SortStrategy` class based on a copy of the `SelectionSortStrategy` class. You will also find this copy already as a finished class – but still unchanged from the original. Have fun with this task.

10.2.3 The Merge Sort

The Merge Sort works on the principle of "divide and conquer". The array to be sorted is divided into two parts. Let's take the following unsorted array:

If you divide this array, you have two parts, the values 17, 45, 21, 99 on the left and 2, 20, 15, 12 on the right. If you divide these two halves again, you have the following four parts:

Obviously, it doesn't make sense to keep dividing the individual lists, so now sort them individually:

Now the sorted sublists are merged in pairs, making sure that the new lists are sorted correctly:

And these lists are now sorted and put together again to the final result.

The algorithm for this can be found in the `MergeSortStrategy` class.

10.2.4 The Quick Sort

The Quick Sort also works on the divide and conquer principle. Next to us the unsorted array from above:

This array is again divided into two parts. You calculate a value, a pivot element, so that about half of the values are smaller and the other half are larger than this value. The smaller values are written to the left list, and the larger values are written to the right list. For demonstration purposes, I'll take the value 40 as the pivot value here, so you have two lists:

"Purely by chance", the right-hand list contains only two values – so there's no point in dividing it again; sort it and you're done. However, consider the list on the left. You could take 18 as the pivot value. Put all values less than 18 on the left, and the others on the right. So you have:

The right list contains "purely by chance" again only two elements, which you sort. You may then merge them with the already sorted values:

You divide the "left list" again according to a given pivot element and so on.

> Both Merge Sort and Quick Sort work recursively. Quick Sort is fast if you manage to compute a pivot value at each step such that there's roughly an equal amount of numbers in each of the left and right lists. In my implementation of the QuickSortStrategy class, I simply pick the first element of the list. There is a lot of literature about sorting algorithms; so much that I don't want to give a preference here. My descriptions here are only very superficial, but also not really relevant to the topic of design patterns per se.

10.2.5 The Context

All sorting algorithms are of type SortStrategy. So you can rely on them to define the sort() method that triggers the sorting process. You declare a variable within the context that holds a reference to the desired strategy. An assignment then specifies the strategy to use. When you want to sort the array, you simply call the strategy's sort method. A snippet from the Context test class:

```
public static void testeLaufzeit() {
    var field size = 100000;
    var value range = 1000000;
    SortStrategy sortStrategy;
    var numbers_1 = createArray(fieldsize, range);
    var numbers_2 = numbers_1.clone();
    var numbers_3 = numbers_1.clone();
    System.out.println("Three arrays containing the " +
                "same unsorted numbers were created");
    sortStrategy = new SelectionSortStrategy();
```

```
        executeStrategy(sortStrategy, number_1);
        sortStrategy = new MergeSortStrategy();
        executeStrategy(sortStrategy, numbers_2);
        sortStrategy = new QuickSortStrategy();
        executeStrategy(sortStrategy, numbers_3);
    }


    private static void executeStrategy(SortStrategy s, int[] z) {
        Instant istart;
        Instant iend;
        Long idifference;
        System.out.println("Start " + s);
        istart = Instant.now();
        s.sort(z);
        iend = Instant.now();
        Duration elapsed = Duration.between(istart, iend);
        idifference = elapsed.toMillis();
        System.out.println("Duration " + s + ": " +
                        idifference + " milliseconds");
    }
```

In Sect. 9.1 we took a first look at the Date and Time API and looked at the LocalDate. Remember the note about it not containing any information about times? In the code above, you can see the counterpart to that: The `Instant` class. This class contains only time information and appropriate methods for calculations accordingly. You can see a simple application here: A look at the starting time of the sort. Then a look at the clock when everything has run, followed by the calculation of the duration (as a separate class `Duration` for the length of time intervals) and its output in milliseconds.

By the way, this benchmarking approach is very naive and only meaningful at first glance. It is enough for us here to make a rough comparison of the different algorithms. But the startup times of the Java Virtual Machine (and also under different environmental conditions) are not taken into account here. If you have serious performance measurements of Java programs in mind, you should look into the "Java Microbenchmarking Harness" (JMH) added in Java 12 with the JEP 230. However, a description of this small collection of tools goes too far here and misses the actual topic of the book.

10.2.6 Evaluation of the Approach and Possible Variations

What do you think of this approach? Surely one advantage jumps right out at you: The context is much clearer! But there are two more advantages:

The project can be extended to include any number of sorting algorithms. If you want to implement the Heap Sort, define a new class that implements the `SortStrategy` interface. The context can use your `HeapSortStrategy` immediately. For the Selection Sort, I suggested an enhancement option. You can also implement that as a variant of a SortStrategy and compare it directly against the Selection Sort I created.

In principle, the context does not even need to know how his problem is solved. But why only "in principle"? You offer a variety of algorithms that all solve the same problem. In order for a programmer to know when to choose which algorithm, you need to document very precisely under which conditions which algorithm is appropriate. In doing so, you will not be able to avoid going into implementation details in the documentation.

In the implementation above, you as the user have specified which strategy you want to use. However, it would also be conceivable that the program asks the strategies how well they can solve a certain task under certain conditions. An algorithm that sorts data in main memory very efficiently might fail if the data is stored in a file and cannot be fully loaded into main memory. So the context could ask the strategy classes, "How well do you solve the task under the condition that the data is stored on disk?" Each strategy class would return a score, say in the range zero to 100, and the context can then select the strategy that returns the highest score.

Another advantage of the Strategy Pattern is the reusability of the algorithms. Imagine you are programming an office suite. Within the spreadsheet, you need to be able to sort data. But you also want to sort data in word processing. After all, the algorithms are the same, so you can reuse them and, in the case of the spreadsheet, limit yourself to the functionality that is typical of the spreadsheet. For word processing, you program only the parts that are typical for word processing. You can reuse the sort algorithm.

In the example above, I have assumed that the data to be sorted is passed to the `sort()` method. This specification certainly makes sense in this constellation. However, think of a family of algorithms where one implementation takes a lot of parameters, but another implementation takes significantly fewer. Because of the common interface, the context would still have to pass all arguments – an avoidable overhead.

10.3   The Strategy Pattern in Practice

Where can the Strategy Pattern be found in the Java class library? In the area of GUI programming, you will find the Strategy Pattern in several places. For example, there are LayoutManagers or the "Look and Feel"; containers are provided with a certain strategy by default, which can, however, be exchanged by the user.

Instances of the `JPanel` class are needed to combine components of a GUI. By default, the FlowLayout is used for this. You can understand this, for example, by executing the following code once in the Java shell:

```
javax.swing.JPanel pnlLayoutTest =
                        new javax.swing.Jpanel();
java.awt.LayoutManager layout =
                        pnlLayoutTest.getLayout();
System.out.println(layout);
```

The   console   will   then   output   `java.awt.` `FlowLayout[hgap = 5,vgap = 5,align = center]`. You can replace the strategy `FlowLayout` by passing a new strategy with `pnlLayoutTest.` `setLayout(layoutManager)`. The variable `layoutManager` must be of type `LayoutManager`.

The `LayoutManger` interface prescribes five methods. The methods `addLayout-Component()` and `removeLayoutComponent()` are needed if you want to address the components of the Jpanel with a string, otherwise the method bodies may remain empty. The `preferredLayoutSize()` method calculates and returns the optimal size of the Jpanel, while `minimumLayoutSize()` calculates and returns the minimum size of the Jpanel. The positioning of the components is done by the `layoutContainer()` method. In this method, horizontal and vertical position as well as width and height are assigned to each component with `setBounds()`.

In the source code for this book, you will find the example project LayoutStrategy, in which I implemented the LayoutManager – the Strategy – `TwoColumnLayout`. When you place components on the Jpanel, they are displayed in two columns. If you drag the GUI to the width, the components in the right column are enlarged accordingly. Figure 10.2 shows you what a GUI you create with TwoColumnLayout might look like.

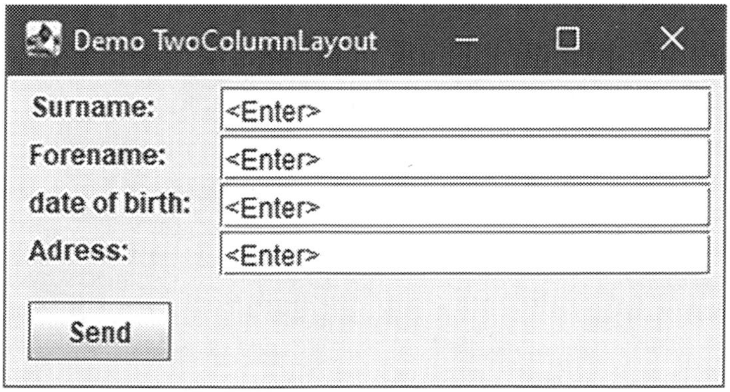

Fig. 10.2 Positioning components with the two-column layout

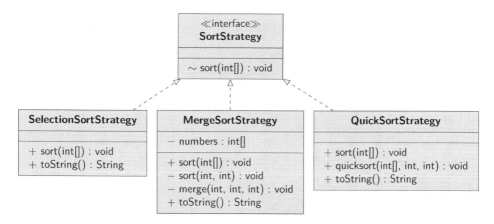

Fig. 10.3 UML diagram of the Strategy Pattern. (Example project Sort)

Please note that the implementation of the TwoColumnLayout is extremely simple – it is certainly far from perfect. I just want to demonstrate with this example how you can design and use your own strategy, your own LayoutManager.

10.4   Strategy – The UML Diagram

From the Sort example project, you can see the UML diagram in Fig. 10.3.

10.5   Distinction from Other Designs

You know the Command Pattern and the State Pattern, and in this chapter, you learned about the Strategy Pattern. All three patterns encapsulate behavior. In fact, the class diagrams of State and Strategy look pretty much the same. You can keep track of them by visualizing the different goals:

The Command Pattern is where you encapsulate commands. You need it to pass different action listeners to all buttons on your GUI. One command opens a file, another saves it. The Command Pattern does not describe the behavior of the calling object.

The Strategy Pattern encapsulates algorithms. Behavior of an object is implemented in different ways: There are many algorithms to compress files, to encrypt or to sort data. But you will only ever need one algorithm. So, out of the multitude of strategies, choose the one that solves your task most efficiently.

You use the state pattern to encapsulate state characteristics. The behavior of an object is based on its state. When an object has a certain state, it exhibits different behavior than when it is in a different state. Think of the open gate – the gate can be closed, but not locked. Only a closed gate can be locked.

10.6   Summary

Go through the chapter again in key words:

- The Strategy Pattern is used when you have multiple algorithms for a task.
- Each algorithm is defined in its own class.
- All Strategy classes implement the same interface.
- The context is programmed against the interface.
- At runtime, an algorithm is passed to the context.
- The context calls the solution strategy, the algorithm, without knowing which algorithm is behind it.
- The algorithm can be reused.

10.7   Description of Purpose

The Gang of Four describes the purpose of the "Strategy" pattern as follows:

> Define a family of algorithms, encapsulate each one, and make them interchangeable. The strategy pattern allows the algorithm to vary independently of clients using it.

Java knows different collections, for example the classes ArrayList and LinkedList. The data is stored differently internally in these classes. However, it is of interest for the client to be able to iterate over the data without knowing the internal structure. In this chapter, you will look at collections in detail and recreate the ArrayList and LinkedList classes. You will also create an interface that allows you to iterate over these classes.

11.1   Two Ways to Store Data

In the following sections, I will show you two ways to create collections.

11.1.1 Storing Data in an Array

The first collection you encountered at some point was most likely the array. In an array, you store any number of elements of a particular data type. With the declaration `int[]`
`numbers = new int[5]`, you create an array that can store five int numbers. You access the individual memory areas very efficiently. An array has the disadvantage that it cannot be enlarged. This is impractical if it turns out that more data is to be stored than it was originally intended.

The basis for our first collection will be an array. The elements in this array will be of the general type Object. Initially, five objects are to be referenced. To be able to store different data types in a type-safe way, create the class generically. In the sample project Collections_1 you will find the following code:

_____

Supplementary Information The online version contains supplementary material available at https://doi.org/10.1007/978-3-658-39829-3_11.

```
public class MyArray<E> {
    private int counter = 0;
    private Object[] elements = new Object[5];
}
```

To insert a new element, define the add() method. It is passed an argument of generic type. This element is stored at the next free position in the array. The counter data field stores this position. If five elements are already stored and a sixth is to be added, the database must be expanded. Since an array cannot be enlarged, the only way left is to redefine the array. In general: If the next free position is equal to the number of elements, the size of the array must be increased by a certain value. In the example, the array size is to be increased by another five elements.

```
public void add(E e) {
    if (counter == elements.length) {
        var tempArray = new Object[counter + 5];
        System.arraycopy(elements, 0, tempArray, 0, counter);
        elements = tempArray;
    }
    elements[counter] = e;
    counter++;
}
```

The client may want to inquire how many items are stored in the collection. For this, it is sufficient that you return the position of the next free item.

```
public int size() {
    return counter;
}
```

The collection only fulfills its purpose when the individual elements can be returned. To do this, you create the get() method, which expects an index as a parameter that describes the location of the element you are looking for in the database. Before the return, the stored value is cast to the generic type.

```
public E get(int index) {
    return (E) elements[index];
}
```

If you want to delete an element, the counter must first be decremented. The element is then deleted by moving the subsequent elements forward one place at a time. However, in order not to throw an "index out of bound" exception, checks on the range between 0 and counter are still required. And to avoid leaving the removed object at the end of the field in memory, it must be overwritten with null.

```
public void remove(int index) {
    if ((index <= counter) && (counter > 0)
                          && (index >= 0)) {
        if (index != counter)
            System.arraycopy(elements, index + 1,
                                    elements, index,
            elements.length - 1 - index);
        elements[counter--] = null;
    }
}
```

By the way, the collection you have just developed corresponds in its methodology to the ArrayList of the class library. It is optimal if you need to access individual elements via their index.

11.1.2 Storing Data in a Chain

You take a completely different approach if you store the individual elements not in an array, but in a chain. Each element knows its successor. It would also be conceivable that an element also knows a predecessor; I won't go into this possibility further – the project would only become unnecessarily extensive without changing the underlying principle.

Strings and any other objects you want to store in your list, I call elements. They are not stored in the collection, but in the instance of an inner class I call node. The Node class has two data fields that store the element you want to store and the subsequent node object. The collection can then restrict itself to referencing the first object (in the header data field).

```
public class MyList<E> {
    private int counter = 0;
    private Node<E> header = null;
    private class Node<E> {
        private final E element;
        private Node<E> nextNode;
        Node(E element, Node<E> next) {
            this.element = element;
            this.nextNode = next;
        }
    }
}
```

Data is inserted into the collection by creating a new node object. This object is referenced by the header variable and displaces the object previously stored as header. The nextNode field of the new header object references the previous header. And finally, the counter must be incremented. When you query the size of the collection, the counter is returned.

```
@SuppressWarnings("unchecked")
public void add(E element) {
    header = new Node(element, header);
    counter++;
}

public int size() {
    return counter;
}
```

To delete an element from the collection, go through the collection with a while loop and check whether the referenced element is the same as the element you are looking for. If so, pass the reference of the subsequent node object to the predecessor of the node object that references the element you are looking for. Then decrement the counter. The local variable `previous` references the predecessor of the node object whose element is currently being checked.

```
public boolean remove(E element) {
    Node<E> previous = null;
    var tempNode = header;
    while (tempNode != null) {
        if (equals(element, tempNode.ELEMENT)) {
            if (previous == null)
                header = tempNode.nextNode;
            else
                previous.nextNode = tempNode.nextNode;
            zaehler--;
            return true;
        }
        previous = tempNode;
        tempNode = previous.nextNode;
    }
    return false;
}
```

The `get()` method is intended to solve the same task as the get method of the `MyArray` class. However, because the database is not index-based, you cannot directly query the xth element in the collection. You must go through the entire collection until you find the xth element.

```
public E get(int index) {
    if (index < 0 || index >= counter)
        throw new NoSuchElementException(index + " Size "
                                              + counter);
    var tempNode = header;
    for (var i = 0; i < index; i++)
        tempNode = tempNode.nextNode;
    return tempNode.ELEMENT;
}
```

By the way, the collection you just developed is similar in methodology to the LinkedList of the class library.

11.2   The Task of an Iterator

When you create a collection, you will certainly want to iterate over all elements. A first approach could be the procedure of the test methods (of the respective main method), which you can find for both classes in the sample project Collections_1. Please analyze them and run them. In both test methods, iterate over the data collection with a for loop.

```
for (var i = 0; i < myList.size(); i++)
    System.out.println(myList.get(i));
```

You access each element of the collection with the get() method. With the MyArray class, this makes perfect sense. However, the performance of the MyList class falls far short of its capabilities when accessing its elements in an index-based manner. So it makes sense to outsource the algorithm of how to iterate over the collection to its own class, the iterator. You can think of the iterator as a bookmark that is pushed through a book page by page. The iterator knows the specific features of a collection and makes the best use of them.

You can design an iterator as an internal iterator or as an external iterator. Internal means that you pass the action of iterating to the iterator, which iterates "independently" over all objects. When you program an external iterator, you have it return the next item at a time and query whether there are any other items you can request; thus, it is the client's job to drive the iterator. You get the most flexibility with an external iterator. In what follows, I will only deal with external iterators. You will find an internal iterator in the composite pattern.

11.3   The Interface Iterator in Java

The class library knows the interface `Iterator`, which is an interface for all conceivable iterators. With `hasNext()` you let yourself return whether there are still further elements in the data collection. The `next()` method returns the next element in the collection. If the client wants to access an element that doesn't exist, throw a `NoSuchElementException`. And finally, `remove()` deletes the current element from the underlying data collection. According to the specification, the `remove()` method does not need to be implemented, it is allowed to throw an `UnsupportedOperation Exception`.

11.3.1 The Iterator of the Class MyArray

The simplest form of an iterator is returned by the `iterator()` method in the `MyArray` class. The iterator internally stores the position at which the bookmark is set. The `next()` method returns the next element in each case, and the `hasNext()` method returns `true` if there are more elements. Take a look at the sample project Collections_2 and there the class `MyArray`.

```
public class MyArray<E> {
    // … abridged
    public Iterator<E> iterator() {
        return new Iterator<E>() {
            private int position = -1;

            @Override
            public boolean hasNext() {
                return (position < size())
                        && elements[position + 1] != null;
            }

            @Override
            public E next() {
                position++;
                if (position >= size()
                        || elements[position] == null)
                    throw new NoSuchElementException("No more data");
                @SuppressWarnings("unchecked")
                var value = (E) elements[position];
                return value;
            }
```

```
                @Override
                public void remove() {
                    throw new
                            UnsupportedOperationException();
                }
            };
        }
        // ... abridged
    }
```

The next section shows how to use the iterator.

11.3.1.1 Test of the Iterator

You first create a collection of type `MyArray` in the main method and store some strings in it.

```
var myArray = new MyArray<>();
myArray.add("String 1");
// ... abridged
myArray.add("String 6");
```

After that, you have an iterator returned and query data in a while loop until there is no more data in the collection. To provoke the exception, you specifically retrieve one more element than is stored.

```
var iterator = myArray.iterator();
while (iterator.hasNext()) {
    String temp = iterator.next();
    System.out.println(temp);
}
// throws an exception
System.out.println(iterator.next());
```

Each string is now output on the console. Afterwards the exception is thrown.

11.3.1.2 Benefits and Variations of the Iterator

Iteration now becomes much easier, and since the client code doesn't change, the lists are interchangeable. You first let it give you an iterator and call the method `next()` as long as the method `hasNext()` returns a `true`. The examples are kept very simple, the method `iterator()` returns the instance of an anonymous class as the iterator. This iterator steps through the database one element at a time from front to back. This simplification should not obscure the fact that you, as a programmer, are free to define the iterator as you need. For example, the iterator could go through the array from back to front.

Alternatively, you could have an iterator that first copies and/or sorts the database before returning the individual elements. Also, if you build your own complex structures (tree structures, …), you can design a "standard" iterator for it according to your needs. Of course, you don't have to define the iterator as an anonymous class – you could also design a class outside the collection's namespace.

11.3.2 The Iterator of the Class MyList

The class `MyList` - also in the project Collections_2 – is internally structured differently. The individual elements are not stored in an array, but linked. What consequence does this have for the iterator? In contrast to `MyArray` no counter is stored as bookmark, but the current element. Initially the current element is set to the header of the list.

If you want to test whether a collection contains more elements, you must ask whether the current element of the iterator is non-null, in which case the `hasNext()` method may return `true`. The `next()` method returns the contents of the current element and advances the pointer to the next element one place.

```
public Iterator<E> iterator() {
    return new Iterator<E>() {
        private Node current = header;
        @Override
        public boolean hasNext() {
            return (current != null);
        }

        @Override
        public E next() {
            if (current == null)
                throw new NoSuchElementException("...");
            @SuppressWarnings("unchecked")
            var value = (E) current.element;
            current = current.nextNode;
            return value;
        }

        @Override
        public void remove() {
            throw new UnsupportedOperationException();
        }
    };
}
```

In the next section we will also test this iterator.

11.3.2.1 Test of the Iterator

To test the iterator, you create an instance of the `MyList` class and store various strings in it. You let it return its iterator and iterate over the complete collection. Of course, I also included one query too many in this test to provoke the exception to be thrown.

```
var myList = new MyList<>();
myList.add("String 1");
// ... abridged
myList.add("String 6");
var iterator = myList.iterator();
while (iterator.hasNext())
    System.out.println(iterator.next());
System.out.println(iterator.next());
```

Again, at first all strings are printed to the console; then an exception is thrown.

11.3.2.2 Benefits of the Iterator

The special features of the two collection classes are now taken into account without the client even noticing. You remember that with the Observer pattern, you saw that iterators are prone to problems resulting from concurrency. Since you can create multiple iterators, it's not at all unlikely that an element will be deleted, added, or replaced during iteration. You are then quickly faced with the situation that an iterator wants to access an element that no longer exists or that it cannot yet access a new element. The collection classes of the class library throw a `ConcurrentModificationException` in such cases.

11.4   The Iterable Interface

A while loop is related to the for loop. Instead of the while loop.

```
while (iterator.hasNext()) {
    // ... Action
}
```

you could also use a for loop:

```
for (var iterator = myList.iterator();
                    iterator.hasNext(); ; ) {
    // ... Action
}
```

Since Java 5, there is the for-each loop. Iterating becomes much easier:

```
for (var tempString : list)
    System.out.println(tempString);
```

How can you prepare your MyList and MyArray collections so that you can use them in a for-each loop? All you need to do is implement the Iterable interface. This interface dictates the iterator() method, whose return value is the collection's iterator. You can see this in the Collections_3 sample project – here using the MyArray class as an example:

```
public class MyArray<E> implements Iterable<E> {
    public Iterator<E> iterator() {
        // ... as before
    }
    // … abridged
}
```

Now you can use the MyArray class in an extended for loop:

```
var myArray = new MyArray<>();
myArray.add("String 1");
// … abridged
myArray.add("String 6");

for (var tempString : myArray)
    System.out.println(tempString);
```

This works accordingly for the MyList. Please have a look at it again independently.

Search the API documentation for the interface Iterable. A subinterface of this is the Collection interface. This interface is implemented by all common collections such as List and Set and by many others. Therefore, you can trust that all collections define the iterator() method, which returns an iterator object.

With a map, the issue is a bit more complicated. As an example, consider a HashMap that consists of three collections: a KeySet for the keys, a Collection for the values, and an EntrySet for the connection between the two collections. No one can know in advance whether the user will want to iterate over the keys or the values; therefore, the HashMap cannot design a "default" iterator.

The for-each loop is a very useful language construct for the programmer. However, although a lot of work is done for the programmer, the compiler has relatively little work to do with it. It rewrites the for-each loop into a while loop before compiling it (code rewriting) and lets you give it the iterator. If you iterate over an array with the for-each loop, the loop is rewritten into a conventional for-next loop and then compiled.

You can see from this example how patterns have found their way into the class library. Not only the name, but also the realization of the pattern corresponds to the description of the GoF.

11.5 Iterator – The UML Diagram

From the example project Collections_3/MyList you can see the UML diagram in Fig. 11.1.

11.6 Summary

Go through the chapter again in key words:

- Collections can be structured internally in very different ways.
- Iterators are bookmarks that are moved from one element to the next.
- They allow you to iterate over the collection without knowledge of the internal structure.
- Internal iterators are responsible for the progress of the iterator itself.
- For external iterators, the client is responsible for advancing.
- An iterator, when following the Java specification, has three methods:
- remove() deletes an element from the collection – the method does not need to be overridden,
- hasNext() returns true if the collection has more elements,
- next() returns the next element in the collection; if there is no element, a NoSuchElementException is thrown.
- The ListIterator is an iterator specialized on lists and has some more methods that allow iteration in both directions.
- The iterator is returned by the iterator() method.
- The programmer can adapt the definition of a custom iterator to the structure of his collection as needed.

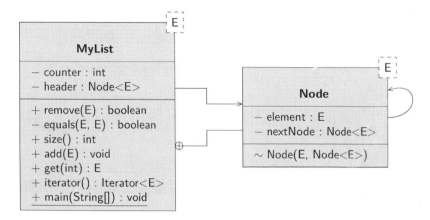

Fig. 11.1 UML diagram of the Iterator Pattern (sample project Collections_3/MyList)

- There can be multiple iterator classes and multiple iterator instances.
- While at least one iterator is active, the database must not be changed.
- If a collection implements the `Iterable` interface, you can iterate over it with the for-each loop.

11.7   Description of Purpose

The Gang of Four describes the purpose of the "Iterator" pattern as follows:

> Provides a way to sequentially access the elements of a composite object without exposing the underlying representation.

Composite

12

The Composite Pattern, which I will now introduce, belongs to the Structural Patterns. It describes how objects are put together to form larger meaningful units. A composite structure is great for displaying in a JTree. So, in this chapter I will also describe how to define your own data models for a JTree.

12.1 Principle of Composite

You have a structure that consists of several units. These units can optionally contain smaller units. You want to be able to call certain methods on all of these units without having to worry about whether or not the unit contains other units. What is meant by this?

If you keep a budget book, write down the individual items of your income and expenses. The income includes your salary from your main job. Maybe you also have a side job, then this is also written under the heading of income. To the expenses belongs certainly your rent or rates for an own real estate. In addition, you also have items that can be subdivided. Under the heading of food, there are various sub-categories: Lunch, Eating out with friends, etc. In these subcategories you have the individual items like "Pizzeria 16.00 €" or "Canteen 4.00 €". You can ask at the lowest level: "How much did the visit to the pizzeria cost?" But you can also add up by asking, "What did I pay in total for food?" And finally, at the top level, you can ask: "What did I take in and spend in total?"

Or think of a company that consists of different departments that are divided into several hierarchical levels; if you ask an employee there about the personnel costs, he will name his own salary. If you ask a department manager for his personnel costs, he will first determine the personnel costs of his subordinate employees, add his own salary and give

Supplementary Information The online version contains supplementary material available at https://doi.org/10.1007/978-3-658-39829-3_12.

you the total sum back. If you ask the owner of the company, he will return the total personnel costs of all departments in addition to his own.

Very practical: The file system of your computer returns the size of a folder as well as of a single file.

In short, the Composite Pattern helps you represent tree structures. Let's clarify some terms! Each item in a tree structure is a node. A node that has no child nodes is a leaf; for example, this is the single item "Pizzeria 16.00 €". A node that has subnodes is called a composite; this is, for example, the item "food". The node at the top of the tree (the company owner) is the root.

There are two different approaches to implement the composite pattern.

12.2   Implementation 1: Security

Leafs and composites must have different behavior; consequently, they must be defined in different classes. However, composites can store both other composites and leafs as nodes; therefore, composites and leafs must have a common interface.

In the sample project Budget_1 you will find a first draft. The class Node is the common interface for leaves and composites. It defines a data field that describes the revenue or spending item; this field is needed for both leaves and composites. And finally, the print() method is prescribed.

```
public abstract class Node {
    protected final String description;
    // … abridged
    public abstract void print(int indentation);
}
```

The class Leaf extends the class Node. It additionally defines a field in which it is stored whether the position is required or whether it is luxury. For revenue, this flag certainly doesn't matter. However, you will certainly think about whether an expense was necessary or not. It also defines a data field that stores the amount of the item. The print method takes an integer value that describes the number of indentations; tabs are inserted according to this number before the value of the item is printed. Items that are required are preceded by an exclamation mark; outputs that are not strictly required are not marked separately.

```
public class Leaf extends Node {
    private final boolean required;
    private double amount = 0.0;
    // … abridged
    @Override
    public void print(int indentation) {
        for (var i = 0; i < indentation; i++)
```

```
            System.out.print("\t");
        System.out.println(this);
    }


    @Override
    public String toString() {
        var prefix = required ? "(!) " : "( ) ";
        var tempAmount =
        NumberFormat.getCurrencyInstance().format(amount);
        return prefix + description + ": " + tempAmount;
    }

}
```

The Composite class defines a list in which the child nodes are stored and the required access methods. This includes, for example, a method that returns the number of child nodes and a method that returns the child at a specified position. The print method is overridden in such a way that, according to the indentation, first the value of the toString method is output and then recursively all child nodes.

```
public class Composite extends Node {
    private final List<node> kinder = new ArrayList<>();
    // ... abridged
    public node getKind(int index) {
        return children.get(index);
    }


    public int getNumberofChildNodes() {
        return kinder.size();
    }


    @Override
    public void print(int indentation) {
        for (var i = 0; i < indentation; i++)
            System.out.print("\t");
        System.out.println(this);
        children.forEach((node) -> {
            node.print(indentation + 1);
        });
    }


    @Override
    public String toString() {
        return description;
    }

}
```

The client creates variables for the root and various expense categories, for example, income and expenses. Among the expenses, there is the category books, where two books are set. I am only printing the listing in abbreviated form.

```
final var root = new Composite("Budget book");
final var january = new Composite("January");
final var income = new Composite("Income");
final var expenses = new Composite("Expenses");
final var books = new Composite("Books");
january.add(income);
january.add(expenses);
root.add(january);
revenue.add(new Leaf("Main job", 1900.00, true));
revenue.add(new Leaf("Side job", 200.00, true));
expenses.add(books);
expenses.add(new Leaf("rent", -600.00, true));
books.add(new Leaf("Design Patterns", -29.9, true));
books.add(new Leaf("trashy novel", -9.99, false));
root.print(0);
System.out.println("Only the expenses: ");
outputs.print(0);
```

The client can now restrict itself to calling `root.print(0)`. Then the income and expenses for January are clearly output to the console:

```
Budget book
    January
        Income
            (!) Main job: 1.900,00 €
            (!) Side job: 200,00 €
        Expenses
            Insurances
                (!) Car: -50,00 €
                (!) ADB: -100,00 €
            Books
                (!) Design Patterns: -29,90 €
                ( ) Trashy novel: -9,99 €
            (!) Rent: -600,00 €
```

It is possible to have only the January expenses printed; to do this, call the print command on the expenses composite: `expenses.print(0)`. This solution works perfectly. However, it proves to be too inflexible in certain places – and you will see and correct this in the following section.

12.3   Implementation 2: Transparency

The client code violates the principle that one should program against interfaces and not against implementations: `final composite root = new composite("Budget book")`. This was unavoidable because the interface node declares only those methods that are actually needed by both leaves and composites. This "lowest common denominator" does not include `add()`. And this is where a huge problem starts to mature – the program from the previous approach could only be made to work with a little "trick". The print method calls itself recursively on all objects. However, if you wanted to access the list with an external iterator or have a single item returned, you would have to work with numerous comparisons (`instanceof composites`) and downcasts. However, downcasts are the programmer's crowbar; if possible, they should be avoided.

To demonstrate the problem, I want to print the list to the console again, but this time using an external iterator. I delete the print method in the sample project Budget_2. Now the client itself has to take care of the iteration. So, the most important change in this project is in the test routine area. First, create some income and expenses as in the previous example. Then, within the test class, call a newly defined print method. In this method, first the required tabs are printed and then the object itself. It then checks whether the item to be printed is a composite. If so, the node object is cast to a composite object. And finally, ask the composite for the number of its child nodes and output each child node to the console.

```
public static void main(String[] args) {
    final var root = new Composite("Budget book");
    final var january = new Composite("January");
    final var february = new Composite("February");
    // ... abridged
    print(root, 0);
}

private static void print(node node, int indentation) {
    for (var i = 0; i < indentation; i++)
        System.out.print("\t");
    System.out.println(node);

    if (node instanceof Composite composite) {
    var numberChildren = composite.getNumberChildNodes();
        for (var j = 0; j < numberChildren; j++) {
            var childNode = composite.getChild(j);
            print(childNode, indentation + 1);
        }
    }
}
```

Do you think the example is a little contrived? Not at all! You're about to see an implementation of the TreeModel interface – where it would be difficult to implement with an internal driver.

Do you notice anything about the instanceof command? Here I used a preview feature newly added in Java 14: Pattern Matching for instanceof, found under the Java Enhancement Proposal JEP 305. You can only use it if you enable preview features in Java 14 or 15 (JEP 375). This is done by the additional compiler option –enable-preview, which you have to add in the compiling project settings of NetBeans or just in the command line call of the Java compiler javac. In Java 16 (JEP 394) this feature is final. But what does this pattern matching actually do?

We get the reference to the node, which can be either a leaf or a composite. If we want to act differently depending on the subclass, we check with instanceof that it belongs to the class Composite and then cast the reference "down" to that class. Previously, in Java, this was two steps: first the check, then the casting. Now it works in a single step. You can see in the code that after the previously used `if (node instanceof Composite)`, there is now another `composite`. This automatically introduces this variable and casts the node to the class composite. The additional line `Composite    composite = (Composite) node;` is thus omitted completely.

Such checks are used very frequently in Java. Pattern matching simplifies them in both programming effort and readability.

The Budget_3 sample project shows how you establish generality. You define the following two methods in the class Node:

```
public abstract class Node {
    protected final String description;

    public Node(String description) {
        this.description = description;
    }

    public node getChild(int index) {
        throw new RuntimeException("No child nodes");
    }

    public int getNumberChildNodes() {
        return 0;
    }
}
```

The class Composite overrides these methods as before. What is new in this realization is that a leaf can now also specify how many children it has – namely none. If a client nevertheless tries to call a child at a specific index, a RuntimeException flies up in its face.

So the client has to make sure that the node to be printed actually has child nodes. The print method in the test class is formulated more generally.

```java
private static void print(node node, int indentation) {
    for (var i = 0; i < indentation; i++)
        System.out.print("\t");
    System.out.println(node);
    for (var j = 0; j < node.getNumberChildNodes(); j++) {
        var childNode = node.getChild(j);
        print(childNode, indentation + 1);
    }
}
```

A leaf object returns 0 as the number of children. The condition of the for loop is therefore not fulfilled, a recursive call of the print method does not take place.

12.4   Consideration of the Two Approaches

The first approach relies on a narrow interface. A leaf can only do what it absolutely must be able to do. Therefore, you will find management methods for the list of child nodes only for composites. Security is the primary concern with this approach. The client has to compare and cast, but it has the guarantee that the methods it calls are executed in a way that makes sense. The AWT, for example, is based on this principle. There is the abstract class Component. In it, methods are defined that use both leaves and composites: Register listeners, change visibility, etc. The various controls (Button, Label, CheckBox, etc.) are derived from Component. In addition, the Container class inherits from Component. It defines methods to manage components as child nodes. Only those classes inherit from Container that must be able to accommodate other components, i.e. Frame and Panel.

The alternative is to use a broad interface: leaves and composites can in principle do anything. Swing is built on this approach. There is the class JComponent, which inherits from Container. All controls inherit from JComponent, including JLabel, JButton, etc. So they all have the method add(), to which you can pass a Component object. Subsequently, it is possible to store a JPanel in a JLabel, which you can check with the following code, e.g. in the Java Shell of NetBeans.

```java
javax.swing.JPanel pnlTest = new javax.swing.JPanel();
javax.swing.JLabel lblTest = new javax.swing.JLabel();
lblTest.add(pnlTest);
int count = lblTest.getComponentCount();
System.out.println("Number of children in JLabel: " + count);
System.out.println("Parent of JPanel: " + pnlTest.getParent());
```

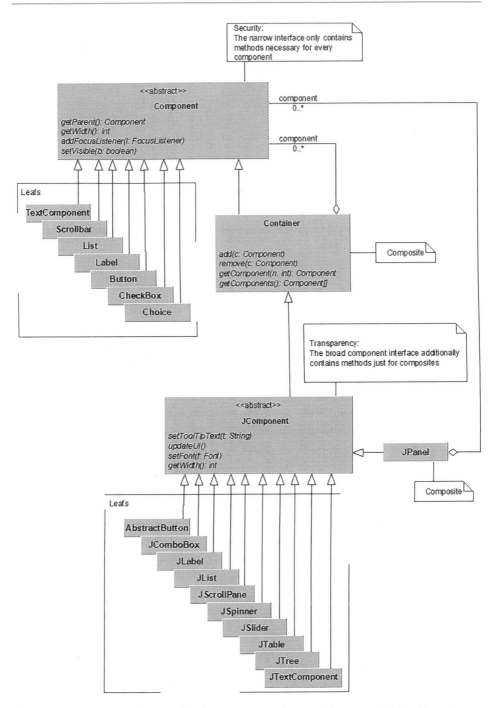

Fig. 12.1 Class diagram AWT and Swing components, borrowed from www.PhilippHauer.de

On the console – shortened – is output:

```
Number of children in JLabel: 1
Parent of the JPanel: javax.swing.JLabel...
```

The interaction of AWT and Swing is shown in Fig. 12.1. I borrowed the diagram from Philipp Hauer. Philipp deals with design patterns, among other things, on his site www. PhilippHauer.de. It is definitely worth visiting his site.

An interface that is too broad is problematic. Take project Budget_3 as a basis. There, you define methods that are specific to a composite in the interface in order to obtain generality. In the test class, you query the number of child nodes and have a child node returned. I'm sure that's not a problem. But it gets tricky when you need to include the addChild() method in the interface. How does the Leaf class implement this method? What does the default implementation look like? One solution might be to have the leaf simply do nothing add(){}. But an empty implementation is not without its problems – the client will certainly want to know that its job cannot be executed. So the client can't avoid making a case distinction up front. Although this approach can be problematic, it is favored in practice, and the GoF also advocates it.

12.5   Going One Step Further

Let's expand the project now.

12.5.1 Creating a Cache

It would be a useful thing if the categories could sum up the individual child items, and this is realized with the example project Budget_4. To do this, you create a cache in the composites that stores the sum of the child nodes. In the interface, you declare an abstract method calculateCache(), which must be overridden by leaves in the same way as by composites. Also, both leaves and composites should be able to return the internally stored value.

```
public abstract class Node {
    // … abridged
    abstract double getValue();
    public abstract void calculateCache();
}
```

The definition in the Leaf class is quite simple – a leaf does not need to create a cache, so the method can be overridden empty. However, a leaf must be able to name the amount stored:

```java
public class Leaf extends Node {
    // ... abridged
    private double amount = 0.0;

    @Override
    public void calculateCache() {
    }

    @Override
    double getValue() {
        return amount;
    }
}
```

The composite class returns the cache when the getValue() method is called. The calculateCache() method is defined so that the cache is first cleared. Then, all children are recursively instructed to calculate their cache. Finally, the stored amount is queried from all children and added to their own cache.

```java
public class Composite extends Node {
    // ... abridged
    private double cache = 0.0;

    @Override
    public void calculateCache() {
        cache = 0;
        for (var node : children) {
            node.calculateCache();
            cache += node.getValue();
        }
    }

    @Override
    double getValue() {
        return cache;
    }

    @Override
    public String toString() {
        var tempCache =
```

```
            NumberFormat.getCurrencyInstance().format(cache);
            return description + " (Sum: " + tempCache + ")";
        }
    }
```

The test of the program differs only minimally from the previous examples. The tree is constructed as before. Then the root node receives the instruction to calculate its cache.

```
final var root = new Composite("Budget book");
// ... abridged
books.add(new sheet("Design Patterns", -29.9, true));
books.add(new sheet("Trashy novel", -9.99, false));
ROOT.calculateCache();
print(ROOT, 0);
```

When you start the program, you get the subtotals of the categories.

```
Budget book (Sum: € 1,310.11)
    January (Sum: € 1,310.11)
        Income (Sum: € 2,100.00)
            (+) Main job: 1,900.00 €
            (+) Side job: 200.00 €
        Expenses (Sum: -789.89 €)
            Insurances (Sum: -150.00 €)
                (+) Car: -50.00 €
                (+) ADB: -100.00 €
            Books (Sum: -€39.89)
                (+) Design Patterns: -€29.90
                (-) Trashy novel: -€9.99
            (+) Rent: -600.00 €
    February (Sum: €0.00)
```

Since the project is very manageable, it would certainly have been reasonable for the categories to recalculate the cache each time getValue() is called. However, a cache makes sense if the call of getValue() in the leaf causes high costs.

12.5.2 Referencing the Parent Components

In the following step, the structure is created as a doubly linked list – the parents know their children, but the children also know their parents. You probably know this from

Swing – you call the method getParent() on a component; the parent node is returned. In the Budget_5 example project, you maintain new income or expenses; the parent category is notified and can update its cache. In the Node class, add the Composite parent field with the appropriate access methods.

```
public abstract class Node {
     // … abridged

     private composite parent = null;


     protected void setParent(Composite parent) {
          this. Parent = parent;
     }

     protected Composite getParent() {
          return this.parent;
     }
}
```

The add() method of the Composite class is extended. A composite passes itself as parent to each newly added child node. If the new child to be added already has a parent, an exception is thrown – because the situation should not occur.

```
public class Composite extends Node {
     // … abridged

     public void add(node child) {
          children.add(child);
          var parent = kind.getParent();
          if (parent == null)
               kind.setParent(this);
          else
               throw new RuntimeException(child + " already has a parent:
               " + parent);
     }
}
```

The introduction of a reference to the parent node does not yet have an effect in this project version. The parent node is used in the sample project Budget_6 to recalculate the cache. If you insert a new leaf or change the value of a revenue or expense item, all affected composites pass this information on to the parent until the message reaches the root. The root node then recursively calls the calculateCache() method on all child nodes, as in the previous project.

You want only the composites to recalculate their caches that are affected. You introduce a flag in the Composite class that indicates whether the cache needs to be recalculated. When a new node is added to a composite, the cache is no longer valid. So add() causes its own cache and the parent node's cache to be recomputed. The same is true when a node is removed. If the calculateCache() method just recalculated the cache, it is certainly correct and the flag may be set to true. The newly added setCacheIs-Valid() method is interesting. If true is passed to it, the flag is corrected. If false is passed to it, the parent node is additionally instructed to mark the cache as invalid. If there is no parent – this only applies to the root node – the child nodes are instructed to recalculate their cache. However, these only recalculate the cache if the flag isValid is set to false.

```java
public class Composite extends Node {
    // … abridged
    private boolean cacheIsValid = false;

    public void add(node child) {
        children.add(child);
        var parent = child.getParent();
        if (parent == null)
            child.setParent(this);
        else
            throw   new   RuntimeException(child   +   "   already   has
            a parent: " + parent);
        this.setCacheIsValid(false);
    }

    public void remove(node child) {
        children.remove(child);
        child.setParent(null);
        this.setCacheIsValid(false);
    }

    void setCacheIsValid(boolean isValid) {
        this.cacheIsValid = isValid;
        if (!isValid) {
            var parent = this.getParent();
            if (parent == null)
                this.calculateCache();
            else
                if (this != parent)
                    parent.setCacheIsValid(isValid);
        }
    }
}
```

```
@Override
public void calculateCache() {
    if (!cacheIsValid) {
        cache = 0;
        for (var node : children) {
            node.calculateCache();
            cache += node.getValue();
        }
        this.setCacheIsValid(true);
    }
}
}
```

I take the same test routine as in the previous project. I can do it without `root.cal-culateCache()` now, because the structure calculates the intermediate values "auto-matically" when new positions are entered. To test the new functions in more detail, I add a retirement provision to the insurances, which costs 1000.00 €. I have the budget book output again and find that the figures are correct. I notice that the retirement provision is not monthly with 1000.00 €, but annually. So, I delete the insurance and have the budget book displayed again – the figures are correct again. I insert the retirement provision again, but this time at the same level as the months, i.e., directly below the root. And again, the correct values are output. The structure of the pattern and the calculation method allow a very easy to use automatic update.

```
final var root = new Composite("Budget book");
// … abridged
print(root, 0);
var retirement = new Leaf("Retirement provisions", -1000.00, true);
insurances.add(retirement);
print(root, 0);
insurance.remove(retirement);
print(root, 0);
root.add(retirement);
print(root, 0);
```

Did you think it was a bit awkward how I moved the retirement provisions? Me too – let's correct that in the next section.

12.5.3 Moving Nodes

The sample project Budget_7 deals with the question of how to move a node to another node. Since both leaves and composites must be moved, the method `changeParent()`

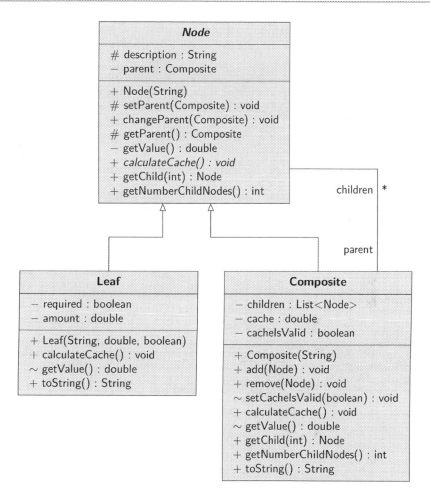

Fig. 12.2 UML diagram of the composite pattern. (Example project Budget_7)

is defined in the class Node, to which you pass a reference to the new parent node. The method returns the current parent and deletes itself there as the child node. With the new parent, the node enters itself as a child node. Since both add() and remove() cause the caches of the composites to be recalculated, the entire tree structure is up-to-date and correctly calculated again.

```
public void changeParent(Composite newParent) {
    var parent = this.getParent();
    parent.remove(this);
    newParent.add(this);
}
```

12.6   Composite – The UML Diagram

From the example project Budget_7 you will find the UML diagram in Fig. 12.2.

12.7   Summary

Go through the chapter again in key words:

- A composite represents hierarchical structures.
- The structures are formed from nodes (leaves and composites).
- The node that has no parent node is called the root.
- Nodes can be nested to any depth.
- Leaves and composites behave identically for the client.
- Leaves and composites inherit from a common interface.
- The width of the interface brings either security or transparency.
- An interface that is too broad will result in designs that are too general.
- Nodes can optionally hold a reference to their parent node.
- Composites can cache values of their child objects.

12.8   Description of Purpose

The Gang of Four describes the purpose of the "Composite" pattern as follows:

> Compose objects into tree structures to represent part-whole hierarchies. The composition pattern allows clients to treat both individual objects and compositions of objects consistently.

Flyweight

13

The Flyweight Pattern is a structural pattern; in order to understand it, the terms intrinsic and extrinsic state must be defined. Therefore, I will present two examples in this chapter. The first example clarifies the principle of the pattern, the second is closer to the example of the GoF and describes these two terms.

13.1 Task of the Pattern

The flyweight has the task of turning an elephant into a mosquito. Imagine programming an application that records all births in a year. Each record consists of an ID1, first name, last name, and birthday. Take a look at the very simple example project Birthrates.

```java
public class Child {
    private final long id;
    private final String forename;
    private final String surname;
    private final Date dob;

    public Child(String forename, String surname, LocalDate dob) {
        this.forename = forename;
        this.surname  = surname;
        this.dob= dob;
        id = (long) (((Long.MAX_VALUE * Math.random())
                          * (forename.hashCode()
                          + surname.hashCode())
                          + dob.getTime())));
    }
}
```

Supplementary Information The online version contains supplementary material available at https://doi.org/10.1007/978-3-658-39829-3_13.

A client creates a large number of children:
A critical look at the client code shows that two children are named Jack. Two others have the last name Miles. And all six were born on the same day. Do these repeating values meet your expectations?

```
public class ApplStart {
    public static void main(String[] args) {
        var child_1 =
            new Child("Jack", "Miles", LocalDate.now());
        var child_2 =
            new Child("Peter", "Smith", LocalDate.now());
        var child_3 =
            new Child("Jack", "Darby", LocalDate.now());
        var child_4 =
            new Child("Frank", "Miller", LocalDate.now());
        var child_5 =
            new Child("Peter", "Burke", LocalDate.now());
        var child_6 =
            new Child("John", "Miles", LocalDate.now());
    }
}
```

According to the Federal Statistical Office, just under 780,000 children were born in Germany in 2019. If we assume that the births are evenly distributed over the year, then over 2100 people have their birthday on the same day. According to the Gesellschaft für deutsche Sprache e.V. (Society for the German Language), about 2.52% of newborn girls had the first name Marie in 2019, which would therefore result in the same new first name being given about 54 times per day. And surname sameness is also certainly likely for newborns on a single day (In Germany, some common family names are Müller, Schmidt, Schneider, Fischer, …).

So the above approach would result in you having over 2100 identical Date objects; also, the previous programming would create thousands of strings with the same first name and same last name. And we're only talking about one birth cohort here. For the entire population in Germany, you would have to manage over 83 million first and last names individually.

In the simple example code shown above, the compiler is intelligent enough to detect this and optimize it, but if the names need to be read from external sources, the compiler cannot detect this in advance. It would not take long for the program to blow up the available memory.

The Flyweight Pattern now describes how objects of the smallest granularity can be reused. Let's look at what is meant by this in the next section.

13.2   The Realization

Take again as a negative example the project births. Let's assume for the sake of simplicity that the majority of children get either fashionable names or traditional names. The number of different first names will be very small in proportion to the 780,000 children. I'm assuming there are 200 different first names given in 2019. It would make sense to not create 780,000 string objects that are almost all the same anyway. It would make more sense to create 200 different string objects. Children with the same first name can share a string object.

The example project Birthrates_Flyweight demonstrates this. First, it is noticeable that the child objects are not called or created directly by the client. The client calls the method getChild() on a factory and passes the data of the child to this method.

```
public static void main(String[] args) {
    var factory = new factory();
    var child_1 =
      factory.getChild("Jack", "Miles", LocalDate.now());
    var child_2 =
      factory.getChild("Peter", "Smith", LocalDate.now());
    var child_3 =
      factory.getChild("Jack", "Darby", LocalDate.now());
    var child_4 =
    factory.getChild("Frank", "Miller", LocalDate.now());
    var child_5 =
      factory.getChild("Peter", "Burke", LocalDate.now());
    var child_6 =
      factory.getChild("John", "Miles", LocalDate.now());
    factory.evaluate();
}
```

The factory keeps a HashSet in which all first names are stored. When a child is to be created, the call to the add method adds the name to the HashSet only if it is not already contained. Surnames and birthdays are handled in the same way.

```
public class Factory {
    private final HashSet<String> forenameSet =
                                    new HashSet<>();
    private final HashSet<String> surnameSet =
                                    new HashSet<>();
    private final HashSet<LocalDate> dobSet =
                                    new HashSet<>();
    Child getChild(String forename,
                        String surname, Date dob) {
        forenameSet.add(forename);
```

```
            surnameSet.add(surname);
            dobSet.add(dob);
            return new Child(forename, surname, dob);
        }
    }
```

Nothing changes in the child class itself. The check to see if an entry already exists in the set is handled here by the add method of the HashSet, so we don't have to worry about that at all. This makes the code very simple.

The advantage of this approach is that you have reduced a large number of identical objects by dividing the objects.

When objects are shared, you need to critically examine whether you define them mutable or better immutable. If a child is renamed from Peter to Paul, the change of name would affect all births that refer to it. However, since strings are immutable, this problem is unnecessary here. With birthdays, the situation would be more problematic; a Date object could be set to a different value with `date.setTime()`. Thus, all child objects referencing the date would suddenly have a different birthday.

This approach is particularly interesting when these split objects are either very large and/or costly to create, for example by querying a database.

This example is extremely simple. In the following section, you will dive a little deeper into the matter.

13.3   A More Complex Project

Now let's look at an example that is a bit more complex. You program a software that takes orders for a pizzeria.

13.3.1 The First Approach

Your first approach might be to define a Pizza Order class that stores the name of the pizza and the table to which it should be delivered. Take a look at the Pizza sample project.

```java
public class PizzaOrder {
    public final String name;
    public final int table;

    public PizzaOrder(String name, int table) {
        this.table = table;
        this.name = name;
        System.out.println("I'll make a " + name);
    }
}
```

The Client creates new order objects and stores them in a list. When each table has placed an order, the pizzas are served.

```
public class ApplStart {
    private static final List<PizzaOrder> orders =
                                new LinkedList<>();

    private static void takeOrder(int table,
                                String pizza) {
        orders.add(new Pizza(pizza, table));
    }

    public static void main(String[] args) {
        takeOrder(1, "Pizza Hawaii");
        takeOrder(2, "Pizza Funghi");
        takeOrder(3, "Pizza Carbonara");
        // ... abridged
        orders.forEach(pizza -> {
            System.out.
            println("Now serving " + pizza.name
                    + " to table " + pizza.table);
        });
    }
}
```

If you analyze the code, you will see that each pizza is ordered multiple times. Of course, in individual cases, it is also possible that two or more orders are placed at one table. Which attribute will you share – the pizza or the table number? It takes a lot of effort to make a pizza. So, since your goal is to save resources in your ordering software, you will share the pizza – but note: only in the software, of course, each guest will end up with the whole pizza of their choice. The number of the table the order comes from will not be shared – the client will be blamed for that right away. So you have two different states: the state that is shared; and the state that the client is held responsible for. **You call the shared state intrinsic; the other extrinsic.** Objects that define the intrinsic state are the fly-weights. They are independent of the context in which they are used.

13.3.2 Intrinsic and Extrinsic State

The PizzaOrder class has two attributes: the description of the pizza and the number of the table to which it should be delivered. You decompose the PizzaOrder class into an intrinsic state and an extrinsic state, where the description of the pizza itself should be the intrinsic state. So, you pull the other attribute out of the class and move it into the context. What remains in the pizza class is only what is necessary to describe the pizza. This is not the baked pizza itself, but the note that it was ordered. In the example project PizzaFlyweight it should be sufficient to define the pizza by its name.

```
public class Pizza implements MenuItem {
    public final String name;

    public Pizza(String name) {
        this.name = name;
    }


    // … abridged
}
```

To allow for more dishes (salad, pasta, …) later on, I introduced the interface MenuEntry right away in this context, which is implemented by the class Pizza. I'll go into this in more detail in a moment; let's look at the client code first.

The client manages the different pizza objects and the table numbers. To enable a unique assignment, the orders are stored in a map; the key of this map is the table number, the value is the ordered menus. In order to represent the situation that a table can place several orders, the menus are stored as arrays.

```
public class ApplStart {
    private static final Map<Integer, MenuItem[]>
                                ORDERS = new HashMap<>();
    private static final MenuFactory
                    MENU_FACTORY = new MenuFactory();

    public static void takeOrder(int table,
                                    String... menue) {
        var order = MENU_FACTORY.getMenu(menu);
        ORDERS.put(table, order);
    }

    public static void main(String[] args) {
        takeOrder(1, "Pizza Hawaii");
        takeOrder(2, "Pizza Funghi");
        takeOrder(3, "Pizza Carbonara");
        takeOrder(4, "Pizza Calzone", "Pizza Carbonara");
        // … abridged
    }
}
```

The code of the factory, which keeps an overview of all ordered variants, is almost identical to the code you already know from the example project "Births". I do not want to go into it any further.

How is the pizza served to the table? The interface `menu` prescribes the method `serve()`, to which you pass the table as a parameter. The GoF describes this by saying, *"If operations depend on extrinsic state, they get it as a parameter."*

```
Public interface MenuItem {
    void serve(int table);
}
```

Now let's introduce the rest of the pizza class, the `serve()` method. It can be limited to outputting the message on the console that the pizza has been served to a specific table.

```
public class Pizza implements MenuItem {
    // … abridged
    @Override
    public void serve(int table) {
        System.out.println("" + name
                + " is served to table " + table + ".");
    }
}
```

Once the client has taken all the orders, he goes through the orders table by table and serves the pizzas.

```
public class ApplStart {
    // … abridged
    public static void main(String[] args) {
        // … abridged
        takeOrder(79, "Pizza Funghi");
        ORDERS.keySet().forEach(tempTable -> {
            var menus = ORDERS.get(tempTable);
            for (var tempMenu : menus)
                tempMenu.serve(tempTable);
        });
    }
}
```

In the following paragraph you can see where the flyweight is used in practice.

13.4   Flyweight in Practice

Where can you find the flyweight pattern in the wild? When you create an integer object using the new operator, you compare the objects' references for equality using ==. Run the following code in a Java shell:

```
Integer value_1 = new Integer(1);
Integer value_2 = new Integer(1);
boolean equality = value_1 == value_2;
System.out.println("Objects are equal: " + equality);
```

The following is output on the console: `Objects are equal: false`.
But for a test, create the objects with `Integer.valueOf()`:
Now output to the console: `Objects are equal: true`.
Obviously, the Integer class stores the values in the sense of the Flyweight pattern – at least if the objects are created using `valueOf`. And this is also the recommended method. The constructor `Integer(int)` is marked as "deprecated" since Java 9. It will not be available in future Java versions at some point.
Does this affect all numbers in the value range of integer? Let's just test this!

```
for (int i = -130; i < 130; i++) {
    Integer value_1 = Integer.valueOf(i);
    Integer value_2 = Integer.valueOf(i);
    boolean equality = value_1 == value_2;
    System.out.println(i + ": Objects are equal: "
                                    + equality);
}
```

If you run this code, you will see that all numbers from −128 to +127 are divided:

```
-130: Objects are equal: false
-129: Objects are equal: false
-128: Objects are equal: true
-127: Objects are equal: true
...
-2: Objects are equal: true
-1: Objects are equal: true
0: Objects are equal: true
1: Objects are equal: true
2: Objects are equal: true
...
126: Objects are equal: true
```

```
127: Objects are equal: true
128: Objects are equal: false
129: Objects are equal: false
```

What happens when you create objects via AutoBoxing, which is the automatic conversion of simple data types to the object-oriented types? Take the test:

```
Integer value_1 = 3;
Integer value_2 = 3;
boolean equality = value_1 == value_2;
System.out.println("Objects are equal when AutoBoxing: "
                                          + equality);
```

Output to the console:

```
Objects are the equal when AutoBoxing: true
```

So, you can work with autoboxing or valueOf.

13.5   Flyweight – The UML Diagram

The UML diagram from the PizzaFlyweight example project can be found in Fig. 13.1.

13.6   Summary

Go through the chapter again in key words:

- You have a large number of objects that are either large, costly to create, or simply consume a lot of system resources due to their number.
- You split these objects into a part that can be split and a part that is not split.
- The attributes that can be shared form the intrinsic state; they are flyweights.
- The extrinsic state is shifted to the context.
- The context manages the intrinsic and extrinsic state.
- Operations are performed by the context passing the extrinsic state as a parameter to a method of the intrinsic state.
- The intrinsic state is independent of its context.

Fig. 13.1 UML diagram of
the Flyweight Pattern.
(Example project
PizzaFlyweight)

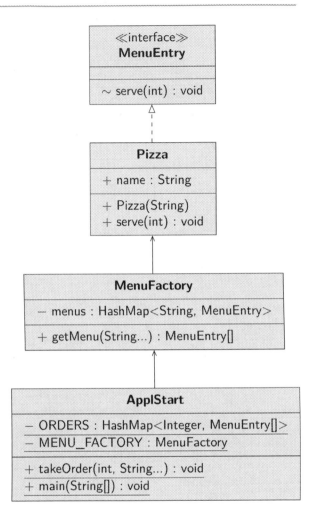

13.7   Description of Purpose

The Gang of Four describes the purpose of the pattern "Flyweight" as follows:

Use objects of smallest granularity together to be able to use large amounts of them efficiently.

Interpreter

14

After the first excursion to the structure patterns Composite and Flyweight, we continue again with a behavior pattern, the Interpreter Pattern. The pattern is not really difficult to understand, but it opens up great possibilities.

14.1 The Task in This Chapter

I would like to give you an impression of where the journey is going right at the beginning. The screenshot in Fig. 14.1 shows the program from the sample project Interpreter, which we will now discuss, in action. The principle is very simple: you type a mathematical expression into the input field. It can be of any length and nested; you end the input with a semicolon. Unary plus and minus, the addition sign, the subtraction sign, the multiplication sign and the division sign are processed. In addition, you can set round brackets to indicate priorities. Square brackets indicate that the result will be processed as an absolute value. You can insert as many spaces as you like. When you click on "Start", the input is scanned, parsed and calculated.

The input field is an editable combo box, in which a few expressions are already stored. The structure of the GUI will not be discussed here; the code is very simple. When you click on "Start", the combo box queries the entered value. This value is passed to a scanner, which returns a list of symbols. You send this list to the parser, which creates the root of an abstract syntax tree. On this root you call the method `calculate()` and get the calculated result.

```
final var input =
                (String) cmbExpression.getSelectedItem();
    try {
```

Supplementary Information The online version contains supplementary material available at https://doi.org/10.1007/978-3-658-39829-3_14.

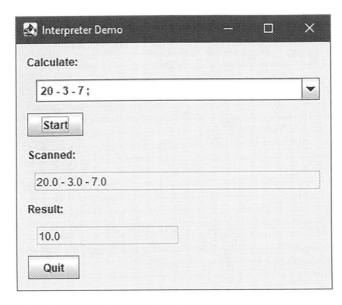

Fig. 14.1 A calculator in action, "Interpreter" project

```
    var scanner = new Scanner(input);
    edtScan.setText(scanner.toString());
    final var symbols = scanner.getSymbols();
    var parser = new Parser(symbols);
    var result = parser.getRoot();
    System.out.println(result);
    final var outcome = result.calc();
    edtResult.setText(Double.toString(outcome));
} catch (IllegalArgumentException ex) {
    JOptionPane.showMessageDialog(null, ex.getMessage());
}
```

This chapter deals with the question of how you prepare an expression that a user enters in such a way that a computer can handle it. The tools of the interpreter pattern, i.e. the abstract syntax tree, the scanner and the parser, are discussed.

The subject of compiler construction is the subject of an independent lecture at the university within the framework of computer science studies. Reference books on this subject contain many hundreds of pages. So, the implementation I will present to you can only be one way of many. I have developed it with the motivation to offer a comprehensible introduction; I have left out questions about efficiency.

14.2   The Scanner

The first processing step is performed by the scanner. It performs the lexical analysis. In this process, the input is broken down into sense units, the tokens, or symbols. Symbols in this example are numbers, spaces, semicolons, the parentheses, and the mathematical operators. For example, suppose you enter 5 + 14;. The scanner recognizes the following symbols:

```
Number( 5 ) Space( ) Plus sign( + ) Space( )
Number( 14 ) Semicolon(;)
```

I want to have the scanner filter out the spaces and the semicolon. So the scanner returns the following symbols:

```
Number( 5 ) Plus sign( + ) Number( 4 )
```

It is important to see that the scanner does not yet perform a syntactic check; it cannot detect whether an opening bracket has also been closed again. In the following paragraph, let's look at how the scanner breaks a string into symbols.

14.2.1 The Defined Symbols

In the package `symbols`, you first create the superclass Symbol. From it, symbol classes are derived to represent the mathematical operators, parentheses, and numbers. Consider the Add symbol-it doesn't have to do anything more than say about itself "I am a plus sign".

```
public class Add extends Symbol {
    @Override
    public boolean isPlus() {
        return true;
    }
}
```

A number is represented by the numeral symbol. It must indicate that it is a numeral. It also stores the value it represents.

```
public class Numeral extends Symbol {
    final double value;
    public Numeral(String number) {
        this.value = Double.valueOf(number);
    }
```

```
    public Numeral(double number) {
        this.value = number;
    }
    @Override
    public boolean isNumeral() {
        return true;
    }
}
```

> If the grammar would allow the input of strings, you would have to introduce a
> literal symbol corresponding to the numeral symbol.

I have not printed the implementation of the toString methods in each case. You can see
that the isNumeral() and isPlus() methods each override a method of the Symbol
superclass. In Symbol, the is... method is negated by default for all derived symbols.

```
public abstract class Symbol {
    // ... abridged

    public boolean isNumeral() {
        return false;
    }

    public boolean isPlus() {
        return false;
    }
}
```

So you can ask any symbol if it is a plus sign, but only the plus sign will actually return
true. In the following paragraph you can see how the scanner generates the symbols.

14.2.2 The Scanner Converts Strings into Symbols

In the class Scanner, it is mapped which character is mapped to which symbol. In addition, a list of symbols is defined, in which all symbols are stored; this list is returned later
by the scanner.

```
public class Scanner {
    private final List<Symbol> symbols =
                                    new ArrayList<>();
    private final Map<Character, Symbol> operators =
```

```
                              new HashMap<>();

    private Scanner() {
        operators.put('+', new Add());
        operators.put('-', new Subtract());
        operators.put('*', new Multiply());
        operators.put('/', new Divide());
        operators.put('[', new AbsoluteStart());
        operators.put(']', new AbsoluteEnd());
        operators.put('(', new LeftParenthesis());
        operators.put(')', new RightParenthesis());
        operators.put('=', new Equals());
    }
    // … abridged
}
```

The constructor is overloaded. You pass the string you entered to it. It removes the spaces and throws an exception if the input is not terminated with a semicolon. It also checks to see if there is more than one semicolon in the input. It then goes through the string character by character and tries to convert the characters into symbols.

```
public Scanner(String input) throws IllegalArgumentException {
    this();
    input = input.replaceAll(" ", "");
    var length = input.length();
    var firstSemicolon = input.indexOf(';');
    if (firstSemicolon != length - 1)
        throw new IllegalArgumentException(" ... ");
    var lastchar = input.charAt(length - 1);
    if (lastcharacter != ';')
        throw new IllegalArgumentException(" ... ");
    else
        for (var i = 0; i < input.length(); i++) {
            // … abridged
        }
}
```

Consider below the work inside the for loop. The indexed character is extracted from the string. Since the semicolon is not taken into account, the scanner only has to act if the current character is **not a** semicolon. The scanner first checks whether the currently indexed character is contained in the list of operators. In this case, the corresponding symbol object is read out and stored in the result list. Then the scanner checks whether the current character is a letter, a literal. You will need a letter if you want to develop the project further and introduce variables or map an assignment: $a = 5 + 7$. In this version, literals are scanned, but will not be parsed correctly. Instead, a usage of a literal may cause an exception.

As soon as the scanner determines that the current character is a number, it creates a buffer. It reads the next character into the buffer in a while loop until the following character is no longer a number. If the next current character is a point or a comma, it is also copied into the buffer – it can be assumed that the user has entered a double value. Provided there are decimal numbers, these are also queried in a while loop and passed to the buffer. Finally, the cache is used to create a numeral symbol that is stored in the result list. Now the work starts again at the beginning of the for loop with the next current character. Here is the code in the for loop that I had cut out above:

```
Character character = input.charAt(i);
if (!character.equals(';'))
    if (operators.containsKey(character))
        symbols.add(operators.get(character));
    else if (Character.isLetter(character))
        symbols.add(new Literal(character));
    else {
        var numberBuilder = new StringBuilder();
        while (Character.isDigit(character)) {
            numberBuilder.append(character);
            character = input.charAt(++i);
        }
        if (character == '.' || character == ',') {
            character = '.';
            numberBuilder.append(character);
            i++;
            character = input.charAt(i);
            while (Character.isDigit(character)) {
                numberBuilder.append(character);
                character = input.charAt(++i);
            }
        }
        symbols.add(new
                Numeral(numberBuilder.toString()));
        i--;
    }
```

This does the work of the scanner. It overrides the toString() method and defines the getSymbols() method, which returns the result list.

14.3   The Parser

If you enter the string *2 + (6 + 4) * 4;*, the scanner will return a series of symbols. These symbols have not yet been checked to see if they are syntactically correct, e.g. if all brackets have been closed. Also, no meaning has been assigned to the symbols yet. Both, syntactic and semantic analysis are the task of the parser.

> The GoF assumes that the expression is already parsed when describing the interpreter pattern. The interpreter operates on the parsed abstract syntax tree. Nevertheless, I describe the parser in this section to introduce you to the interpreter's tools, the expressions.

14.3.1 Abstract Syntax Trees

Scanner and parser have the task to create an abstract syntax tree. What is meant by this? A syntax tree has the task of representing a sentence in the defined grammar as a tree structure. If you were to include all spaces and the semicolon in the tree, you would have a *concrete syntax tree*. A concrete syntax tree is not efficient to manage. Therefore, to generate an abstract syntax tree, you go one step further and remove all symbols that are not required for execution.

The spaces and the semicolon are already removed by the scanner. What about operators and numerals? Each operator and numeral is represented by objects that are the nodes of the syntax tree. The edges of the tree describe the composition of the nodes. Take the example from above; the user types: 5 + 10;. The scanner removes the spaces and semicolon and returns number (5) plus sign (+) number (10). The diagram in Fig. 14.2 illustrates how the expression is converted into a syntax tree whose nodes are the operators and numerals.

The priority of the point calculation over the dash calculation can be taken into account by the position in the syntax tree. The input *10 + 5 * 4;* would produce the syntax tree in Fig. 14.3.

Brackets can change the priority. The changed priority is taken into account in the syntax tree, so that the brackets can be removed. For example, the user enters: *(10 + 5) * 4;*. This input can be represented by the syntax tree in Fig. 14.4.

In the next section, we'll look at how to convert a sequence of symbols into a syntax tree.

Fig. 14.2 Abstract syntax tree
of the expression 5 + 10

Fig. 14.3 Abstract syntax tree
of the expression 10 + 5 * 4

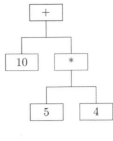

Fig. 14.4 Abstract syntax tree
of the expression (10 + 5) * 4

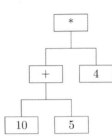

14.3.2 Expressions for the Parser

Operators and numerals are nodes of the syntax tree. To be able to treat them the same, it
is necessary that both are of the same type. Group numerals and operators under the interface Expression, which the method `calculate()` prescribes.

```
public interface Expression {
    double calc();
}
```

A numeral does not reference any other expressions. It may be limited to storing and
returning the value when `calculate()` is called.

```
public final class TerminalExpression implements Expression {
    private final double value;

    public TerminalExpression(double value) {
        this.value = value;
    }

    @Override
    public double calc() {
        return value;
    }
}
```

Operators operate on two expressions. They are non-terminal and are grouped under the abstract class `NonTerminalExpression`.

```
public abstract class NonTerminalExpression implements Expression {
    protected final Expression left;
    protected final Expression right;

    protected NonTerminalExpression(Expression left, Expression right) {
        this.left = left;
        this.right = right;
    }
}
```

To add two numbers, derive the `PlusExpression` class from this class. You pass the two expressions to be added to it. The `calc()` method is implemented so that the PlusExpression asks the two expressions to return their values. These values are added together and the sum is returned.

```
public class PlusExpression extends NonTerminalExpression {
    public PlusExpression(Expression left, Expression right) {
        super(left, right);
    }

    @Override
    public double calc() {
        return left.calc() + right.calc();
    }
}
```

At the beginning, your grammar should be limited to the fact that two or more numbers can be added.

14.3.3 Parse Stroke Calculation

The sample project Interpreter_1 is a slimmed down version of the project Interpreter. The parser stored here is limited to adding any number of numbers. Let's have a look at the procedure. You pass the list of symbols generated by the scanner to the constructor. The parser lets itself be given the iterator from this. The method `nextSymbol()` determines the next symbol from this list, which is stored in the attribute `currentSymbol`. If there are no further symbols, an EndSymbol is passed to `currentSymbol`. The constructor passes an expression to the `root` field, which is returned by the `parseExpression()` method. The client can query `root` with `getRoot()`.

So we actually already use several patterns in combination here: The iterator you saw
in Ch. 11 and the composite known from Ch. 12. Feel free to look it up again and try to
find these structures here.

```
public final class Parser {
    private final iterator<symbol> iterator;
    private final Expression root;
    private symbol currentSymbol;

    public Parser(List<Symbol> symbols) {
        iterator = symbols.iterator();
        nextSymbol();
        root = parseExpression();
    }

    private void nextSymbol() {
        currentSymbol =
            iterator.hasNext()
                ? iterator.next()
                : new EndSymbol();
    }
    // ... abridged
}
```

The method parseExpression() is the entry point for the parser. It calls the
method parseAddition(), which returns an object of type Expression.

```
private Expression parseExpression() {
    return parseAddition();
}
```

The method parseAddition() queries the first summand in the first step and calls
the method parseNumber() for this purpose. If parseNumber() determines that
currentSymbol is not a number, the method throws an exception; otherwise, the value
of currentSymbol is passed to a TerminalExpression and returned. Before that, currentSymbol is updated to the next symbol in the list of symbols. The variable expression in parseAddition() now references a TerminalExpression. The
parseAddition() method now loops to check if currentSymbol is a plus symbol.
If this is the case, the symbol is no longer needed, the next symbol from the list of symbols
can be passed to currentSymbol. From parseNumber() the next number, a terminal expression, is queried. With the two expressions a PlusExpression is created and passed
to expression. The variable expression is finally returned.

```
   private Expression parseAddition() {
       var expression = this.parseNumber();
       while (currentSymbol.isPlus()) {
           nextSymbol();
           var right = this.parseNumber();
           expression =
                   new PlusExpression(expression, right);
       }
       return expression;
   }

   private Expression parseNumber() {
       if (! currentSymbol.isNumeral())
           throw new IllegalStateException("Current  symbol  is  not  a
number: " + currentSymbol);

       var value =
               Double.parseDouble(currentSymbol.toString());
       nextSymbol();
       return new TerminalExpression(value);
   }
```

In the sample project Interpreter_2 I renamed the method `parseAddition()` to `parseAddSub()` and implemented the subtraction also. So, new in this version is also the class `MinusExpession`.

```
   private Expression parseAddSub() {
       var expression = this.parseNumber();
       while (currentSymbol.isPlus()
                           || currentSymbol.isMinus()) {
           var add = currentSymbol.isPlus();
           nextSymbol();
           var right = this.parseNumber();
           expression = add
               ? new PlusExpression(expression, right)
               : new MinusExpression(expression, right);
       }
       return expression;
   }
```

> **Tip**
> If you type 5 + 7–2;, the parser generates a series of expressions that are partially nested. Using a debugger or suitable console output, try to see that the expressions are nested as follows:
>
> ```
> MinusExpression (
>     PlusExpression (
>         Terminal ( 5.0 ) Terminal ( 7.0 )
>     )
>     Terminal ( 2.0 )
> )
> ```
>
> The abstract syntax tree for this can be found in Fig. 14.5.

In the next section we add the point calculation, which must be considered before the dash calculation.

14.3.4 Parse Point Calculation

The version in the sample project Interpreter_3 includes the multiplication and division. Two expressions are added: the MultExpression and the DivExpression. Accordingly, the parser knows the method `parsePunktrechnung()`, which is structured similarly to `parseMultDiv()`. Multiplication and division have priority over addition and subtraction. To establish this precedence, the `parseAddSub()` method must first call `parse-MultDiv()` before checking whether to add or subtract.

```
private Expression parseAddSub() {
    var expression = this.parseMultDiv();
    while (currentSymbol.isPlus()
                    || currentSymbol.isMinus()) {
```

Fig. 14.5 Abstract syntax tree
for the expression 5 + 7–2

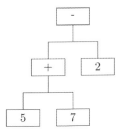

```
                var add = currentSymbol.isPlus();
                nextSymbol();
                var right = this.parseMultDiv();
                expression = add
                        ? new PlusExpression(expression, right)
                        : new MinusExpression(expression, right);
        }
        return expression;
    }
    private Expression parseMultDiv() {
        var expression = this.parseNumber();
        while (currentSymbol.isMultiply()
                            || currentSymbol.isDivide()) {
            var mult = currentSymbol.isMultiply();
            nextSymbol();
            var right = this.parseNumber();
            expression = mult
                    ? new MultExpression(expression, right)
                    : new DivExpression(expression, right);
        }
        return expression;
    }
```

Tip

Try to reproduce, either with a debugger or with console output, that *5 * 2 + 3;* is parsed into the following expression:

```
PlusExpression {
    MalExpression {
        Terminal ( 5.0 ) Terminal ( 2.0 )
    }
    Terminal ( 3.0 )
}
```

The input *5 + 2 * 3;* is parsed into another expression:

```
PlusExpression {
    Terminal ( 5.0 )
    MalExpression {
        Terminal ( 2.0 ) Terminal ( 3.0 )
    }
}
```

Now let's move on to the Interpreter_4 sample project. Here you will first consider a sign-minus and a sign-plus. Does a sign-plus make sense? No idea – but in any case, it is mathematically correct, and our grammar should allow it. In priority, the sign still comes before the multiplication and division. So you need to check it before division and multiplication. The `parseMultDiv()` method, when called, must first pass the call to the new `parseLeadingSign()` method. If `parseLeadingSign()` detects that a sign-minus is set, the next TerminalExpression is wrapped in a UnaryExpression. The code isn't much more complicated than the previous versions of the project; so I won't explain it in detail. Just look at the mentioned methods in the parser class.

14.3.5 Consider Brackets

In this section, parentheses are introduced. Now we come full circle and back to the Interpreter sample project from the beginning of this chapter. Round brackets set the precedence of a calculation; square brackets cause the bracketed expression to be positive. Parentheses have a higher precedence than the sign, so they must be parsed beforehand. The `parseAbsolute()` method parses an expression that is enclosed in square brackets, and the `parseParenthesis()` method parses round brackets. The first change is found in the `parseLeadingSign()` method: When a parenthesis is placed around an expression, that expression can be a NumeralExpression or a nested expression that can consist of addition, subtraction, multiplication, and division. Thus, an UnaryExpression may only be created if the following symbol represents a number.

```
private Expression parseLeadingSign() {
    Expression expression;
    var minus = currentSymbol.isMinus();
    if (currentSymbol.isMinus()
                        || currentSymbol.isPlus())
        nextSymbol();
    if (currentSymbol.isNumeral())
        expression = this.parseNumber();
    else
        expression = parseAbsolute();
    if (minus)
        expression = new UnaryExpression(expression);
    return expression;
}
```

The method `parseAbsolute()` creates a variable `Expression expression` and first checks whether `currentSymbol` is an opening square bracket. In this case, this symbol is "used up" and no longer needs to be observed. Now `parseAbsolute()` calls the method `parseExpression()`, which returns an expression. This expression is wrapped into an AbsoluteExpression and returned. The AbsoluteExpression has the task of determining the amount of the referenced expression. In the above test, if the `currentSymbol` is not an opening square bracket, `parseAbsolute()` asks the `parseParenthesis()` method for an Expression object.

```
private Expression parseAbsolute() {
    Expression expression;
    if (currentSymbol.isAbsoluteStart()) {
        nextSymbol();
        expression = this.parseExpression();
        expression = new AbsoluteExpression(expression);
        if (!currentSymbol.isAbsoluteEnd())
            throw new RuntimeException("...");
        nextSymbol();
    } else
        expression = parseParenthesis();
    return expression;
}
```

If the input is syntactically correct, `currentSymbol` **must be** an opening round bracket when `parseParenthesis()` is called; if `currentSymbol` is any other character, the method throws an exception. The procedure of `parseParenthesis()` is the same as that of `parseAbsolute()`: The `parseExpression()` method is called recursively to get an expression from there. This expression is returned.

14.4   Interpreter – The UML Diagram

From the example project Interpreter_4 we have to split the UML diagram a bit due to its size.

In Fig. 14.6 you first see the classes from the package symbols.

The classes from the package expressions can be found in Fig. 14.7.

And the classes from the package interpreter itself can be found in Fig. 14.8.

14.5   Discussion of the Interpreter Pattern

I wrote at the beginning that the GoF in describing the interpreter pattern assumes that the expression already exists as a finished parse tree. So, what is the basic principle of the interpreter?

They have the common interface Expression. Terminal and non-terminal classes are derived from this interface. Each non-terminal class represents a rule in the grammar; the operands – numbers in the example above – are stored in instances of terminal classes. The

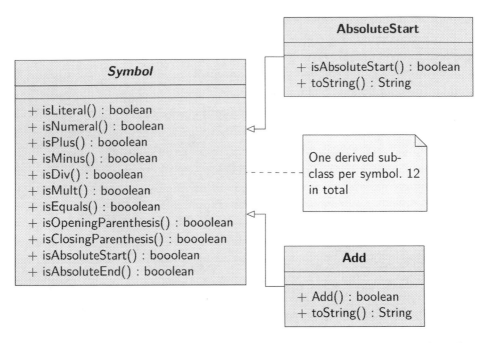

Fig. 14.6 UML diagram of the interpreter pattern. (Example project Interpreter_4, package symbols)

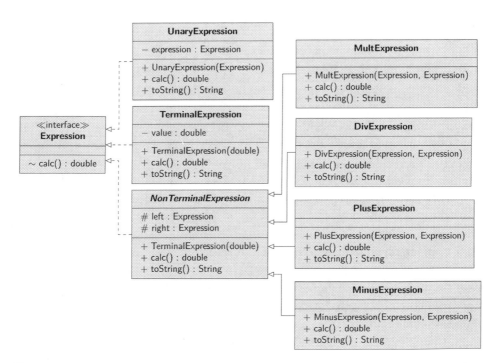

Fig. 14.7 UML diagram of the interpreter pattern. (Example project Interpreter_4, package expressions)

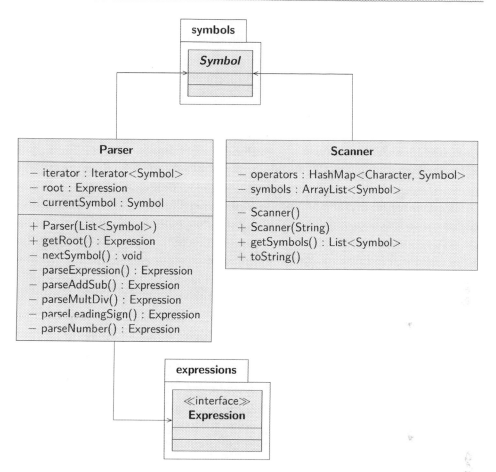

Fig. 14.8 UML diagram of the interpreter pattern. (Example project Interpreter_4, package interpreter)

nonterminal classes reference subexpressions that are themselves either terminal or non-terminal. It follows that any expression to be interpreted must be able to be represented as an abstract syntax tree. The syntax tree is composed of instances of the defined terminal and non-terminal classes.

The client calls the method defined in the common interface at the root of the syntax tree. Each nonTerminalExpression calls the same method on the referenced expressions, processes the response of the expressions, and returns the result. Does this approach look familiar from the Composite Pattern? The similarity is striking, isn't it? The GoF describes Composite and Interpreter as having "many implementation aspects in common". On the Internet and in the literature, you will occasionally even read the opinion that Interpreter is just a special case of Composite. However, you will notice differences in purpose and implementation. The composite is a structure pattern that can map a tree structure, whereas the interpreter is a behavior pattern that performs processing across the structure in our examples.

14.6   Summary

Go through the chapter again in key words:

- You have a simple grammar.
- An expression in this grammar can be represented as an abstract syntax tree.
- The syntax trees are composed of terminal and non-terminal expressions.
- Each non-terminal expression represents a rule in the grammar.
- To create an abstract syntax tree, the input must be scanned and parsed.
- The scanner converts the input string into a sequence of tokens – symbols.
- The parser checks the syntactical correctness of the input and builds the syntax tree.

14.7   Description of Purpose

The Gang of Four describes the purpose of the "Interpreter" pattern as follows:

> For a given language, define a representation of the grammar and an interpreter that uses the representation to interpret sentences in the language.

Abstract Factory (Abstract Factory)

15

Do you remember the singleton pattern from Chap. 3? You created an object without using the new operator. Instead, the client could use a static access method to get the instance of the class. The abstract factory delegates the creation of objects to a method, so that you, the user, can do without the actual creation with `new`.

Using two examples, let's take a closer look. We start with a beautiful garden.

15.1 Create Gardens

In our example there are different types of gardens; first we have monastery gardens where herbs are planted. But there are also ornamental gardens where roses grow. The respective enclosure is different, of course. The monastery garden is surrounded by a stone wall, while the ornamental garden is framed by a nicely cut hedge. The ground is also different in each case: in the monastery garden there are stone slabs, while in the ornamental garden you walk on fresh grass. The monastery garden and the ornamental garden are therefore two different *product families*. Each product family has the same characteristics (plants, fencing, soil), but each has a different design; the respective characteristics are called *products* in the abstract factory.

15.1.1 The First Attempt

Let's start with the example project Abstract_Garden, with the package Trial1, where we define a class Garden, where the garden is created and maintained. Like this:

Supplementary Information The online version contains supplementary material available at https://doi.org/10.1007/978-3-658-39829-3_15.

```java
public class Garden {
    private enum garden type {
        MonasteryGarden, OrnamentalGarden
    };

    private GardenType garden =
                        GardenType.MonasteryGarden;

    public void layFloor() {
        switch (garden) {
            case MonasteryGarden -> {
                // lay old flagstones
            }
            default -> {
                // Sowing grass
            }
        }
    }

    public void plant() {
        switch (garden) {
            case MonasteryGarden -> {
                // Planting herbs
            }
            default -> {
                // Set roses
            }
        }
    }

    public void enclose() {
        // ... as with the previous two methods.
    }
}
```

You can guess that this approach seems somehow wrong. But why are you bothered by it? Quite simply: You have three methods in which a switch query is needed. If you want to create another garden – for example a kitchen garden with tomatoes – you have to change a switch query in three methods. This is not very maintenance-friendly, but all the more error-prone.

The garden certainly also needs to be managed: The plants want to be watered and pruned; you also need to weed regularly. I will not print the methods for managing the garden here. However, you have a violation of the Single Responsibility Principle here:

you put the creation of the garden and its maintenance into one class. True, I had written that it is okay to violate it if you are aware of it and have a good reason. But that good reason is exactly what is missing here. Violating the SRP could be problematic, though, because both creating and managing the garden are very costly; these two tasks had better not be mixed. So the approach above implements a lot of code in a single class that, in case of doubt, is not needed at all. If you redefine a responsibility, both responsibilities need to be retested. Neither of the responsibilities can be reused. Here, the cohesion is decidedly weak and that is an indication of inappropriate design.

15.1.2 The Second Attempt – Inheritance

Perhaps the problem would be solved if you used inheritance? In the Trial2 package, you define an abstract class `AbstractGarden`, from which the subclasses `MonasteryGarden`, `KitchenGarden`, or `OrnamentalGarden` inherit. The garden is created in the constructor of the subclass.

```
public class MonasteryGarden extends AbstractGarden {
    MonasteryGarden() {
        super.layFloor(new OldStonePlate());
        super.plant(new Herbs());
        super.enclose(new StoneWall());
    }
}
```

This solution looks cleaner, but in fact it doesn't solve the dual responsibility problem: you still have an object that lavishly creates the garden and manages it. Moreover, this approach violates a principle that I consider much more essential than the SRP: prefer composition to inheritance. So let's find an alternative!

15.1.3 The Third Approach – The Abstract Factory

In the Trial3 package you have different gardens (*product families*) each with different *products*, i.e. different types of plants, soil types and enclosures. The products vary and are now encapsulated. I mentioned earlier that it makes sense to program against interfaces. This gives you the greatest possible flexibility. How can the products be abstracted? Both herbs and roses are plants; both the stone wall and the hedge are enclosures; both the flagstones and the lawn are soil. So design the interfaces, the different abstract products, and the implementations, the different concrete products. As an example, let me show the plants.

```
public interface Plant {
    // the abstract product "plant
}
```

There are at least two implementations of plants:

```
public class Rose implements Plant {
    // the concrete product Rose
}
public class Herbs implements Plant {
    // the concrete product herb
}
```

To create the different gardens, define a factory. For a monastery garden, implement a
MonasteryGardenFactory and for the ornamental garden, implement an
OrnamentalGardenFactory. You expect both factories to provide the same methods
and create the same products. To ensure this, you define an interface (abstract class or
interface), the abstract factory, from which the concrete factories inherit. And in it are the
methods that must be implemented in each of the concrete factories.

```
public interface AbstractGardenFactory {
    Plant plant();
    Floor layFloor();
    Enclosure enclose();
}
```

The MonasteryGardenFactory returns the elements typical of a monastery garden.

```
public class MonasteryGardenFactory
                    implements AbstractGardenFactory {
    @Override
    public Plant plant() {
        return new Herb();
    }

    @Override
    public Floor layFloor() {
        return new Flagstone();
    }

    @Override
    public Enclosure enclose() {
        return new StoneWall();
    }
}
```

And how can the client who wants to have a garden deal with this? It creates an instance of the desired garden factory and gets the individual elements from it. In the following example, we create the elements for a monastery garden.

```
public class Gardenin {
    Gardening() {
        AbstractGardenFactory factory =
                            new MonasteryGardenFactory();
        var floor = factory.layFloor();
        var enclosure = factory.enclose();
        var plant = factory.plant();
    }
}
```

Note that I explicitly specify the superclass `AbstractGardenFactory` for the declaration of the variable `fabrik`. Using `var.` for this declaration would create a factory of type `MonasteryGardenFactory,` which I explicitly do not want here.

Let's look at what we gain from this.

15.1.4 Advantages of the Abstract Factory

For a better overview, the class diagram Fig. 15.1 only shows the project in abbreviated form – the floor classes end interface are left out here.

The abstract garden factory knows the abstract declaration of the individual products, i.e., the interfaces floor, enclosure and plant. The client creates a variable of the abstract factory type that references an instance of a concrete factory: `AbstractGardenFactory factory = new OrnamentalGardenFactory()`. The concrete factory knows its specific products: In the example, the ornamental garden knows only the lawn, rose, and hedge – it has no reference to the flagstones, herb, or stone wall. When the client requests floor, plants, and enclosure, the factory is able to return its special products. Since the client

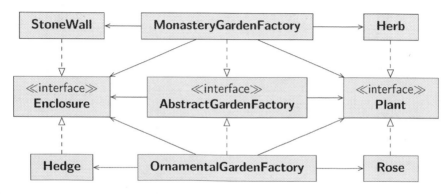

Fig. 15.1 Abbreviated class diagram of the garden project

relies on abstractions, i.e. the interfaces, it has no idea what specific products it will receive –
and thanks to polymorphism, it doesn't have to worry about the runtime type of the object.

The client is free to instantiate a different factory and thus be given completely different
products. A single line of code changes the nature of the garden:

```
AbstractGardenFactory factory =
                           new MonasteryGardenFactory();
```

The client is independent of changes to existing factories. If lilies are to be planted in
the ornamental garden instead of roses, this change can be made in the
`OrnamentalGardenFactory`; the client will not even notice this change, it does not
have to be tested again.

With this solution, you ensure that the garden is consistent. You purchase the individual
products from a specific factory. The factory uniformly supplies only products for either a
monastery garden or an ornamental garden. The gardens are now consistent; it is ensured that
no roses grow in the monastery garden and no herbs are planted in the ornamental garden.

15.1.5 Defining a New Garden

You have a cohesive family of products and you can add new families very easily. What
would have to happen if you wanted to create a new garden, for example an allotment or
garden plot? First, you need a new concrete factory that implements the
`AbstractGardenFactory` interface. Take a look at the example project GardenPlot:

```
public class GardenPlotFactory
                    implements AbstractGardenFactory {
    @Override
    public Plant plant() {
        return new Tomato();
    }

    @Override
    public layFloor() {
        return new ConcreteApron();
    }

    @Override
    public Enclosure enclose() {
        return new ChainLinkFence();
    }
}
```

You now still create the concrete products, the classes `Tomato`, `ConcreteApron`, and `ChainLinkFence`, which must correspond to the interfaces of the abstract products, `Floor`, `Enclosure`, and `Plant`.

> Why is the pattern called "Abstract Factory"? Because both the factories and the products rely on abstraction.

15.2   Discussion of the Pattern and Practice

You will use the abstract factory whenever you need a set of individual products that all correspond to a certain type. The products form the product family. In the previous example you got to know the product families of the gardens. However, the following example would also have been conceivable: You are programming an address management system. When you code the postal code, you plan five digits for Germany. But the structure of a postal code will be different in America or in Russia. Likewise, the length of the telephone number varies from country to country. Maybe there is even a different structure or a certain pattern for it? So, when you instantiate a contact, you need a consistent set of products for each country: a country-specific postal code and a country-specific phone number. The `AmericaFactory` will provide these products, just like the `RussiaFactory`, but customized for that country. The contact generated by the factory, if the factory is programmed correctly, is consistent. Furthermore, the client can be written in such a general way that its code is valid for all conceivable product families.

Where do you find the abstract factory in practice? Think of the different look and feels that Java provides. You can set a specific look and feel and change it at runtime. Each component is drawn uniformly with the chosen look and feel. Third party developers can develop their own look and feel. And since all created objects come from the same family, they can interact with each other if necessary. One pitfall must be addressed, however: Once you've determined the products, stick to them. Imagine that you also want to create a pond in your garden. The `AbstractGardenFactory` interface must dictate a corresponding factory method `getPond()`. Then, all concrete factories must define a method that returns a pond object. In our small example, this is certainly not a problem. However, if you have created a large framework for which your clients have already created their own garden factories, then this change can become very high-maintenance and therefore very expensive.

15.3   Chasing Ghosts

Imagine you get the order to create a game in which you have to hunt ghosts and open magic doors in an old house. Remember the old text adventures that were popular in the early days of home computing and still have fans today? We're doing something similar.

15.3.1 The First Version

The first version you create should be quite simple. You have a house created and explore it with a few simple commands. The commands you enter will be marked with the greater than sign, which should appear after the description of the game situation. Example:

Example

```
You are in the hallway
You see
      to the North: a closed door
      to the South: a wall
      to the West: a closed door
      to the East: a wall
> open door west
The door will be opened
> enter door west
You are in the bathroom
> look
You are in the bathroom
You see
      to the North: a wall
      to the South: a wall
      to the West: a wall
      to the East: an open door
> exit
```

The first version has nothing to do with factories yet. It is intended to introduce you to the logic of the game and the approach to programming. We start with the example project House_1.

15.3.1.1 The Player
The Player class has the task of storing the current position of the player. If the player enters another room, the data field is changed.

```
public class Player {
    private Room currentRoom;

    public void setCurrentRoom(Room room) {
        currentRoom = room;
    }

    public room getCurrentRoom() {
        return currentRoom;
    }
}
```

15.3.1.2 The Four Cardinal Points

You have seen in the short excerpt above that the four cardinal directions play an essential role. You must always explicitly specify which of four possible doors you want to enter or open. The cardinal directions are stored in an enumeration. I print the source code in the following only abbreviated – you will find the example project House_1 in the source files and some extensions in it. For example, the opposite direction plays an important role: If you find a door in a room in northern direction and cross this door, the door in the new room must necessarily be in southern direction. There is also a static method that maps the user's input strings to an object in the enumeration. However, I urge you to explore these details for yourself.

```
public enum direction {
    NORTH("to the North"),
    SOUTH("to the South"),
    WEST("to the West"),
    EAST("to the East"),
    UNKNOWN("unknown direction");

    private final String description;
    private Direction oppositeDirection;

    private Direction(String description) {
        this.description = description;
    }

    private void setOppositeDirection(
                    Direction oppositeDirection) {
        this.oppositeDirection = oppositeDirection;
    }

    // ... abridged
    @Override
    public String toString() {
        return description;
    }
}
```

15.3.1.3 Building the House

A house consists of doors and walls and thus forms rooms. The class Component describes the components. Please note that this class is not an abstract product and will not become one in later versions. The only purpose of this common class is to declare the enter() and describe() methods.

```
public abstract class Component {
    protected abstract void enter(Player player);
    protected abstract String describe();
}
```

A wall cannot be entered – at least in my version; but you might want to elaborate the project further and create walls that can be moved and clear the way to a mysterious passage. For my version, the wall can be limited to emitting an error message when the enter() method is called. However, it must be able to describe itself.

```
public class Wall extends component {
    @Override
    public void enter(Player player) {
        System.out.println("You step into a wall.");
    }

    @Override
    protected string describe() {
        return " a wall.";
    }
}
```

A door receives references to the two rooms it connects in the constructor. If the door is open, it can also be entered, i.e., the user walks through it.

```
public class Door extends Component {
    private boolean isOpen = false;
    private final Room room1;
    private final Room room2;

    Door(Room room1, Room room2) {
        this.room1 = room1;
        this.room2 = room2;
    }

    void open() {
        System.out.println("The door is opened");
        isOpen = true;
    }

    @Override
    public void enter(player player) {
        if (isOpen) {
            var currentRoom = player.getCurrentRoom();
```

```
                    var newRoom = currentRoom == room1
                                        ? room2 : room1;
                    newroom.enter(player);
                } else
                    System.out.println("The door is closed.");
        }


        @Override
        protected string describe() {
            return isOpen
                    ? " an open door" : " a closed door.";
        }
        // … abridged
    }
```

The class Room expects a name and a description in the constructor. Both are needed to generate meaningful text output. In an EnumMap, the directions are stored as keys; the values are components attached to a side: Doors or Walls. The overloaded method addComponent() allows to insert a door or a wall at a side of the room. When a room is created, all sides are initially pre-populated with walls, and a door can only be subsequently placed at a location where there are walls in both rooms.

This is physically not quite correct, because the wall between two rooms exists only once. Here in the example, we look at it from each room individually.

```
public class Room extends Component {
    private final String description;
    private final String name;
    private EnumMap<direction, component> directions =
                        new EnumMap<>(direction.class);

    void addComponent(Direction direction, Wall wall) {
        if (directions.get(direction) == null)
            directions.put(direction, wall);
        else
            System.out.println("Cannot put a wall here");
    }

    void addComponent(Direction direction, Door door) {
        var oppositeDirection =
                        direction.getOppositeDirection();
        var neighbor = door.getNeighbor(this);
        var mySide = directions.get(direction);
        var oppositeSide =
                neighbor.directions.get(oppositeDirection);
```

```
            if (oppositeSide instanceof Wall
                              && mySide instanceof Wall) {
                directions.put(direction, door);
                neighbor.directions.put(oppositeDirection,
                                                  door);
            } else
                System.out.println("Cannot put a door here");
        }
    }
```

Of course, you can also enter a room. The method outputs a description of the current room and informs the player about his current position.

```
@Override
public void enter(Player player) {
    System.out.println("You are now " + description);
    player.setCurrentRoom(this);
}
```

The other methods of the class describe the room. If you want to expand the project further, you can provide trap doors or a staircase or even a chimney through which the room can be changed, according to this procedure.

15.3.1.4 The "House" Class for Controlling the Game

The House class controls the game. The enter() method asks for your input in a while loop and reacts to it. With the *look* command you look around. The *exit* command ends the game. To open a door, type *open door* and the direction the door is in, for example, *open door north*. To go into another room, *enter* the door with *enter door north*. Of course, you can only go through an open door. Our game does not need more commands.

The main method creates an instance of the House class and calls its constructor. The constructor calls the method createHouse(). In this method, rooms, walls, and doors are created. Then, the components are assembled and the hallway is defined as the entry point.

And by the way: You are completely free with the directions between the rooms. Nobody forces you to construct an arrangement of rooms that is physically possible at all. Look at the rooms and their arrangement in the example code, and then simply construct another door from the pantry eastward into the bathroom. From each room there is at most one door in each direction to exactly one other room, and from this room there is only one door in the opposite direction back to the original room. But whether the library to the north may still contain a door into the kitchen or the living room is up to you as the "creator". Confuse the player at will.

When the construction is complete, the main method calls the enter() method, which starts the game. The player first looks around and the hallway is described. After that, a while loop reads and processes the player's commands.

When processing the commands, you resort to the Command pattern. There is the `Command` interface, which specifies the `matches()` and `handle()` methods. The `matches()` method is passed the entered line; the method checks whether the entered string `matches` the Command object. The entered command is represented by the static inner class `CmdLine`, which internally tokenizes the command.

```java
public static class CmdLine {
    private final String[] tokens;

    public CmdLine(String nextLine) {
        this.tokens = nextLine.split(" ");
    }

    public boolean startsWith(String... tokens) {
        if (this.tokens.length < tokens.length)
            return false;
        for (var i = 0; i < tokens.length; i++)
            if (!this.tokens[i].
                            equalsIgnoreCase(tokens[i]))
                return false;
        return true;
    }

    public boolean hasDirection(int index) {
        try {
            var r =
                direction.getDirection(tokens[index]);
        } catch (Exception e) {
            return false;
        }
        if (d == Direction.UNKNOWN)
            return false;
        return true;
    }

    public Direction getAsDirection(int index) {
        return Direction.getDirection(tokens[index]);
    }
}
```

The `handle()` method of the Command interface describes the action to be performed by the `command`. As an example, I print the source code of the `exit command`. But please also have a look at the sample code to see how the system reacts to missing directions for the commands "open door" and "enter door".

```
public class Exit implements Command {
    @Override
    public boolean matches(CmdLine cmdLine) {
        return cmdLine.startsWith("exit");
    }

    @Override
    public void handle(CmdLine cmdLine, Player player) {
        System.exit(0);
    }
}
```

The while loop mentioned above passes the command entered to an object of the class CmdLine. Subsequently, all commands are checked in a for-each loop to see whether they correspond to the command entered. If they do, the command is executed.

```
private void enter() {
    System.out.println(input.describe());
    var player = new Player();
    entry.enter(player);

    var scanner = new Scanner(System.in);
    String command;
    System.out.print("> ");
    while (!((command = scanner.nextLine()) == null)) {
        var cmdLine = new CmdLine(command);
        for (var cmd : commands)
            if (cmd.matches(cmdLine)) {
                cmd.handle(cmdLine, player);
                break;
            }
        System.out.print(">");
    }
}
```

Please make sure to analyze the complete source code of the class House in the example project House_1.

15.3.2 The Second Version of the Project

The second version of the project is primarily intended to resolve the complexity of the class House of the first version. The class has three tasks: It must obtain the components of the house, it must assemble the components, and it must provide game control. The multiplicity of tasks violates the SRP! In fact, it should be enough for the class to know which room the player is currently in in order to apply the currently entered command to him.

To break the complexity, the construction process is outsourced in this version of the program, which you can find in the example project House_2. There is a class ComponentFactory whose task is to create rooms, new walls and new doors from the components.

```
public class ComponentFactory {
    CreateRoom(String name, String description) {
        return new Room(name, description);
    }
    // Doors and walls accordingly
}
```

In addition, in this program version there is the new class Architect, which knows the factory and gets rooms and doors from there to construct the house and assemble it from the individual components. If the floor plan is stored in a file that needs to be read and parsed, the Architect class can become quite complex. The architect gets a reference to a ComponentFactory in the constructor. From this factory it gets the components and assembles them. Afterwards, it returns the room that you defined as the entry point.

```
public class Architect {
    private final componentFactory factory;

    // ... abridged
    Room buildHouse() {
        var corridor = factory.createRoom("corridor",
                                          "in the corridor");
        var hallway = factory.createRoom("hallway",
                                          "in the hallway");
        // ... abridged
        var door = new Door[7];
        door[0] = factory.createDoor(hallway, corridor);
        // ... abridged
        door[6] = factory.createDoor(livingroom, study);
        board.addComponent(direction.NORTH, door[0]);
        // ... abridged
        return hallway;
    }
}
```

The House class has now become very lean. It can limit itself to creating an architect, parameterizing it with a component factory and having it build a house. The class House only needs to know the entrance and the architect tells it.

```
public class House {
    private final room entry;
    private final Architect architect;

    private House() {
        architect =
            new Architect(new ComponentFactory());
        entrance = architect.createHouse();
        / ... abridged
    }

    private void enter() {
        System.out.println(input.describe());
        var player = new Player();
        entry.enter(player);
        var scanner = new Scanner(System.in);
        String command;
        System.out.print("> ");
        // Wait for command input (Enter)
        while (!((command = scanner.nextLine()) == null))
            {
                // ... abridged
            }
    }
}
```

In this version, we have introduced one factory; in the following section, we create a
second factory.

15.3.3 Version 3 – Introduction of Another Factory

In the third version you will find the principle of the Abstract Factory Pattern again.
However, the abstract factory is not so abstract at all, as you will see in a moment. Now
take a look at the example project House_3.

15.3.3.1 Spells
New in this version is a class that defines a door that can only be opened with a spell. When
you try to open a door, it will ask you a question. For example, you may want to open a
door and it will tell you to "Speak FRIEND and enter". Of course, if you are familiar with
the relevant literature, you will know to type *mellon*. The question and your answer are
stored in the static inner class question.

```
public static class Question {
    public final String question;
    public final String answer;
```

```
      private question(String question, String answer) {
          this.question = question;
          this.answer = answer;
      }
  }
```

15.3.3.2 The New Factory for Doors with Spells

The class `EnchantedDoorFactory` inherits from the class `ComponentFactory` and only overwrites the method `createDoor()`. This method randomly decides whether a door shall be enchanted or not. In addition, the factory has the task of generating a list of questions. If an enchanted door is to be created, a question and the associated password are selected from this list.

```
  public class EnchantedDoorFactory
                                extends ComponentFactory {
      public static class Question {
          // ... see previous source text
      }

      private final List<question> ask = new ArrayList<>();
      {
          questions.add(new  Question("SPEAK  FRIEND  AND  ENTER  ",
"mellon"));
          // more
      }

      @Override
      CreateDoor(Room room1, Room room2) {
          var number = (int)(Math.random() * 10);
          if (number > (questions.size() - 1))
              return new Door(room1, room2);
          else
              return new EnchantedDoor(room1,
                        room2, questions.get(number));
      }
  }
```

So, the factory class is very unspectacular. Now let's look at the door with spell.

15.3.3.3 The New Component: A Door with a Magic Spell

The class `EnchantedDoor` inherits from the class `Door` and overwrites the method `open()`. To the constructor you pass both the affected rooms and the question. The rooms are passed to the superclass, the question is stored in a data field.

```java
public class EnchantedDoor extends Door {
    private final question question;
    EnchantedDoor(Room room1, Room room2,
                                    Question question) {
        super(room1, room2);
        this.question = question;
    }

    @Override
    void open() {
        if (super.isOpen())
            System.out.println("… ");
        else {
            var scanner = new Scanner(System.in);
            System.out.print(question.question + " >> ");
            var input = scanner.nextLine();
            if (input.equalsIgnoreCase(question.answer))
                super.open();
            else
                System.out.println("… ");
        }
    }
}
```

In the next version, you will introduce another factory that will generate rooms where you will encounter ghosts.

15.3.4 Version 4 – The Haunted House

Our goal is to program a haunted house. There are doors that have to be opened with a spell. There are also some rooms where ghosts can be found. So, to program the last version, create the class `HauntedHouseFactory`, which inherits from the class `EnchantedDoorFactory`. That is, randomly create doors with spells. You apply the same logic again to create rooms where ghosts can randomly appear. A static data field is used to store how apparitions can appear. You can find the code in the example project House_4.

```java
public class HauntedHouseFactory
                        extends EnchantedDoorFactory {
    @Override
    CreateRoom(String name, String description) {
        var number = (int) (Math.random() * 10);
        if (number > 5)
            return new Room(name, description);
        else
```

```
                    return new HauntedRoom(name, description);
        }
   }
```

The factory should be able to create a room with a ghost. The class `HauntedRoom`
extends the class `Room`. When you enter the room, it is randomly decided whether the
ghost appears or not. A static data field stores how the apparitions can appear.

```
public class HauntedRoom extends Room {
        private static final List<String> ghosts =
                                    new ArrayList<>();
    static {
        ghosts.add("A ghost flits through the door.");
        ghosts.add("You're hearing strange noises.");
    }
    HauntedRoom(String name, String description) {
        super(name, description);
    }
    @Override
    public void enter(Player player) {
        super.enter(player);
        var number =
            (int) (Math.random() * (ghosts.size() * 2));
        if (number < ghosts.size() - 1) {
            System.out.println("\t*******************");
            System.out.println("\t"
                            + ghost.get(random number));
            System.out.println("\t*******************\n");
        }
    }
}
```

At the end of the project I would like to mention a difference to the garden project.
There, we had abstract products, the interfaces `Plant`, `Floor` and `Enclosure`.
In the Ghost House project, the abstract products, the classes `Door`, `Room` and
`Wall`, are also concrete products. Further concrete products are derived from these
products, e.g. the enchanted door or the haunted room. In the same way, the
`ComponentFactory` is an abstract and a concrete factory at the same time – new
factories are derived from this factory. This is also a possible implementation of the
Abstract Factory Pattern. I use inheritance instead of composition because this is
actually extending behavior of an existing class. A `HauntedRoom` **is** a `Room`.

15.4   Abstract Factory – The UML Diagram

Figure 15.2 shows the UML diagram from the example project House_4.

15.5   Summary

Go through the chapter again in key words:

- With the abstract factory, you create a product family that consists of various individual products.
- The products together form a unit, e.g. a uniform look and feel.
- During implementation, an interface for a factory is created: the abstract factory.
- The client programs against abstractions of products, that is, against abstract products.
- The abstractions can be abstract classes or interfaces.
- A concrete factory produces the concrete products that belong to a particular family.
- The bond between the products and the client is loosened.
- As a result:
- An entire product family can be replaced without affecting the client code,
- A specific product can be changed without affecting the client code,
- New product families can be added,
- Products can be reused, e.g. in other product families,
- The products can communicate with each other because they know their mutual interfaces.
- One disadvantage is that it is difficult to expand a product family with additional members.

15.6   Description of Purpose

The Gang of Four describes the purpose of the "Abstract Factory" pattern as follows:

Provide an interface for creating families of related or interdependent objects without naming their concrete classes.

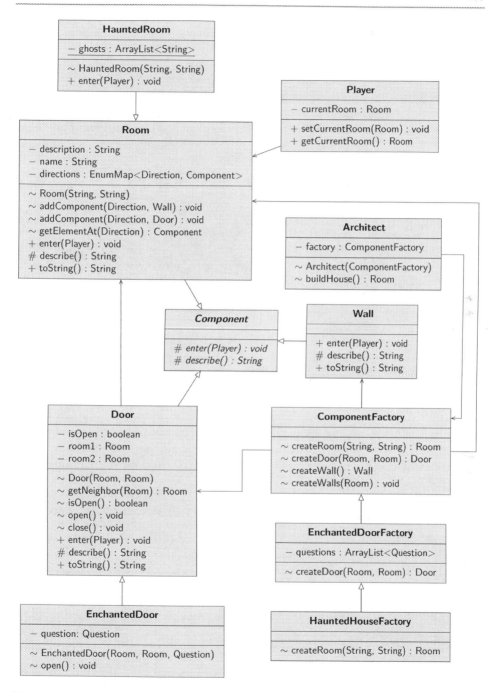

Fig. 15.2 UML diagram of the Abstract Factory Pattern. (Example project House_4)

Factory Method

16

In Chap. 15 you got to know the abstract factory. If you now work on the factory method pattern, you can transfer many structures and arguments from there. While both patterns are about creating objects, they differ in their goals; the abstract factory creates unified product families, while the factory method creates only a single product. They also differ in structure – the Abstract Factory is based on object composition, the Factory Method is based on inheritance, as you'll see in a moment.

16.1 A First Example

For the first, introductory example, meals are to be prepared. Since everything is kept very simple at the moment, there are only the classes `Doner` and `Pizza`. Both implement the interface `Meal`. Fittingly, there is a `Pizzeria` and a `Takeaway`. Both inherit from the abstract class `Restaurant`. The abstract class defines the `order()` method, which dictates that the guest should first be asked for their request, then the requested meal is prepared, and finally it is served. This method is called by the guest when he wants to order a meal. The method `prepareMeal()` is a factory method. Its job is to create a specific product. The actual execution is delegated to subclasses, i.e. `Takeaway` and `Pizzeria`. Note that while the `takeOrder()` method is also defined by the subclasses, this is irrelevant to the discussion of the pattern; I intended this coding to ask the guest for their pizza request at the pizzeria and their doner request at the takeaway. You can find the complete code in the sample project Meal.

Supplementary Information The online version contains supplementary material available at https://doi.org/10.1007/978-3-658-39829-3_16.

```
public abstract class Restaurant {
    protected abstract String takeOrder();

    protected abstract Meal prepareMeal();


    private void serveMeal(Meal meal) {
        System.out.println("Meal is here! It's " + meal);
    }

    public final Meal order() {
        var order = takeOrder();
        var meal = prepareMeal();
        serveMeal(meal);
        return meal;

    }

}
```

Takeaway and pizzeria create either a doner or a pizza – each varied according to customer preferences. All meals implement the same interface. The guest – in the example the test class – creates the instance of a subclass of the class Restaurant and calls the method order() on it.

```
public class Test {
    public static void main(String[] args) {
        Restaurant mammaMia = new Pizzeria();
        mammaMia.order();
        Restaurant istanbul = new Doenerbude();
        istanbul.order();
    }
}
```

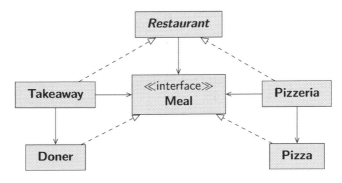

Fig. 16.1 Class diagram of the sample project Meal

The following text is output on the console:

```
Dinner's ready! There is Pizza Margharita
Dinner's ready! There is kebab with everything
```

If the guest wants to eat a pizza, he creates an instance of the class `Pizzeria`, otherwise an instance of the class `Takeaway`. At no point is there an `if` query. Just by selecting the "right" subclass, the desired product is created.

Figure 16.1 shows you the class diagram of the project. In the terminology of the pattern, the interface `Meal` is a product. The derived classes `Doner` and `Pizza` are concrete products. The interface `Restaurant` is a producer and the concrete localities (pizzeria and takeaway) are concrete producers.

16.2   Variations of the Example

The factory method can optionally be parameterized. The project is already prepared for this variation. The method `takeOrder()` returns a string with the order. The previous project version ignores the customer request, which is not very friendly. In the new version, the order is passed to the factory method as a parameter, which then creates the desired meal. The pizza example demonstrates this procedure. The following code from the MealVariation sample project shows the parameterized factory method of the pizzeria.

```
protected Meal prepare(String order) {
    if (order == null || order.isEmpty())
        return new Pizza();
    else
        return switch (order) {
            case "Calzone" -> new Calzone();
            case "Hawaii" -> new Hawaii();
            default -> { System.out.
                println("We don't offer this pizza!");
                yield null;
        }
    }
}
```

Note that I added a switch expression to the return statement in the else branch, and then I don't have to write another `return` in every single case, but give the result expression of every case distinction to the return statement. In the above example you can also see that firstly you can have multiple statements executed in a case distinction (here the default case), and secondly the keyword `yield` which is used instead of a return. A `return` is intended exclusively for terminating a method. The termination of a command sequence within a switch expression is done with `yield` and returns the subsequent value as the value of the expression.

With a parameterized factory method, you can easily introduce new products. Without parameters, you would have to rely on creating a new concrete producer for each new concrete product. However, since the production effort for the different pizzas is similar and calzone even inherits from pizza, it makes sense to parameterize the factory method.

16.3   Practical Application of the Pattern

You have already seen the pattern in practical use.

16.3.1 Recourse to the Iterator Pattern

In Chap. 11, you created iterators. To use a collection in an extended for-each loop, it must implement the `Iterable` interface. The interface prescribes the `iterator()` method, which returns an object of type `Iterator`. The Iterable is implemented by the `ArrayList` class, for example, but the two collections you created in the Iterator Pattern chapter also have this interface implemented. All of these classes must be able to return a product, an object of type `Iterator`; the Iterator prescribes three methods that you can use to iterate element-by-element through the collection. In most cases, it might be convenient to define the iterator as an anonymous class, that is, `return new Iterator{...}`. The diagram in Fig. 16.2 shows this interaction.

You define an interface, the `Iterable` interface, which prescribes a method for creating objects: `iterator()`. This method is the factory method. An object of the type of the interface `Iterable` must return an object of the type `Iterator`, which works together with its own specification. In the diagram, I have helpfully named this object `MyIterator`. The example project Iterator shows this (rough) structure.

> If the `iterator()` method is a factory method because it returns an object, then you could say that any method that returns an object is a factory method, which is not uncommon in object-oriented programming. A factory method is characterized by the fact that subclasses decide on the exact specification of the object. The client does not know by which class the object it receives was created.

The factory method pattern is useful when you want to write general-purpose code. A for-each loop, which I mentioned in the last example, has no idea from which class the

Fig. 16.2 Class diagram
Factory Method Pattern

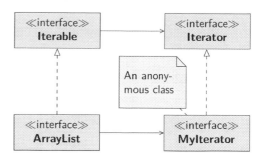

object of type Iterable was instantiated – it doesn't even need this knowledge. Similarly, the for-each loop has no interest in which concrete product it is working with. Since the binding of the concrete iterator object to the for-each loop is very loose, you can define any collection classes and use them in the for-each loop. The concrete creator is responsible for creating a matching concrete product.

If you create a new object with the new operator, you must always call a constructor of the class. When you define a factory method, on the other hand, you can choose any identifier you want. For example, consider the procedure of the Color class. Here, there are numerous static methods whose only task is to create a Color object from certain parameters. There is, for example, the method getHSBColor(), which describes its purpose much more succinctly.

> If you compare the Factory Method pattern up to this point with the Abstract Factory, you'll notice that the Abstract Factory is much more complex. In fact, many projects start with the Factory Method and end up with the Abstract Factory.

16.3.2 At the Abstract Factory

In the Abstract Factory chapter, when you programmed the Haunted House, you referred back to the Factory Method several times. There was the creator, the class ComponentFactory. In this class, there are the methods createRoom(), createDoor(), and createWall(), which all create doors, rooms, and walls that have no special feature, that is, neither a ghost nor an enchantment. This class is the interface and there is nothing wrong with defining the interface to bring default behavior. Therefore, other classes, called concrete creators, were derived from this class; one class creates doors with spells. The other class creates doors with spells and rooms with ghosts. The derived classes override certain create methods of the superclass. These are exactly the "factory methods". It looked similar with the products. Products were the classes door, room and wall. From these, other concrete products were derived: Doors with spells and Rooms with ghosts.

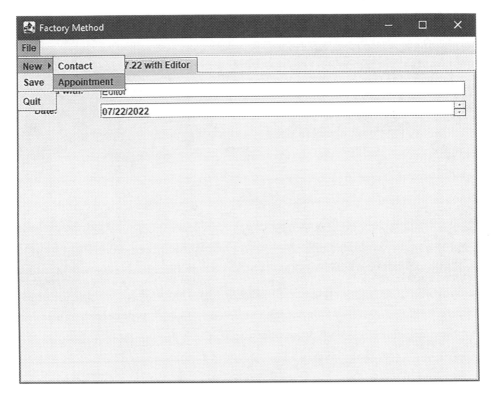

Fig. 16.3 Screenshot of the finished sample project AddressBook

16.4   A Larger Example – A Framework

The Factory Method finds practical application in the creation of frameworks.

16.4.1 And Another Calendar

You create a framework that manages appointments and contacts. In the screenshot in Fig. 16.3, you can see that I have created several contacts. I also have an appointment with my editor on July 22, 2022 – I must not forget it!

The frame of the program provides a blank interface and the menu. You can create entries (appointments and contacts). If you have created a new entry, it will be displayed on a new tab. The program should remain flexible to be able to display new entries such as e-mails or entire address books in a further expansion stage. You can guess that it's all about the frame and the entries being separated from each other and having only loose interfaces.

Let's take a closer look at the connection between the frame and the entry. Entries are certainly responsible for their own data. A contact consists of first and last name and a date of birth. An appointment consists of the name of the other participant and the date of the appointment. The question now is which entity composes the controls for each data. If you delegate this task to the frame, this assumes that the frame knows all the dates of all conceivable entries. You are restricting yourself in that an existing entry may not get any additional data, because otherwise the frame would have to be modified. Also, implementing new entries would be extremely costly because the new controls would have to be coded in the frame. However, the frame has already been extensively tested and delivered to the customer – you will never want to touch it again under any circumstances. So the responsibility for designing the editor must be delegated to the class that best knows the controls you need: the entry itself.

You can find the following code in the AddressBook sample project.

16.4.2 The Interfaces for Entries and Their Editors

The entries implement the interface `Entry`. It prescribes two methods; one requests a textual description from the entry, the other retrieves an object of type `EntryPanel`. The returned `EntryPanel` can be optimized for either an appointment or a contact – this is like the iterator returned by any list with its own specifics.

```
public interface Entry {
    EntryPanel getEntryPanel();
    String getDescription();
}
```

The editor of an entry is of the type of the interface `EntryPanel`. This interface again prescribes two methods. One method asks the editor to save the entry. The other method returns a `JPanel` on which the controls are arranged.

```
public interface EntryPanel {
    void save();
    JPanel getEditor();
}
```

The following section shows how these interfaces are implemented.

16.4.3 The Class "Contact" as an Example of an Entry

Next, I would like to introduce the Contact class as an example of a possible entry. The class stores the first name, last name, and date of birth in its data fields. In addition, the class creates an object of type `EntryPanel`. This object is an instance of an inner class, which will be described below.

```
public class Contact implements Entry {
    private String firstname = "<first name>";
    private String lastname = "<last name>";
    private LocalDate birthday = LocalDate.now();
    private final EntryPanel entryPanel = new MyEditor();

    @Override
    public EntryPanel getEntryPanel() {
        return entryPanel;
    }

    private class MyEditor implements EntryPanel {
        // … abridged
    }
}
```

In the constructor of the inner class, the editor panel is assembled. Here I use the TwoColumnLayout that you developed in the chapter about the Strategy Pattern. Further, I've given the input fields a FocusListener that highlights all the text when you click in the field. And finally, the JSpinner, where the date of birth is entered, gets its own date editor and date model. Please analyze the code of the project. Of course you could also use a DatePicker instead of the simple spinner, this is not available natively in the JDK, but in many free libraries, of which you can choose one. For the demo here, however, the JSpinner serves its purpose. You can also overwrite the date manually instead of tediously "spinning" back and forth day by day.

The input fields are saved as data fields. When the user gives the command to save the data, the editor transfers the values from the input fields and from the JSpinner to the data fields of the outer class. If you extend the project further, you could, for example, provide the functionality that the class gets serialized. The getEditor() method returns the panel built in the constructor.

```
private class MyEditor implements EntryPanel {
    private final JPanel pnlEntry = new JPanel();
    private final JTextField edtfirstname =
                        new JTextField("<First Name>");
    private final JTextField edtlastname =
                        new JTextField("<Last Name>");
    private final JSpinner spnBirthday = new JSpinner();

    MyEditor() {
        // … abridged
    }

    @Override
    public void save() {
```

```
            firstName = edtFirstName.getText();
            lastName = edtLastName.getText();
            birthday = (Date) spnBirthday.getValue();
        }


        @Override
        public JPanel getEditor() {
            return pnlEntry;
        }
    }
```

How does the client handle these classes?

16.4.4 The FactoryMethod Class as a Client

In this class there is a list where all entries are stored. Each new entry gets its own tab in a JTabbedPane on the GUI. When the user clicks Save on the menu, an object of type Action compares each entry in the list with each entry with the components of the JTabbedPane. From the currently selected component, the editor is determined and the save() method is called on it. The constructor assembles the controls and displays the GUI on the screen.

```
public class FactoryMethod {
    // ... abridged
    private final JMenuItem mnSave = new JMenuItem();

    private final Action saveAction =
                            new AbstractAction("Save") {
        @Override
        public void actionPerformed(ActionEvent e) {
            listEntries.forEach((tempEntry) -> {
                Object selectedPanel =
                        tbbMain.getSelectedComponent();
                if (tempEntry.getEntryPanel().getEditor()
                                == selectedPanel) {
                    tempEntry.getEntryPanel().save();
                    var index =
                            tbbMain.getSelectedIndex();
                    tbbMain.setTitleAt(index,
                            tempEntry.toString());
                }
            });
        }
    };
}
```

Most of the tricky bits in this class are in the Swing programming area. What is important for the factory method pattern is that the coupling of the client to the entries is loose, which allows you to develop more entries very easily.

> You can see the power of the factory method in this example: the client does not need to know from which class the object of type `EntryPanel` was instantiated. It is enough that it calls the factory method `getEntryPanel()` on the object of type `Entry`. Since interfaces are classes with only abstract methods, you can say that the entry (contact or inheritance) has delegated the responsibility for creating the EntryPanel to a subclass.

16.5   Difference to Abstract Factory

Finally, let's look at the differences with Abstract Factory. At first glance, the difference seems relatively clear: The abstract factory creates a family of products; think of a unified look and feel or a specific garden. The factory method creates a single product. However, since nowhere does it say that a family must necessarily consist of two or more products, the difference should not be based on this alone.

The more important difference, in my opinion, is that the Abstract Factory is object-based, while the Factory Method is class-based. Object-based patterns rely on the interaction of objects selected by the client. Class-based patterns involve inheritance; the superclass calls the "right" method.

> **Background Information**
> I told you in Sect. 1.2 that patterns are divided into three categories: Creation Patterns, Behavior Patterns, and Structural Patterns. However, the GoF has made two further distinctions within these three categories: by scope.
> Class-based patterns are the template method and the interpreter. In the case of the adapter, there are two types – one object-based and one class-based. All other patterns are object-based. So the GoF follows its own postulate that composition is preferable to inheritance. An overview of the pattern categories can be found in Table 1.1.

16.6   Factory Method – The UML Diagram

From the example project Address Book you can find the UML diagram in Fig. 16.4.

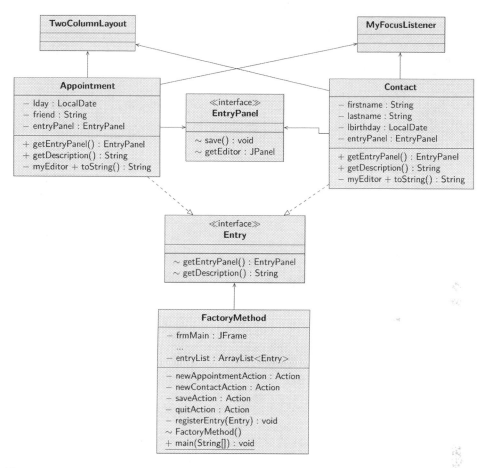

Fig. 16.4   UML diagram of the Factory Method Pattern (example project Address Book)

16.7   Summary

Go through the chapter again in key words:

- The Factory Method supports SRP: object creation and object usage are separated.
- The object creation is outsourced to a separate class.
- The creator delegates object creation to a subclass.
- To do this, it calls the factory method that gives it its name: e.g. `createCar()`.
- The subclass must define this method in its own unique way.
- The subclass decides which concrete product/object is created.

- Producers and products rely on abstractions and are therefore interchangeable for the client.
- Three variations are conceivable:

  - In addition to the Factory Method, the producer can define other methods that are applied to all generated products before they are returned,
  - The creator can provide a default implementation in the factory method,
  - The factory method can be parameterized.

16.8   Description of Purpose

The Gang of Four describes the purpose of the "Factory Method" pattern as follows:

Define a class interface with operations to create an object, but let subclasses decide which class the object to be created is from. Factory methods allow a class to delegate object creation to subclasses.

Prototype

The Prototype Pattern belongs to the category of generation patterns. You have a certain number of products that do not differ significantly. You create a prototype of a product. When variations are requested, you clone the prototype and vary it. Example: you offer different types of pizzas. To cope with the volume of orders, you make a prototype of a Pizza Margherita. When a Hawaiian pizza is ordered, you clone the prototype, top it with ham and pineapple, and serve the finished pizza. That actually explains the pattern. In this chapter, I present more details and address the question of how to clone objects in Java.

17.1 Cloning Objects

The Prototype Pattern is not really difficult to understand – the problem is more about how to clone an object. Take a look at the example project car factory. There we have the class `Motor` with the attributes `id` (of the block), `hp.` (horsepower), and (cubic) `capacity` and the respective access methods. The class `Car` holds a reference to an engine instance, `Car` stores the number of seats and finally the special edition of the car. The class also implements the interface `Cloneable` and overrides the method `clone()` of `Object`.

```
public class Auto implements Cloneable {
    private Engine engine;
    private Edition edition;
    private final int numberSeats;

    Auto(Engine engine, Edition edition, int numberSeats)
        {
            this.engine = engine;
```

Supplementary Information The online version contains supplementary material available at https://doi.org/10.1007/978-3-658-39829-3_17.

```
            this.edition = edition;
            this.numberSeats = numberSeats;
    }
    // ... abridged

    @Override
    public Object clone()
                throws CloneNotSupportedException {
        return super.clone();

    }

}
```

The main method of the test class demonstrates the use of the project. First, an engine is created and installed in the car designed as a prototype. The prototype is to be created in the TINY edition.

```
var engine = new Engine("General Motors", 100, 1.6);
var prototype = new Car(engine, Edition.TINY, 4);
System.out.println("Prototype: " + prototype);
var newCar = (car) prototype.clone();
System.out.println("New car: " + newCar + "\n");
```

The following text is output on the console:

```
Prototype: 4-seater passenger car, Edition TINY, Engine:
    General Motors with 100 hp and 1.6 liters capacity
New car: 4-seater passenger car, edition TINY, engine:
    General Motors with 100 hp and 1.6 liters capacity
```

So you created a clone from the prototype.

17.1.1 Criticism of the Implementation

The solution works, but it is not unproblematic. Look critically at the first approach.

17.1.1.1 The Cloneable Interface

The method `clone()` of the class `Object` has the visibility `protected`. It must therefore first be made `public` by a subclass. What is the role of the interface `Cloneable`? Please comment out the interface in the project as a test:

```
public class Auto {// implements Cloneable {
    // … abridged
    @Override
    public Object clone()
                    throws CloneNotSupportedException {
        return super.clone();
    }
}
```

The project continues to compile without errors. Now call the test method again. You will see that a `CloneNotSupported` exception is thrown. The default implementation of the `clone()` method first checks whether the object to be `cloned` is of type `Cloneable`. The interface is purely a marker interface – it does not impose a method. If the object to be cloned is not of this type, the default implementation throws the exception. If the object to be cloned is of type `Cloneable`, a bitwise copy of it is created and returned. The type of the clone is the same as the type of the original.

The documentation for the `Object.clone()` method recommends that the original object and the clone have the following relationships:

- The objects have different references `prototype != clone`
- The classes are identical: `prototype.getClass() == clone.getClass()`
- The objects are equal in the sense of `clone.equals(prototype) == true`

The main method of the test class checks these conditions.

```
System.out.println("Test for reference identity (==): "
                    + (newcar == prototype));
System.out.println("Class prototype: "
                    + prototype.getClass());
System.out.println("Class new car: "
                    + newCar.getClass());
System.out.println("Test for equality (equals): "
                    + newCar.equals(prototype));
```

The console outputs:

```
Test for reference identity (==): false
Class prototype: class car
Class new car: class car
Test for equality (equals): true
```

The default implementation of the equals method in the `Object` class checks for reference equality of the objects being compared (`prototype == clone`). However, since prototype and clone have different references, if you override `clone()`, you will also override `equals()`. If you override `equals()`, you should also override `hashCode()`. The documentation for `Object.equals()` says:

> The equals method for class Object implements the most discriminating possible equivalence relation on objects; that is, for any non-null reference values x and y, this method returns true if and only if x and y refer to the same object (x == y has the value true).

> Note that it is generally necessary to override the hashCode method whenever this method is overridden, so as to maintain the general contract for the hashCode method, which states that equal objects must have equal hash codes.

17.1.1.2 The Problem of Equal References

In the last code section, the main method returns the engine of the prototype and sets a different identifier there. Again, have the data of the vehicles output to the console.

```
motor = prototype.getEngine();
motor.setId("Marshall Motors");
System.out.println("Prototype: " + prototype);
System.out.println("New car: " + newCar);
```

The console now outputs (abbreviated):

```
Prototype: (…) Engine: Marshall Motors with 100 hp (…)
New car: (…) Engine: Marshall Motors with 100 hp (…)
```

A change that you have made to the prototype is reflected in the clone. You have to critically question whether this is intentional. All employees of a company – the prototypes and the clones – have the same employer, and if he is called "Dr. Z" today and "Dr. Q" tomorrow, this affects all employees. Here, a change to a referenced object of a prototype is certainly important for all clones. However, the reverse case is also conceivable: Dolly[1] and the prototype sheep may have the same DNA. However, it must never happen that you shear Dolly and the original sheep then also stands shaven on the meadow. In this case, changes to the clone or the prototype must have no effect on the other specimen. But first let's look at why the engine is the same on both cars, even though you only made the change to one.

---

[1] https://de.wikipedia.org/wiki/Dolly_(sheep).

17.1.1.3 What Happens During Cloning

I delegated the cloning to the default implementation of the clone() method in the example above:

```
public Object clone() throws CloneNotSupportedException {
    return super.clone();
}
```

This standard implementation copies the object to be cloned bit by bit. The contents of the variables are copied unchanged. What happens to a variable with a primitive data type? At the point where you create an int variable, for example, the value of the number is stored after an assignment. The variable simply makes it easier for you to access the memory location within the object. When you assign a new value to the variable, the memory location within the object is overwritten. This assignment has no effect on the clone, which has its own memory area. If you have a variable with a complex data type, a reference to the assigned object is stored in the location of the variable. The object is stored on the heap. And that reference is copied just like the value of the primitive variable. So two objects independently hold a reference to the same object. This is not critical if you are referencing immutable objects. If the clone and prototype reference the same String object, and you change that String on either the clone or prototype, a new String object is created and referenced there. The bitwise copy procedure is called shallow copy. When you clone arrays or collections, you always get a shallow copy. The Test_Collections sample project demonstrates the shallow copy using several examples.

This may be desired as in the joint employer example. But it may also be that you do not want to have two shorn sheep standing in the meadow. You can only put one engine in one car. So it makes sense to change the depth of the copy and create a deep copy. To do this, you recursively trace all referenced objects and create copies of them.

The class Object defines the protected method clone(). Subclasses make this method public; they override the method with super.clone(). The default implementation of the method in Object requests memory for the object's runtime type. The object is then copied one bit at a time. If the object to be cloned is not of type Cloneable, the default implementation throws an exception. You as the programmer are responsible for overriding the clone() method in a meaningful way. In particular, this also means deciding whether to create deep or shallow copies. The caller of the clone method you override cannot tell whether you are copying deep or shallow. You should therefore always document your procedure in the JavaDoc so that no uncertainties arise for the user with regard to the copying behavior.

17.1.2 Cloning in Inheritance Hierarchies

It is entirely up to you how you implement the clone method. The following solutions are therefore also conceivable. The clone method of the Car class could create a new Car object with the new operator. The number of seats and the reference to the enum are copied; a new engine (no clone here!) is created.

```
@Override
public Obect clone() throws CloneNotSupportedException {
    var newEngine = new Engine("Bishop Motors", 80, 1.4);
    var car = new Car(newEngine, Edition.TINY, 4);
    return car;
}
```

You can achieve a similar effect with a CopyConstructor. Here, too, a new car instance is created; the prototype then passes itself as an argument to the private constructor when cloned. You can find this code in the sample project CarFactory_CopyConstructor:

```
public class Car implements Cloneable {
    private Engine engine;
    private Edition edition;
    private final int numberSeats;

    Auto(Engine engine, Edition edition, int numberseats)
        {
        this.engine = engine;
        this.edition = edition;
        this.numberSeats = numberSeats;
    }

    private Car(Car car) {
        this.engine =
                    new Engine("Bishop Motors", 80, 1.4);
        this.numberSeats = auto.numberSeats;
        this.edition = auto.edition;
    }

    @Override
    public Object clone() throws CloneNotSupportedException {
        return new Auto(this);
    }
    // ... abridged
}
```

Please look at these two approaches very skeptically they are not without problems. Assume that at some point you will have to deal with inheritance – car should be super-class for roadster, for example. How are the sub classes cloned? Roadster might try to request a clone with `super.clone()` - just as it did in the previous version. The clone method of Car would return an object of dynamic type Car, and that cannot be cast to a subtype, say Roadster; an appropriate cast would throw a ClassCastException.

It would be conceivable to query the dynamic type and call the corresponding constructor:

```
@Override
public Object clone() throws CloneNotSupportedException {
    if(car.getClass() == roadster.getClass())
        return new Roadster(this);
    else
        return new Car(this);
}
```

Each new subclass of Auto would get a new if branch – that's horror! But you have to make sure that the clone matches the type of the subclass, because a clone should satisfy the condition `prototype.getClass() == clone.getClass()`. Thus, if a class may have subclasses, so it is not final, it must implement the clone method differently. Since a superclass can never know all subclasses, it must not be its job to determine the runtime type of the object to be cloned. Only the default implementation of Object. clone() can take the runtime type into account. So a class that is not final should request the object to be returned with super.clone().

It is possible, of course, that a superclass must modify private data fields before returning the clone. In the example project CarFactory_Superclass, the Roadster class inherits from Car. In addition, you want the Roadster to get a new engine of its own when cloned. How do you achieve this goal? In this project version, I have removed the setEngine method. So a new car can only get a new engine in three ways: Either the constructor is parameterized appropriately, another car object changes the motor, or the object changes its motor itself. You won't call a constructor. So there must be another solution. Now take a look at the example project CarFactory_Superclass .

The client calls the clone method of the Roadster class, which in turn calls the clone method of the superclass. In the Roadster class you will find:

```
@Override
public Object clone() throws CloneNotSupportedException {
    return super.clone();
}
```

And in the car class then:

```
@Override
public Object clone() throws CloneNotSupportedException {
    var clone = super.clone();
    var carClone = (Car) clone;
    var newEngine = new Engine("Roadster Star", 80, 1.4);
    carClone.engine = newEngine;
    return carClone;
}
```

The clone method of Car first calls the clone method of Object. It gets back an object of dynamic type Roadster – you remember: Object.clone() returns the runtime type. This object is cast to type Car; this is allowed by Liskov's substitution principle – a subclass should be able to replace its base class. Now the Car instance has access to the private data field engine and assigns a new engine. After that, the cloned object is returned. The client receives an object of dynamic type Roadster with a brand new engine.

How is this done in practice? In practice, it makes sense for classes from which other classes are derived to override the clone method only protected and not implement the interface Cloneable. Subclasses are then free to support cloning or not.

Previously, the clone method was implemented according to the signature of the Object class: The return value is of type Object; also, the CloneNotSupportedException is propagated. Let's look at these two points in more detail.

When a method returns an object of a particular type, the client must first cast it to the expected type. Since Java 5, covariant return types are allowed; thus, the clone method is allowed to return a Car-object, as the following code snippet shows.

```
@Override
public Car clone() throws CloneNotSupportedException {
    var clone = super.clone();
    var carClone = (Car) clone;
    var newEngine = new Engine("Roadster Star", 80, 1.4);
    carClone.Engine = newEngine;
    return carClone;
}
```

However, if you make this change in the Car class, you must also do so in the Roadster subclass. There, too, the return value must be of type Car, not of type Roadster.

The other issue, the CloneNotSupportedException is passionately argued about in the forums; the prevailing opinion in the literature is not happy about this exception. On the one hand, there is a method clone() that is overridden by the class; on the other hand, this very method says that it may not support cloning at all. The CloneNotSupportedException is thrown when the default implementation of the clone() method determines that the object to be cloned is not of type Cloneable. However, this case is only relevant if none of the superclasses in an inheritance hierarchy implements the interface Cloneable.

However, this error can be detected and cured at compile time; it is therefore dispropor-
tionate to propagate a checked exception. For practical purposes, it is therefore a good idea
to catch the exception within the clone method and throw an AssertionError instead:

```
public Auto clone() {
    try {
        var clone = super.clone();
        var carClone = (Car) clone;
        var newEngine =
                new Engine("Roadster Star", 80, 1.4);
        carClone.Engine = newEngine;
        return carClone;
    } catch (CloneNotSupportedException exc) {
        throw new AssertionError();
    }
}
```

In the following section, you design a larger project that builds on prototypes.

17.2   A Major Project

You draw different colored circles and connect them with lines. Both circles and lines are
graphics. You can delete both circles and lines. Lines that no longer connect two graphics
after deletion are also deleted. Figure 17.1 shows the program in action.

17.2.1 Discussion of the First Version

Right-click to open the context menu and choose to either draw a line or add a circle or
select a graphic. You have different circles at your disposal: red, blue, green and so on. If
you choose to draw a line, click either a circle or a line and drag a line to the target graphic,
which can also be either a line or a circle. If you select Select a graphic, you can select
either a circle or a line. Once you have made a selection, choose "Edit..." and "Delete
selected" from the main menu. The selected graphic will then be deleted, with all affected
connections – lines – also being deleted. If you have selected a circle, you can also move it.
   You can model the highway network of Germany, the metro map of Paris or whatever
with this version of the graphics editor. In further expansion stages, you could add boxes
in addition to circles and turn the framework into a small UML editor. Before I show you
the essential classes of the sample project GraphEditor_1, it's best to open it with NetBeans
and familiarize yourself with the handling.
   The program is started with the main method in the ApplStart class. This method
creates a JFrame and adds the main menu and the drawing area, an instance of the

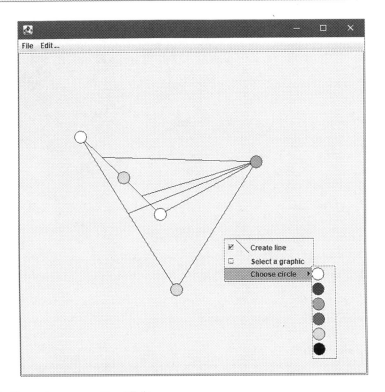

Fig. 17.1   Example program GraphEditor

PanelCanvas class, there. The PrototypeManager class creates the prototypes of the circles to be drawn. In practice, this class can grow to any size; extensive initialization routines to create the prototypes are offloaded there. The class Diagram is the data model of the editor. Here, the graphics are stored and managed in a list. The interface GraphicIF defines methods that must be implemented by all graphics (circles and lines). The interface RelationIF, which is derived from this, describes methods that only have to be implemented by lines. The Circle and Relation classes implement these interfaces and define the prescribed methods. For example, each graphic must be able to describe the rectangle enclosing it and store a specific color and its position. Perhaps most importantly, a graphic must be able to draw itself and, most importantly, clone itself. Lines always connect two other graphics, so they must also be able to store and return the start and end graphics.

The diagram is drawn on the PanelCanvas. The MouseAdapter overrides some EventHandlers. The PanelCanvas also defines some actions: The Create_Line_Action sets a flag that a line should be drawn. The Select_Action specifies that a graphic can be selected. The actions are passed to JCheckBoxMenuItem instances and hooked into the panel's context menu. The actions are combined into a ButtonGroup so that only one can be selected at a time.

```
private final ButtonGroup group = new ButtonGroup();
// … abridged
group.add(mnCreateLine);
group.add(mnSelect);
```

In the constructor, the prototype circles are also created as menu items. First, the prototype manager queries all prototypes. Then a separate menu item is created iteratively for each prototype; when called, the prototype is passed to the data field `nextGraphic`.

```
public PanelCanvas(Diagram) {
    // … abridged

    for (final GraphicIF tempGraphic :
                    PrototypeManager.getPrototypes())
        addPrototype(tempGraphic);
        // … abridged
}
    // … abridged

private void addPrototype(final GraphicIF prototype) {
    final var drawAction = new AbstractAction() {
        @Override
        public void actionPerformed(ActionEvent event) {
            createLine = false;
            nextGraphic = prototype;
        }
    };

    var mnNewGraphic = new JCheckBoxMenuItem(drawAction);
    mnCirclePrototypes.add(mnNewGraphic);
    group.add(mnNewGraphic);
    var icon = prototype.getIcon();
    mnNewGraphic.setIconTextGap(0);
    mnNewGraphic.setIcon(icon);
}
```

If you have selected a circle and click on the drawing area, the event handler `mouse-Clicked` is called, which requests the prototype from the data field `nextGraphic`, clones it and saves the clone in the diagram.

```
@Override
public void mouseClicked(MouseEvent event) {
    mousePosition = event.getPoint();
```

```
if (nextGraphic != null)
try {
    var newGraphic = (GraphicIF) nextGraphic.clone();
    selected = newGraphic;
    diagram.add(newGraphic, mousePosition);
} catch (CloneNotSupportedException ex) {
    new ErrorDialog(ex);
}
else
    // Search for a graphic object
    // at the mouse position and select
    selected = diagram.findGraphic(mousePosition);
repaint();
}
```

These are the essential points of the program. Everything else are gimmicks that facilitate the handling of the program. Please analyze the code of the program independently.

17.2.2 The Second Version – Deep Copy

In the second version (sample project GraphEditor_2) it should be possible to clone the
whole diagram. Two canvas instances are placed on the JFrame. If you click on Clone
Diagram in the File menu item, the diagram is copied from the left side to the right side.
You can now modify both diagrams independently. Figure 17.2 shows you the interface of
the new version.

The menu item is defined in the `Appl Start` class and hooked into the menu. It queries for the diagram at the left panel and inserts it at the right panel. The `PanelCanvas`
class defines the `getDiagramAsClone()` method in this version. First, the
`ByteArrayOutputStream` baos is created and passed to the `ObjectOutputStream`
oos. Into the baos the diagram is serialized. Then you create the `ByteArrayInputStream`
bais. The data of the baos is passed to this. The bais is passed to the `ObjectInputStream`
ois, which deserializes the serialized diagram. The resulting object is cast to a diagram
and returned. Serialization and deserialization cause the objects, including the objects they
reference, to be independent of each other.

```
public Diagram getDiagramAsClone() {
    Diagram clone = null;
    try {
        this.nextGraphic = null;
        this.selected = null;
        this.createLine = false;
        ObjectOutputStream oos;
```

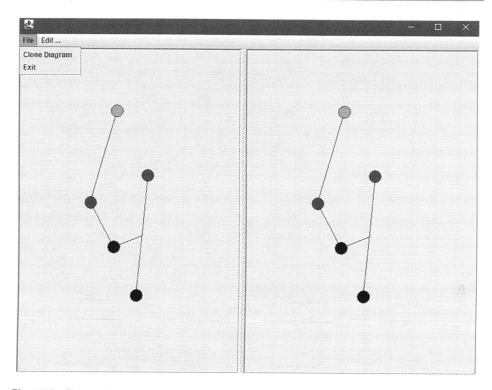

Fig. 17.2 Cloned diagram

```
ByteArrayInputStream bais;
ObjectInputStream ois;
try ( var baos = new ByteArrayOutputStream()) {
    oos = new ObjectOutputStream(baos);
    oos.writeObject(diagram);
  bais =
    new ByteArrayInputStream(baos.toByteArray());
    ois = new ObjectInputStream(bais);
    clone = (diagram) ois.readObject();
}
oos.close();
bais.close();
ois.close();
} catch (IOException ex) {
    new ErrorDialog(ex);
} finally {
    return clone;
}
}
```

In the latest version of the program you will design your own prototypes.

17.2.3 Defining Your Own Prototypes

A special feature of the Prototype Pattern is that you can develop and add your own prototypes at runtime. The example project GraphEditor_3 is based on the first project version.
So you already know most of the functionality. There is a new menu item New Prototype
in the Edit menu. When you select this menu item, a color selection dialog appears. Select
a color and click Ok. A circle with the desired color is now available as a prototype in the
context menu. In the class `ApplStart` the action `newPrototypeAction` is defined,
which calls the method `createPrototype()` on the drawing area. Within the method
a JColorChooser is called. With the return value a new circle is created and added as prototype to the context menu as well as to the prototype manager.

```
public void createPrototype() {
    var newColor =
            JColorChooser.showDialog(PanelCanvas.this,
            "New Circle", Color.cyan);
    if (newColor != null) {
        GraphicIF newPrototype = new Circle(newColor);
        addPrototype(newPrototype);
        PrototypeManager.add(newPrototype);
    }
}
```

17.3   Prototype – The UML Diagram

From the example project GraphEditor_3 you can see in Fig. 17.3 first the UML diagram
of the packages graphics and prototype, and then in Fig. 17.4 the UML diagram of the
package delegate and the actual application.

17.4   Summary

Go through the chapter again in key words:

• The prototype pattern hides object creation from the client.
• You want to have different objects (products) at runtime.
• A prototype of each product is created, which is cloned when a new object is requested.
• The prototypes are managed by the Prototype Manager.

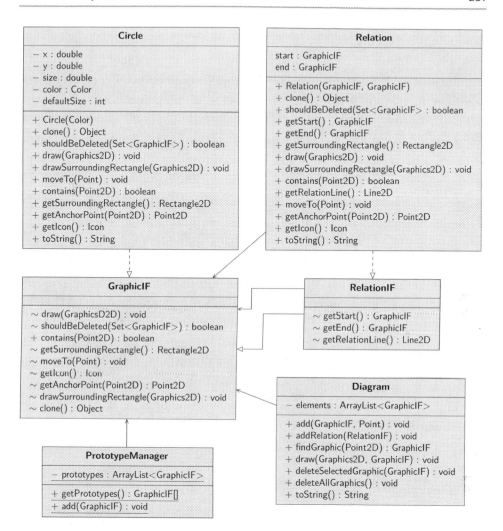

Fig. 17.3 UML diagram of the prototype pattern (sample project GraphEditor_3, packages graphics and prototype)

- Each prototype must override the clone() method when using the cloneable interface.
- The method clone() is defined in Object with the visibility protected.
- The default implementation of this method results in a flat copy of the object; referenced objects are not cloned.
- Collections also clone as a flat copy by default.
- Superclasses should override clone() at least in a protected manner to allow subclasses to be implemented in a meaningful way.

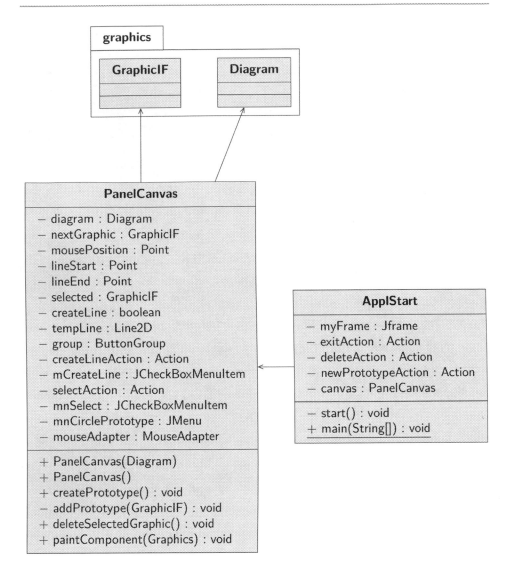

Fig. 17.4 UML diagram of the Prototype Pattern (example project GraphEditor_3, package delegate and application)

17.5   Description of Purpose

The Gang of Four describes the purpose of the "Prototype" pattern as follows:

> Determine the types of objects to create by using a prototypical copy, and create new objects by copying that prototype.

From the set of generation patterns, you know the singleton pattern, the two factories, and the prototype pattern. The Builder Pattern is the last pattern you use to create objects without using the new operator. With the builder pattern, you have an object that is complex or complicated to construct. This object cannot be created in one pass, but goes through an elaborate construction process.

18.1 An Object Creates Other Objects

To get started, let's start with a simple example. If you want to book a trip online, you can specify a variety of search parameters. The most important parameters are probably the time period and the number of days you want to travel. It is also interesting to know how many people you will be traveling with and how many children (under 14) you will be taking with you. You will certainly also want to specify how many stars your accommodation should have. And important are the rating of the accommodation and the recommendation rate. Maybe you want to be on the safe side and only want to see hotels that have already been rated by at least x guests. You save all these search parameters in the data fields of a travel object.

18.1.1 Telescoping Constructor Pattern

Take a look at the Telescoping_Constructor_Pattern sample project. You pass the search parameters to the constructor.

Supplementary Information The online version contains supplementary material available at https://doi.org/10.1007/978-3-658-39829-3_18.

```
public class Trip {
public final LocalDate startDate;
public final LocalDate endDate;
public final int duration;
public final int numberTravellers;
public final int numberKids;
public final int minimumStars;
public final int minimumRecommendations;
public final int rating;
public final int minimumNumberRatings;

Trip(LocalDate startDate, LocalDate endDate,
         int duration, int numberTravellers,
         int numberKids, int minimumStars,
         int minimumRecommmendations,
         int rating, int minimumNumberRatings)
    {
         this.startDate = startDate;
         this.endDate = endDate;
         this.duration = duration;
         this.numberTravellers = numberTravellers;
         this.numberKids = numberKids;
         this.minimumStars = minimumStars;
    this.minimumRecommendations = minimumRecommendations;
         this.rating = rating;
         this.minimumNumberRatings = minimumNumberRatings;
    }
}
```

Calling this constructor is sheer horror! The main method of the `ApplStart` class demonstrates this:

```
public static void main(String[] args) {
    var trip = new Trip(LocalDate.now(), LocalDate.now()
                    , 7, 2, 3, 3, 80, 5, 30);
    System.out.println(travel);
}
```

The problem is not only that you have to pass a lot of parameters – they are of the same type. You will never find out what each parameter stands for without documentation. Errors will creep in very reliably with such a call. One solution might be to overload the constructor. If the client doesn't require a rating or even a minimum number of ratings, it should be allowed to omit them. The new constructor calls the one just presented with this() and passes default values:

```
Trip(LocalDate startDate, LocalDate enddate,
        int duration, int numberTravellers,
        int numberKids, int minimumStars,
        int minimumRecommendations) {
    this(startDate, enddate, duration, numberTravellers,
            numberKids, minimumStars,
            minimumRecommendations, 0, 0);
}
```

The client now creates a travel object with a slightly shorter parameter list:

```
public static void main(String[] args) {
    var trip = new Trip(LocalDate.now(), LocalDate.now(),
                        7, 2, 3, 3, 80);
    System.out.println(travel);
}
```

Is this call more appealing or clear? No! This solution, called the Telescoping Constructor Pattern, has made its way into the list of antipatterns. It's never a good idea to have to pass too many parameters to a method – even more so when they are of the same type. Let's look at another solution.

18.1.2 JavaBeans Pattern

In Java introductions you will find the advice that data fields must be encapsulated and may only be read and modified via getters and setters – and the version in the sample project JavaBeans_Pattern is oriented to this. Information that cannot be dispensed with during construction, i.e. time frame, duration, and number of travelers, is stored in final data fields that are initialized by the constructor. The remaining information is preset with default values and can optionally be overwritten with setters.

```
public class Travel {
    public final LocalDate startDate;
    public final LocalDate endDate;
    public final int duration;
    public final int numberTravellers;
    private int numberKids = 0;
    private int minimumStars = 0;
    private int minimumRecommendations = 0;
    private int rating = 0;
    private int minimumNumberRatings = 0;
```

```
Trip(LocalDate startDate, LocalDate endDate,
                int duration, int numberTravellers) {
    this.startDate = startDate;
    this.endDate = endDate;
    this.duration = duration;
    this.numberTravellers = numberTravellers;
}

public void setNumberKids(int numberKids) {
    this.numberKids = numberKids;
}

// … abridged
}
```

The client can now create an instance of the Trip class much more clearly.

```
public static void main(String[] args) {
    var trip = new Trip(LocalDate.now(),
                    LocalDate.now().plusDays(14), 14, 2);
    trip.setMinimumStars(3);
    trip.setMinimumRecommendations(80);
    System.out.println(trip);
}
```

The code is indeed much more speaking now. However, the other data fields are not final and cannot be. Subsequent modification of the values is therefore allowed, even if it may not be desired. The approach is not quite the same as the JavaBeans specification, but merely adopts the essential principle. The JavaBeans specification requires that you always define a default constructor. Incidentally, you will also occasionally come across opinions in the literature that relegate the JavaBeans specification to the realm of antipatterns – for the reasons just mentioned.

18.1.3 Builder Pattern

Since the toolbox of OOP does not allow a satisfactory solution, it is time for a pattern. The Builder Pattern assumes an object whose task is limited to constructing another object. In the version in the Builder_Pattern sample project, you now realize the travel class by storing all information in final data fields. As with Singleton, the constructor is private, so that an object can only be created within the class. The constructor expects an object of type Builder as parameter.

```
public class Trip {
    // ... abridged
    private final LocalDate startDate;
    private final LocalDate endDate;
    public final String start;
    public final String end;
    public final int duration;
    public final int numberTraveller;
    public final int numberKids;
    public final int minimumStars;
    public final int minimumRecommendations;
    public final int rating;
    public final int minimumNumberRatings;

    private Trip(Builder builder) {
        this.startDate = builder.startDate;
        this.endDate = builder.endDate;
        var formatter =
            DateTimeFormatter.ofPattern("MM/dd/YYYY");
        start = formatter.format(startDate);
        end = formatter.format(endDate);
        this.duration = builder.duration;
        this.numberTravellers = builder.numberTravellers;
        this.numberKids = builder.numberKids;
        this.minimumStars = builder.minimumStars;
        this.minimumRecommendations =
                        builder.minimumRecommendations;
        this.rating = builder.rating;
        this.minimumNumberRatings =
                        builder.minimumNumberRatings;
    }
}
```

The `Builder` type is defined as the static inner class of the trip. The data fields of the trip are also declared here. The important data fields are initialized in the constructor, the others get default values. For each data field, there is a setter that, contrary to language convention, only repeats the name of the field. Inside the setter, the corresponding data field is assigned a value; finally, the setter returns the builder instance.

```
public static class Builder {
    private LocalDate startDate;
    private LocalDate endDate;
    private int duration;
    private int numberTravellers;
    private int numberKids = 0;
```

```
        private int minimumStars = 0;
        private int minimumRecommendations = 0;
        private int rating = 0;
        private int minimumNumberRatings = 0;

        public Builder(LocalDate startDate,
                       LocalDate endDate, int duration,
                       int numberTravellers) {
            this.startDate = startDate;
            // ... abridged
        }

        public Builder numberKids(int numberKids) {
            this.numberKids = numberKids;
            return this;
        }

        public Builder minimumStars(int minimumStars) {
            this.minimumStars = minimumStars;
            return this;
        }

        // ... abridged
    }
```

The build() method then finally creates the journey object and passes the builder object to its constructor for this purpose.

```
public journey build() {
    return new Trip(this);
}
```

In the first step, the client creates a builder, supplies it with the relevant data – if required – and only then has a trip object returned.

```
public static void main(String[] args) {
    var builder = new Trip.Builder(LocalDate.now(),
                                   LocalDate.now(), 15, 2);
    var trip = builder
            .minimumStars(3)
            .rating(5)
            .numberKids(0)
            .build();
    System.out.println(trip);
}
```

This first realization of the Builder Pattern should give you a sense that it can be useful to have objects whose functionality is limited to creating other objects. Please don't be surprised that for simplicity reasons I have given `LocalDate.now()` for the startDate as well as for the endDate in the first examples; in practice it is of course impracticable to have 15 days of vacation in the time "from today to today".

Somewhat unattractive is still the new Trip.builder in the main method. You can still create a builder in the trip class with a static method:

```
public class Trip {
    // ... abridged
    public static Trip.Builder builder(
            LocalDate startDate, LocalDate endDate,
            int duration, int numberTravellers) {
        return new Trip.Builder(startDate,
                endDate, duration, numberTravellers);
    }
}
```

If you then want to do without a separate builder variable in the main method, the following code (which you will also find in the example) will also work:

```
public static void main(String[] args) {
    var trip = Trip.builder(LocalDate.now(),
                    LocalDate.now().plusDays(15), 15, 2)
            .minimumStars(3)
            .rating(5)
            .numberKids(0)
            .build();
    System.out.println(trip);
}
```

18.2 A More Complex Design Process

The purpose of the Builder Pattern is to outsource the construction process to a separate class. This always makes sense if the construction of an object is complex or should be replaceable. In the following example, I would like to take up the budget book from the last chapter. To do this, open the sample project BudgetBuilder. In practice, you probably don't want to store the various items and categories in the source code, as I showed you with the composite pattern in Chap. 12. You may want to read the data from an XML file and display it in a JTree. The Builder Pattern is ideally suited for this, since a node in the JTree cannot be created in one pass; only when it has no further subnodes can the object creation be completed.

The XML shortened file in the example looks like this:

```
<?xml version="1.0" encoding="UTF-8"?>
<!DOCTYPE Budgetbook
[
    <!ELEMENT Budgetbook (Item*, Month+)>
    <!ELEMENT Month (Category*)>
    <!ELEMENT Category (Item| Category)*>
    <!ELEMENT Item EMPTY>

    <!ATTLIST Budgetbook description    CDATA #REQUIRED>
    <!ATTLIST Month description         CDATA #REQUIRED>
    <!ATTLIST Category description      CDATA #REQUIRED>
    <!ATTLIST Item  description         CDATA #REQUIRED
                    amount              CDATA #REQUIRED
                    required (yes|no)      "yes" >
]>
<Budgetbook description = "Budgetbook 2022">
    <Item description="Life insurance"  amount = "-1600" required
= "yes"/>
    <Month description = "January">
        <Category description = "Income">
            <Item description = "Main job" amount = "2000" required
= "yes"/>
            <Item description = "Lectures" amount = "5000" required
= "yes"/>
        </Category>
        <Category description = "Expenses">
            <Category description = "Rent">
                <Item description = "Apartment" amount = "-700"/>
                <Item description = "Garage" amount = "-150" required
= "no"/>
            </Category>
            <Category description = "Insurances">
                <Item description = "Car" amount = "-34.50"/>
            </Category>
        </Category>
    </Month>

    … abridged


</Budgetbook>
```

Your task will now be to turn the XML document into a TreeModel and display it in a JTree.

18.2.1 Converting XML Files into a TreeModel

I first took the last project version of the chapter about the composite pattern. In this, I created a new package `builder`, where you can find the abstract class `Builder`. Builder inherits from `org.xml.sax.helpers.DefaultHandler` and forces its subclasses to define the `startElement()` and `endElement()` method. When an element of the XML document is opened or closed, one of these methods is called. If the XML data is not valid, the `warning()`, `error()`, or `fatalError()` methods emit appropriate error messages. The client first lets an instance of the `Builder` type create an object and then fetches the finished product from this instance; each subclass must therefore also offer the `getProduct()` method.

```
public abstract class Builder extends DefaultHandler {
    public abstract Object getProduct();

    @Override
    public abstract void startElement(String uri,
                        String localName, String name,
                        Attributes attributes);

    @Override
    public abstract void endElement(String uri,
                        String localName, String name);

    @Override
    public void warning(SAXParseException exception) {
        System.err.println("-> warning: " +
                            exception.getMessage());
    }

    @Override
    public void fatalError(SAXParseException exception) {
        System.err.println("-> FATAL ERROR: " +
                            exception.getMessage());
    }

    @Override
    public void error(SAXParseException exception) {
        System.err.println("-> error: " +
                            exception.getMessage());
```

```
        }
    }
```

The first concrete builder you will create is the TreeModelBuilder. It has two data fields: the root node and a list where all nodes are temporarily stored. The startElement() and endElement() methods are responsible for the actual construction process. When an element is opened, the startElement() method first checks if the element is called "Item". If so, the attributes are retrieved and a new leaf is created; otherwise, a new composite is created. If the root is null, that is, only for the very first element, the currently created element is passed to the root data field. If the root data field is not null, that is, starting with the second element, the new element is appended to the last composite stored in the list as a child node. The node is then stored in the list.

```
public class TreeModelBuilder extends Builder {
    private Composite root;
    private final LinkedList<Node> stack =
                                new LinkedList<>();

    @Override
    public void startElement(String uri,
                String localName, String name,
                Attributes attributes) {
        Node node;
        if (name.equalsIgnoreCase("Item")) {
            var tempDescription =
                    attributes.getValue("description");
            var tempAmount = Double.
            parseDouble(attributes.getValue("amount"));
            var tempRequired =
                    attributes.getValue("required").
                    equalsIgnoreCase("yes");
            node = new Leaf(tempDescription, tempAmount,
                                    tempRequired);
        } else {
            var tempDescription =
                    attributes.getValue("description");
            node = new Composite(tempDescription);
        }
        if (root == null)
            root = (Composite) node;
        else {
            var tempNode = (Composite) stack.peekLast();
            tempNode.add(node);
        }
```

```
        stack.add(node);
    }

    // … abridged
}
```

The method `endElement()` is called when the element is closed. It can be limited to removing the last element stored in the list there. The method `getProduct()` creates a MyTreeModel with the data field `root` and returns it.

```
@Override
public void endElement(String uri, String localName,
                                    String name) {
        stack.pollLast();
}


@Override
public TreeModel getProduct() {
    return new MyTreeModel(root);
}
```

The client first creates a builder instance, in this project a TreeModelBuilder. It passes this builder to the `build()` method, which first reads the XML file, converts it into a string and parses it with the builder as handler.

```
Budget() {
    var builder = new TreeModelBuilder();
    build(builder);
    var treeModel = (TreeModel) builder.getProduct();
    var frmMain = new JFrame("Builder Pattern Demo");
  frmMain.setDefaultCloseOperation(JFrame.EXIT_ON_CLOSE);
    var trvBudgetBook = new JTree(treeModel);
    trvBudgetBook.setCellRenderer(
                            new MyTreeCellRenderer());
    trvBudgetBook.setEditable(true);
    trvBudgetBook.setCellEditor(new MyTreeCellEditor());
    var scrTree = new JScrollPane(trvBudgetBook);
    frmMain.add(scrTree);
    frmMain.setSize(500, 500);
    frmMain.setVisible(true);
}
public void build(Builder builder) {
```

```
var filePath = Paths.get(file);
try {
    var content = Files.readString(filePath);
    var factory = SAXParserFactory.newInstance();
    factory.setValidating(true);
    var saxParser = factory.newSAXParser();
    saxParser.parse(new InputSource(
        new StringReader(content)),builder);
} catch (IOException | ParserConfigurationException |
                                SAXException ex) {
    ex.printStackTrace();
}
}
```

Background Information

If you critically review the example, you will notice one disadvantage of the pattern: The builder is strongly tied to the object being created. Since it queries whether an element is called "position", this builder is bound to the given DTD. Likewise, the builder must have precise knowledge of the construction of leaf and composite classes.

On the other hand, you can see the big advantage: You can pass any XML file that conforms to the DTD to the Builder – you will always be able to generate a suitable TreeModel from it.

Your program is now much more modularized. As a result, the routine that reads the XML document can be replaced by a routine that obtains the XML document from another source, such as the network. This change has no effect on the Builder.

In the next section, you will define a new builder that will bring the data into HTML format.

18.2.2 Displaying XML Files as HTML

The following example extends the project with a new builder. It should be possible to generate and display the XML file as an HTML document. Follow the necessary steps in the sample project BudgetBuilder_Ext. In the first step, you create a new builder, the HTMLBuilder, which inherits from the Builder class. Nothing changes in the startElement() and endElement() methods. The getProduct() method generates an HTML string from the information in the root and returns it.

```
@Override
public String getProduct() {
    html.append("<html><body><h1 align=\"center\">");
    html.append(root.getDescription());
    html.append("</h1>");
    html.append("<b>" + "Annual items:</b><br/>");
    for (var i = 0; i < root.getNumberOfChildNodes();
                                                    i++) {
        var tempNode = root.getIndex(i);
        if (tempNode.getClass() == Leaf.class) {
            html.append(" ");
            var item = (Leaf) tempNode;
            formatLeaf(item);
            html.append("<br/>");
        } else {
            html.append("<p>");
            appendElements(tempNode, 0);
            html.append("</p>");
        }
    }
    html.append("</body></html>");
    return html.toString();
}
```

In this method, the `appendElements()` method is called, which recursively traverses all nodes and expands the HTML string.

```
private void appendElements(Node node, int tab) {
    html.append("<br/>");
    for (var i = 0; i < tab; i++)
        html.append(" ");
    if (node.getClass() == Leaf.class)
        formatSheet((sheet) node);
    else {
        if (tab == 0)
        html.append("<b>");
        html.append(node);
        if (tab == 0)
            html.append("</b>");
    }
    for (var j = 0; j < node.getNumberofChildNodes();
                                                    j++) {
        var childNode = node.getIndex(j);
        appendElements(childNode, tab + 1);
    }
}
```

Both methods call the `formatLeaf()` method, which checks an output item to see if it was required. If not, the display text is colored red.

```
private void formatLeaf(Leaf item) {
    if (!item.expenseIsRequired())
        html.append("<font color=\"#FF0000\">");
    double amount = item.getValue();
    html.append(item
            .getDescription())
            .append(": ")
            .append(NumberFormat
                .getCurrencyInstance()
                .format(amount));
    if (!item.expenseIsRequired())
        html.append("</font>");
}
```

The client creates a builder and gets the HTML string from there. This is displayed in a JEditorPane:

```
Budget() {
    var builder = new HTMLBuilder();
    build(builder);
    var html = builder.getProduct();

    var frmMain = new JFrame("Builder Pattern Demo");
    frmMain.setDefaultCloseOperation(JFrame.EXIT_ON_CLOSE);
    System.out.println(html);
    var editorPane = new JEditorPane();
    editorPane.setContentType("text/html");
    editorPane.setText(html);
```

```
var scrTree = new JScrollPane(editorPane);
frmMain.add(scrTree);
frmMain.setSize(500, 500);
frmMain.setVisible(true);
}
```

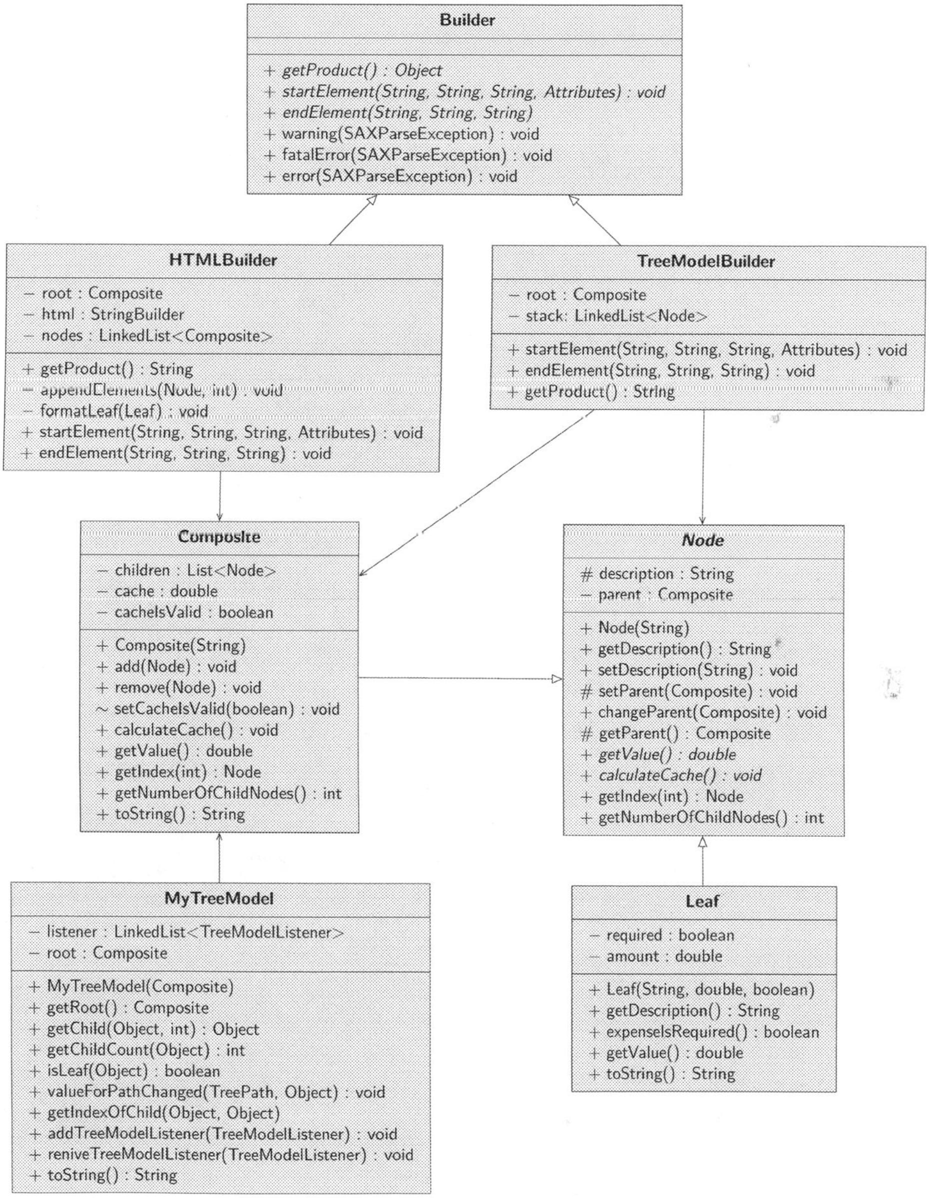

Builder

+ *getProduct() : Object*
+ *startElement(String, String, String, Attributes) : void*
+ *endElement(String, String, String)*
+ warning(SAXParseException) : void
+ fatalError(SAXParseException) : void
+ error(SAXParseException) : void

HTMLBuilder

− root : Composite
− html : StringBuilder
− nodes : LinkedList<Composite>
+ getProduct() : String
− appendElements(Node, int) : void
− formatLeaf(Leaf) : void
+ startElement(String, String, String, Attributes) : void
+ endElement(String, String, String) : void

TreeModelBuilder

− root : Composite
− stack: LinkedList<Node>
+ startElement(String, String, String, Attributes) : void
+ endElement(String, String, String) : void
+ getProduct() : String

Composite

− children : List<Node>
− cache : double
− cacheIsValid : boolean
+ Composite(String)
+ add(Node) : void
+ remove(Node) : void
~ setCacheIsValid(boolean) : void
+ calculateCache() : void
+ getValue() : double
+ getIndex(int) : Node
+ getNumberOfChildNodes() : int
+ toString() : String

Node

description : String
− parent : Composite
+ Node(String)
+ getDescription() : String
+ setDescription(String) : void
# setParent(Composite) : void
+ changeParent(Composite) : void
# getParent() : Composite
+ *getValue() : double*
+ *calculateCache() : void*
+ getIndex(int) : Node
+ getNumberOfChildNodes() : int

MyTreeModel

− listener : LinkedList<TreeModelListener>
− root : Composite
+ MyTreeModel(Composite)
+ getRoot() : Composite
+ getChild(Object, int) : Object
+ getChildCount(Object) : int
+ isLeaf(Object) : boolean
+ valueForPathChanged(TreePath, Object) : void
+ getIndexOfChild(Object, Object)
+ addTreeModelListener(TreeModelListener) : void
+ reniveTreeModelListener(TreeModelListener) : void
+ toString() : String

Leaf

− required : boolean
− amount : double
+ Leaf(String, double, boolean)
+ getDescription() : String
+ expenseIsRequired() : boolean
+ getValue() : double
+ toString() : String

Fig. 18.1 UML diagram of the Builder Pattern (sample project HaushaltsBuilder_Ext)

By the way, you can also "stagger" builders if, for example, you need a very specific sequence in the creation process of the finished object. However, you must then name the corresponding builders individually. For example, for an SQL statement, this could be a selectBuilder, a fromBuilder, and a whereBuilder, each of which can only return the subsequent builder in its last build step. This then leads to chained builders, so-called "NestedBuilders" and also works, for example, for the construction of composite objects.

18.3   Builder – The UML Diagram

You can find the UML diagram from the sample project HaushaltsBuilder_Ext in Fig. 18.1.

18.4   Summary

Go through the chapter again in key words:

- A Builder is an object whose task is to build other objects-.
- The design process is isolated in the Builder.
- Usually the construction process of the objects to be built is complex or complicated; often several steps are required.
- Builders can also be chained together and thus made dependent on each other.
- Since the data is independent of the object creation, many similar objects can be created.
- Typically, builders are used to build a composite.

18.5   Description of Purpose

The Gang of Four describes the purpose of the "Builder" pattern as follows:

Separate the construction of a complex object from its representation, so that the same construction process can produce different representations.

When you work with the Visitor, another behavioral pattern, you are always dealing with a collection of objects with different interfaces. Related operations are to be performed on all objects, which are grouped together in their own class, the Visitor.

19.1 A Simple Example

A car is an aggregate; it consists of wheels, an engine and the chassis. The car as well as its components are grouped under the interface Element.

19.1.1 The Power Unit

Please analyze the classes in the package `visitordemo.car` of the sample project Visitor. You will find that each element has its own data fields and methods. Besides, the methods `getDescription()` and `accept()` are prescribed in the interface. One method will return a short description, the other will provide an interface for a Visitor object. Take the `Wheel` class as an example. The wheel can store its position – for example, front left. It can also store and return the air pressure. The `accept()` method is overridden so that the `visit()` method is called on the Visitor object passed in, and passing over its own instance – `this`.

```
public class Wheel implements Element {
    private final Position position;
    private final double pressure = 2.0;
```

Supplementary Information The online version contains supplementary material available at https://doi.org/10.1007/978-3-658-39829-3_19.

```
public double getPressure() {
    return pressure;
}

public wheel(Position position) {
    this.position = position;
}

@Override
public void accept(VisitorIF visitor) {
    visitor.visit(this);
}

@Override
public String getDescription() {
    return "- Wheel " + position;
}
}
```

On the chassis, the wheels are mounted. When the accept method is called on it, in the first step it calls the visit method on the Visitor and passes itself as a parameter. In the second step, the visit method is called for each wheel.

```
public class Chassis implements Element {
    private final wheel[] wheels;

    public Rad[] getWheels() {
        return wheels;
    }

    Chassis(wheel[] wheels) {
        this.wheels = wheels;
    }

    @Override
    public void accept(VisitorIF visitor) {
        visitor.visit(this);
        for (var wheel : wheels)
            wheel.accept(visitor);
    }

    @Override
    public String getDescription() {
        return "- Chassis";
    }
}
```

The car should also still be described in the required brevity. It stores the information whether the tank is full, whether there is enough oil and whether blinker water (this innovative concoction is here representative for any other possible consumption liquid) was refilled. There are corresponding access methods to these attributes. The constructor installs a new engine, creates the chassis and attaches the wheels to it.

```
public class Car implements Element {
        private final List<Element> parts =
                                    new ArrayList<>();

        // … abridged


        public Car() {
            parts.add(new Engine());
            parts.add(new Chassis(new Wheel[] {
                new Wheel(Position.FL),
                new Wheel(Position.FR),
                new Wheel(Position.RL),
                new Wheel(Position.RR)
            }));
        }
}
```

The accept() method calls each component's visit method and passes them a reference to the visitor. Then the visit method is called on the Visitor and the car passes itself over as a parameter. I won't print the Engine class here – it follows the same logic as the previous classes.

19.1.2 The Visitor

I define the Visitor class in a separate package, visitordemo.visitor. A visitor is described by the interface VisitorIF. Every class that should be able to act as a visitor must override the methods declared in it; this concerns the method visit(), which is overloaded four times, once for each element.

The Visitor inheritance hierarchy is tightly bound to the Element classes. It must have precise knowledge of the interfaces of the objects to be visited, as you will see in a moment. Conversely, the element classes only need to know the Visitor interface.

```
public interface VisitorIF {
void visit(wheel wheel);
void visit(Engine engine);
void visit(Chassis chassis);
void visit(Car car);
}
```

A concrete Visitor is the `PartsVisitor`. It compiles a list of the descriptions of all parts. To do this, it overwrites the method `visit()` so that the method `getDescription()` is called on the parameter passed, i.e. a wheel, an engine, a chassis or a car. The descriptions of all the individual parts are combined by a StringBuilder. The method `getParts()` returns a string with the list of all parts.

```
public class PartsVisitor implements VisitorIF {
        private final StringBuilder builder =
                                        new StringBuilder();
        public String getPartsList() {
            return "Components: \n" + builder.toString();
        }

        @Override
        public void visit(Wheel wheel) {
            builder.append(wheel.getDescription()).
                                        append("\n");
        }

        @Override
        public void visit(Engine engine) {
            builder.append(engine.getDescription()).
                                        append("\n");
        }

        // ... abridged


}
```

How can the client now use this construction?

19.1.3 The Client

The client creates an instance of the Auto class and a component Visitor. It then calls the `accept()` method with the Visitor as a parameter. The resulting string is output to the console.

```
public class ApplStart {
        public static void main(String[] args) {
                var car = new Car();
                var visitor = new PartsVisitor();
                car.accept(visitor);
                var parts = visitor.getPartsList();
                System.out.println(parts);

                // … abridged
        }
}
```

The list of components compiled by the Visitor is displayed on the console:

```
Components:
- motor
- chassis
- Wheel front left
- Wheel front right
- Wheel rear left
- Wheel rear right
- Car (remaining components)
```

19.1.4 Another Visitor

When you drive to the workshop because of an irregularity on your vehicle, a person there hooks up a diagnostic device to a defined interface in the car and can shortly afterwards say precisely whether the car has a defect, and if so, in which element. This situation is mapped by the Diagnose Visitor. It works very similarly to the Component Visitor. It queries certain information on each element and evaluates it. There are two different procedures. The car can measure by itself if the tank is full and if the oil level is correct; therefore, it returns a boolean value with the appropriate access methods. I assume that very few cars measure the air pressure in their tires independently, although this is technically possible.

Here the visitor gets the current value and evaluates it. At the end it can give information whether the car is ready to drive. Please analyze the DiagnoseVisitor independently – the class is not complicated.

19.1.5 Criticism of the Project

It becomes clear what I meant at the beginning by related operations: There are a number of classes on each of which a diagnosis is to be performed. Instead of defining the diagnostic methods in the respective classes, they are combined in a separate class. This has two advantages: First, the classes are not "polluted" by code that is not part of their actual core business. In addition, the newly defined operations can be maintained much more easily; they are located in a single class and do not have to be maintained separately in umpteen classes.

The classes involved do not have to have a common interface. In the "Visitor" project, both the car and the components were subclasses of the Element interface. However, this is not mandatory in the sense of the Visitor pattern.

A disadvantage of the Visitor Pattern is that the visited object must have a sufficiently extensive interface to be able to query all relevant data. For example, the wheel class must be able to provide information about air pressure, the engine must be able to name its state, and so on. You may even need to use the Visitor Pattern to provide access to data that you intended to encapsulate.

Another disadvantage is that you will have extensive maintenance on all concrete Visitor classes when a new element is inserted. Imagine that you additionally define the class Brake – the interface Visitor must declare a corresponding visit method, which must be overridden by all concrete Visitor classes. The Visitor pattern is always best used when new operations are needed rather than changing the object structure more frequently.

> The Visitor Pattern is an excellent example of the Open-Closed Principle. You have a set of classes that are closed against change. But they leave the door ajar for extensions by providing an interface that allows other objects to define new behavior.

One last aspect should be addressed: the type of iteration. In the project you have just worked on, you will find an internal driver – you call the `accept()` method on the Car object, which ensures that iteration is performed over all components. You could also conceivably define an external iterator. The solution with an internal iterator does not have to be the one you find practical.

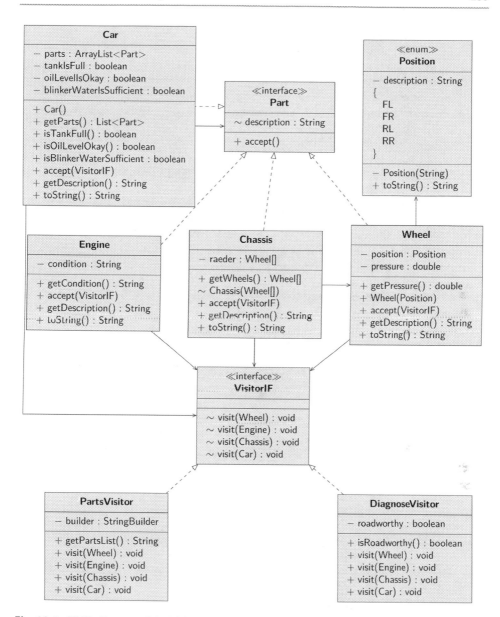

Fig. 19.1 UML diagram of the Visitor pattern (example project Visitor)

19.2   Visitor – The UML Diagram

You can see the UML diagram from the Visitor sample project in Fig. 19.1.

19.3   Summary

Go through the chapter again in key words:

- You are dealing with objects with different interfaces.
- Related operations – a diagnosis – should be performed on all objects.
- The operations are combined in a single class, the Visitor.
- Each object provides an interface that the Visitor can call.
- The object calls the visitor's overloaded visit method on the visitor and passes itself as a parameter.
- The Visitor defines a visit method for each object in the collection.
- According to the rules of polymorphism, the appropriate visit method for the object is called.

19.4   Description of Purpose

The Gang of Four describes the purpose of the "Visitor" pattern as follows:

Encapsulate an operation to be performed on the elements of an object structure as an object. The visitor pattern allows you to define a new operation without changing the classes of the elements it operates on.

Memento

20

Encapsulation is a central theme of object-oriented programming. Every object has attributes that it must not make known to the outside world. Instead, it offers the narrowest possible interface. In the last chapter, with the Visitor pattern, I addressed this conflict – there, access methods had to be created specifically for the Visitor. Encapsulation is also an issue for the Memento Pattern.

20.1 Task of the Memento Pattern

The starting point is to be any object A whose state you want to store externally in order to be able to restore it later. How can the state be determined and stored? First, it is obvious to take an object B that reads the data from A and stores it. But how could the storing object B get at the data of the object A to be stored?

20.1.1 Public Data Fields

A first approach could be to make the data fields publicly available.

```
public class Memento {
    public int answer = 42;
    public String password = "Ken sent me";
}
```

Supplementary Information The online version contains supplementary material available at https://doi.org/10.1007/978-3-658-39829-3_20.

© The Author(s), under exclusive license to Springer Fachmedien Wiesbaden
GmbH, part of Springer Nature 2023
O. Musch, *Design Patterns with Java*, https://doi.org/10.1007/978-3-658-39829-3_20

Now another object could read and store the state. But why won't you pursue this approach? The data fields are publicly viewable and modifiable, which goes against the principle of data encapsulation, information hiding.

20.1.2 The JavaBeans Pattern

Most Java implementations implement the principle of data encapsulation by having methods that can read and write to the data fields, which is more or less like the JavaBeans specification.

```
public class Memento {
    private int answer = 42;
    private String password = "Ken sent me";

    public int getAnswer() {
        return answer;
    }

    public void setAnswer(int answer) {
        this.answer = answer;
    }

    // ... abridged
}
```

Now the data is encapsulated, but nothing has changed compared to the approach with the public fields – anyone can still read and write to the data, albeit via the detour of the access methods.

20.1.3 Default Visibility

Conceivably, you could set the fields – or the access methods – to default visibility (package-private); then only classes in the same package could access the data. Consequently, an object that is to store the state of another object must be defined in the same package. But even this approach is not optimal. Packages should help to group classes into meaningful units. For example, all classes that display data on the screen go into one package, while data that describes the data model is defined in another package. In my opinion, it would be excessive to create a package just to store a class and its data store in it.

The previous suggestions were not convincing – it seems like a bad idea to try to read the data. So, take a different approach: the object whose state is to be stored is itself made responsible for creating its data store.

20.2   A Possible Realization

Before I introduce you to the project, I would like to define a few terms. The object whose state is to be stored is the *originator*; in the German translation of the GoF book it is also called "Urheber". The object that stores the state of another object is the *memento*. Finally, the *caretaker* maintains a list of mementos. The example project Memento_Simple implements the pattern in a very clear way. The caretaker is the class `Stack`. It stores the different memento objects. As stack I didn't take the Java implementation, but developed my own class. The memento is defined as an empty marker interface.

```
public interface Memento {
}
```

You want to save the state of a car object. It has the attributes `speed` and `current-FuelConsumption`. The speed can be influenced; there are corresponding access methods for this. The fuel consumption can only be influenced indirectly via the speed.

```
public class Car {
    // ... abridged

    private int speed = 0;
    private int currentFuelConsumption = 0;

    public void driveFaster() {
        speed++;
        calculateFuelConsumption();
    }

    public void driveSlower() {
        if (speed > 0) {
            speed--;
            calculateFuelConsumption();
        }
    }

    private void calculateFuelConsumption() {
        // ... abridged
    }
}
```

Now I am looking for a way to be able to store all the data fields. For this, I create an inner class AutoMemento which is suitable to copy the data fields. Every time you create an instance of the AutoMemento class, the data fields of the AutoObject are copied.

```
public class Car {
    private class CarMemento implements Memento {
        private final int tempo = speed;
        private final int thirst = currentFuelConsumption;
    }

    private int speed = 0;
    private int currentFuelConsumption = 0;

    // ... abridged
}
```

You pass the responsibility of creating a memento to the car class. There you request a memento; moreover, the car is also responsible for restoring an old state from a given memento.

```
public class Car {
    // ... abridged

    public Memento createMemento() {
        return new CarMemento();
    }

    public void setMemento(Memento memento) {
        var myMemento = (CarMemento) memento;
        this.currentFuelConsumption = myMemento.thirst;
        this.speed = myMemento.tempo;
    }
}
```

The client creates a stack, the caretaker, and an auto object. Then it performs some operations that affect the speed and thus the fuel consumption, and saves the state in a memento after each change. The memento is placed on the stack; any change can now be undone. The main method of the ApplStart class demonstrates this procedure. Please analyze the code on your own.

How do you evaluate this solution? On the one hand, the attributes of neither the originator nor the memento can be read – so they are very consistently encapsulated. However, you buy the encapsulation at the price that the class itself is responsible for creating and restoring the memento; the code is "polluted" in this respect. If this solution appeals to you, please note that the example is extremely simple. The attributes are of the primitive type int. If you have mutable objects, they must be cloned – the problem of copied references, which you learned about in the Prototype chapter on cloning, is encountered again here.

In the next example we will use the graphic editor of the Prototype Pattern again.

20.3   A Major Project

In the second expansion stage of the GraphicEditor in the chapter about the Prototype Pattern, you cloned a diagram by serializing and deserializing it. Exactly this procedure can also be interesting for the Memento. For the following example project Memento, I took the GraphEditor_2 as a template and modified it. The advantage now is that in the class PanelCanvas the method getMemento() is defined – it creates and returns a cloned diagram as a deep copy, the Memento.

```
public Diagram getMemento() {
    Diagram clone = null;
    try {
        ObjectOutputStream oos;
        ByteArrayInputStream bais;
        ObjectInputStream ois;
        try ( var baos = new ByteArrayOutputStream()) {
            oos = new ObjectOutputStream(baos);
            oos.writeObject(diagram);
            bais = new ByteArrayInputStream(baos.
                                    toByteArray());
            ois = new ObjectInputStream(bais);
            clone = (diagram) ois.readObject();
        }
        oos.close();
        bais.close();
        ois.close();
    } catch (IOException ex) {
        new ErrorDialog(ex);
    } finally {
        return clone;
    }
}
```

The setDiagram() method takes a Diagram object and fills the drawing area with its data.

```
public void setDiagram(Diagram clone) {
    selected = null;
    this.diagram = clone;
    repaint();
}
```

In the main method of the `ApplStart` class, the `undoAction` action is defined, which requests the last diagram from the caretaker and passes it to the drawing area. This action is passed to a MenuItem. The caretaker is an instance of the `Stack` class, which you know from the last example. You pass the same instance to the drawing area.

```
private final PanelCanvas canvas =
                        new PanelCanvas(caretaker);
// ... abridged

private final Action undoAction =
                        new AbstractAction("Undo") {
    @Override
    public void actionPerformed(ActionEvent e) {
        myFrame.setTitle("Memento Demo");
        if (!caretaker.empty()) {
            Diagram diagram = caretaker.pop();
            canvas.setDiagram(diagram);
        }
        else
            myFrame.setTitle("...");
    }
};
```

You could trigger most actions via mouse clicks: Moving circles, creating lines or circles, and selecting graphic elements. You deleted graphic elements via the menu. All the methods you called this way were defined in the PanelCanvas class – either as a standalone method or as an EventListener. These methods are supplemented so that a snapshot is created and saved at the same time as the defined action.

```
public void deleteSelectedGraphic() {
    if (selected != null) {
        createMemento();
        diagram.deleteSelectedGraphic(selected);
        selected = null;
        repaint();
    }
}

private void createMemento() {
    var tempDiagram = getMemento();
    caretaker.push(tempDiagram);
}
```

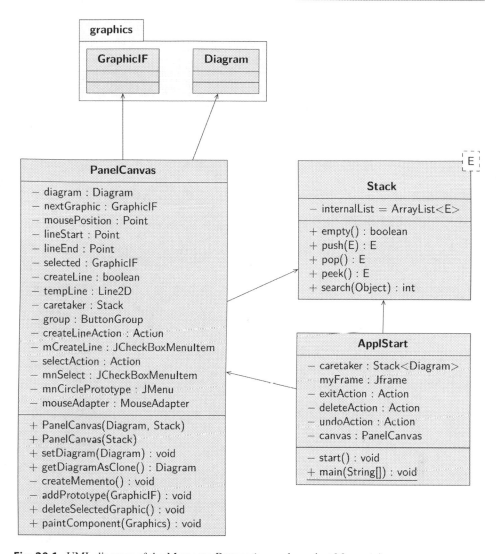

Fig. 20.1   UML diagram of the Memento Pattern (example project Memento)

In this realization, you store an object of type `Diagram` in the caretaker. Alternatively, you could have stored the serialized object in the caretaker.

20.4   Memento – The UML Diagram

In Fig. 20.1, I show you only some of the classes involved in the Memento sample project. I have not shown the graphics and prototype packages again here. You can find their representation in the UML diagram for prototype in Sect. 17.3.

20.5   Summary

Go through the chapter again in key words:

- The goal is to store the state of an object externally.
- The attributes of the object must be accessed.
- The encapsulation should not be weakened if possible.
- To implement the pattern, have the originator create a memento.
- The Caretaker stores the mementos.

20.6   Description of Purpose

The Gang of Four describes the purpose of the pattern "Memento" as follows:

> Capture and externalize the internal state of an object without violating its encapsulation, so that the object can later be restored to that state.

21

The facade belongs to the structure patterns; it describes how you can access a complicated or complex subsystem in an uncomplicated way.

21.1 An Example Outside IT

Imagine that you have a complex or complicated system – for example, an SLR camera. When you take a portrait, you want the depth of field to cover only a small area. You open the aperture as wide as possible, so choose a small f-number. This allows more light to fall on the film or the processor. To prevent the image from becoming too bright, you need to reduce the exposure time.

Maybe you don't want to take a portrait later, but a landscape. There, the depth of field should be as large as possible; you select a large f-stop number and thereby close the aperture. Now there is less light reaching the processor, so you have to increase the exposure time. However, the exposure time cannot be increased indefinitely; experience shows that a picture can only be taken handheld if the exposure time is shorter than 1/focal length. If the exposure time is longer, you run the risk of blurring the image. So you need to increase the film speed, the ISO number.

Does that sound complicated? I think it is! And most camera manufacturers see it the same way. Modern compact cameras, but also (digital) SLR cameras, come with scene programs. All you have to do is tell the camera: "I want to take a portrait!" or: "I want to take landscapes!". The camera automatically sets the aperture and exposure time so that the result is optimal.

This actually explains the principle of the facade: You have a complicated or complex system. To make it easier for you to access the system, a facade is created. As a user or

Supplementary Information The online version contains supplementary material available at https://doi.org/10.1007/978-3-658-39829-3_21.

photographer, you no longer need to concern yourself with the details. It should be enough that you tell the facade – the subject program "Portrait" – what you want to have. The "how" is realized by the facade. You will still have access to the individual components of the system: you do not have to use the facade, you can still set the aperture and exposure time manually.

In the following section, after this short excursion, you will again be introduced to an example from IT.

21.2   The Facade in a Java Example

Take a look at the example project facade. It consists of the packages demo1 to demo4 and the package trip. In this example, you will create a journey. For a trip, you must first take the train to the airport. From there, you fly to your vacation destination. After you arrive at the far airport, the transfer service will take you to the hotel. At the hotel, you will be provided with either all-inclusive or half board or breakfast only. Optionally, you can take a rental car, which must be insured and refueled. In the package trip all necessary classes can be found. You can see how this project looks in the development environment in Fig. 21.1.

If a client wants to create a trip, it must create all components. Look at the client code in the package demo1.

```java
public class Client {
    public static void main(String[] args) {
        System.out.println("A client:");
        var railAndFly = new RailAndFly();
        railAndFly.board();
        var flight = new Flight();
        flight.checkBaggage();
        flight.identify();
        var transfer = new Transfer();
        transfer.loadBaggage();
        var hotel = new Hotel();
        hotel.rentSafe();
        var halfboard = new HalfBoard();
        halfboard.orderBeer();
        // ... . abridged
    }
}
```

If the customer also needs a rental car, they must also first create a rental car object and then call the insure() and refuel() methods on it. So on the one hand, you have many components that you have to serve. On the other hand, you have different configuration options – in one case it is sufficient to create objects, in the other case you have to call methods on the objects in addition. Does this look like a complex system to you?

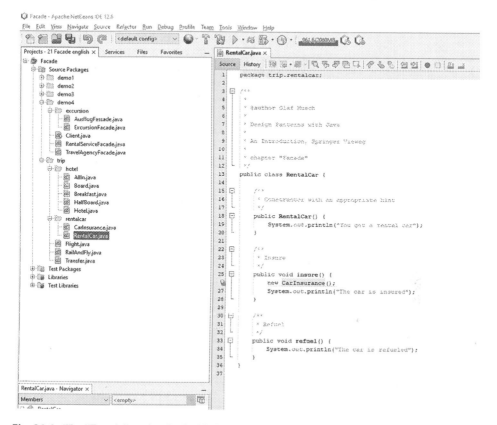

Fig. 21.1 The "Facade" project in the NetBeans development environment

```java
public class Client {
    public static void main(String[] args) {

        // … abridged

        System.out.println("\nAnother Client:");
        railAndFly = new RailAndFly();
        transfer = new Transfer();
        hotel = new Hotel();
        halfBoard = new HalfBoard();
        var rentalCar = new RentalCar();
        rentalCar.insure();
        rentalCar.refuel();
    }
}
```

You must have noticed that the flight was forgotten in the upper listing. But maybe you know the problem from practice: Errors in extensive configurations can only be found after an even more extensive test procedure. So the code from above is error-prone – in the next section you will learn a solution to this dilemma.

21.2.1 Introduction of a Facade

You introduce a facade whose only task is to provide a simplified handling for the client on the one hand, but on the other hand to master the complex interrelationships of the system. In the package demo2, you will find the class TravelAgencyFacade, which offers the method bookTrip(). You give this method a truth value as a parameter that specifies whether a car should be rented.

```
public final class TravelAgencyFacade {
    public void bookTrip(boolean withRentalCar) {
        var railAndFly = new RailAndFly();
        var flight = new Flight();
        var transfer = new Transfer();
        var hotel = new Hotel();
        var halfboard = new HalfBoard();
        if (withRentalCar) {
            var rentalCar = new RentalCar();
            rentalCar.insure();
            rentalCar.refuel();
        }
    }
}
```

The client class in the package demo2 can now call the method very easily.

```
public class Client {
    public static void main(String[] args) {
        System.out.println("A Client:");
        new TravelAgencyFacade().bookTrip(false);

        System.out.println("\nAnother Client:");
        new TravelAgencyFacade().bookTrip(true);
    }
}
```

It is now much easier for the client to book a trip. Let me point out one thing: In practice, you will just call the class TravelAgency. I only added the addition TravelAgencyFacade for clarification.

21.2.2 A Closer Look at the Term "System"

The term "system" is important for the facade: They provide a simplified access to a sub-system. The term system or subsystem is to be interpreted broadly. It can mean an arbitrarily large unit; but it can also mean access to a single class. In the package demo3, I have considered the car rental as a separate system and moved it to a separate package. I also defined the Car Rental facade, which has a single static method that can be used to rent a car: Access to this (sub)system is now only possible through the facade.

```java
public class CarRentalFacade {
    public static void rentCar() {
        var rentalCar = new Rentalcar();
        rentalCar.insure();
        rentalCar.refuel();
    }
}
```

The travel agency now has simplified access to this subsystem.

```java
public class TravelAgencyFacade {
    public void bookTrip(boolean withRentalCar) {
        var railAndFly = new RailAndFly();
        var flight = new Flight();
        var transfer = new Transfer();
        var hotel = new Hotel();
        var halfboard = new HalfBoard();
        if (withRentalCar)
            CarRentalFacade.rentCar();
    }
}
```

The client can either rent a car from the travel agency or directly from the car rental company. By the way, in the implementation I've presented to you here, it's not a problem that the client still accesses the individual elements of the subsystem. The facade does not restrict, nor does it introduce any new logic – it merely simplifies access to a subsystem.

An alternative procedure is demonstrated by the package demo4. Here there is the subsystem (subpackage) excursion. This system is represented in a simplified way by the class Excursion. The class and its methods are package-private, so that access is only possible through the facade. Please analyze demo4 from this point of view. It is also conceivable that the facade not only mediates between client and subsystem, but that it defines its own logic.

Fig. 21.2 Message generated
by "JOptionPane"

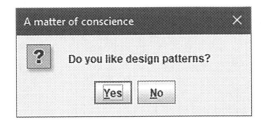

> The advantage of the facade is obvious: access is simplified, the dependency of
> client and subsystem is loosened. This avoids client code breaking when the subsystem
> is changed or replaced. It is even possible to replace a complete subsystem.

In the next section, let's look at where the facade can be found in the Java class library.

21.3   The Facade in the Class Library

I would like to show you an example from the Java class library. You have created a graphi-
cal user interface and want to display a message to the user. You could now design a
JDialog that has a BorderLayout. On BorderLayout.WEST, you place an icon
that displays a warning exclamation point. On BorderLayout.CENTER, display the message. BorderLayout.SOUTH contains a JButton labeled "Ok." When the user clicks on
it, the EventListener will cause the JDialog to close.

Alternatively, you could make do with the facade of the JOptionPane class, which
brings various static methods that you can pass different parameters to in order to config-
ure the dialog. Consider the following lines of code.

```
String question = "Do you like design patterns?";
String title = "A matter of conscience";
javax.swing.JOptionPane.showConfirmDialog(null, question,
            title, javax.swing.JOptionPane.YES_NO_OPTION,
            javax.swing.JOptionPane.QUESTION_MESSAGE);
```

When you run this code, you will be presented with a message, as shown in Fig. 21.2.

The facade requires a large number of classes that it calls. To give you an idea of the
large number of classes involved, I am printing an overview in Fig. 21.3, which I have
borrowed (and slightly adapted in layout) from Philipp Hauer.[1]

I think this example makes the meaning of the phrase "simplified access to a subsystem" pretty clear.

---

[1] https://www.philipphauer.de/study/se/design-pattern/facade.php

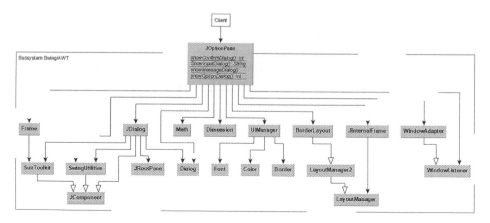

Fig. 21.3   Extract from the API Doc of the JOptionPane Class

21.4   The "Law of Demeter"

In Chap. 2 I showed you some design principles. Now I will address another design principle. It is about the "Law of Demeter",[2] which says – in short – that objects should limit their communication to close friends. The facade shows you one way to make this happen as easily as possible. So what exactly does Demeter's Law say? Objects should only communicate with close friends. Close friends are:

- Attributes and methods of its own object, that is, everything called `this`,
- Methods of objects passed as parameters,
- Methods of objects that the method itself creates,
- Global objects.

If you look at the travel example from above, you can see that the client only needs to access one friend – the facade. The facade gives the client the option of not having to deal with strangers, i.e. additional classes. The facade is an illustrative example of the realization of the principle. I found a detailed description of the LoD on Matthias Kleine's blog. If you want to look further into object-oriented design principles and principles of software engineering, this page is a good starting point for your research:

   http://prinzipien-der-softwaretechnik.blogspot.com/2013/06/das-gesetz-von-demeter.html

   You can also find the (german) text as "LoD.pdf" in the directory of sample projects for this chapter.

---

[2]Demeter in Greek mythology is the mother of Persephone and the unwilling mother-in-law of Hades. She provides seasons, fertility and growth.

In the chapter on object-oriented design patterns, I felt it was important to say that you, the programmer, are not there to satisfy the laws. Rather, the laws are there for you-they are there to make your job easier. Therefore, even with Demeter's law, *nulla regula sine exceptione*, or *No Rule Without Exception*, applies. You may break the law if you are clear about it and can justify the breach. If you want to print some text on standard output, keep coding `System.out.println()`. And if you want to know the name of a class, the statement `myObject.getClass(). get-Name()` is still allowed. However, be careful whenever you access objects that are not part of Java's standard class library.

I would like to offer you an introduction to design patterns with my book. Therefore, I limit myself to a few design principles. However, I hope that I can motivate you to deal with the topic in your own research.

21.5   Facade – The UML Diagram

Figure 21.4 shows the UML diagram for the example project Facade, package demo4.

21.6   Summary

Go through the chapter again in key words:

- The initial situation is a complicated system that you want to work with.
- Access to the system is simplified by a facade.
- The client accesses the facade and does not necessarily know the details of the system.
- The facade can either contain business logic or simply forward requests to the appropriate system object.
- The system becomes interchangeable.
- Dependencies between systems are simplified or dissolved.
- Optionally, a client can still access the system.
- The Demeter law is implemented.

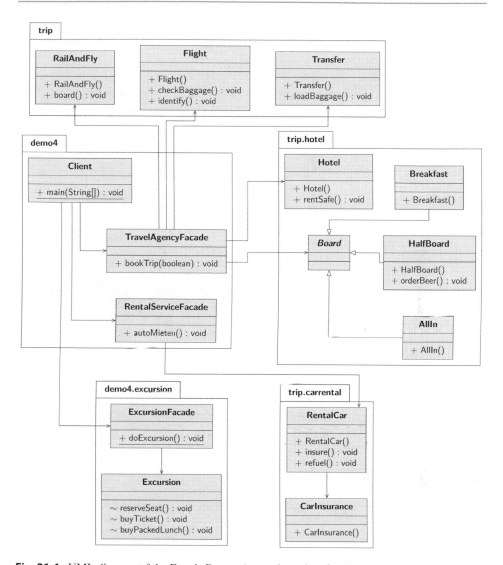

Fig. 21.4 UML diagram of the Facade Pattern (example project facade, package demo_4)

21.7   Description of Purpose

The Gang of Four describes the purpose of the "Facade" pattern as follows:

Provide a unified interface to a set of interfaces of a subsystem. The facade class defines an abstract interface that simplifies the use of the subsystem.

Adapter

22

You are going to London and want to plug your hairdryer into the socket – since the German plug does not fit into the British socket, you need an adapter. I present you the pattern on the level of single classes. In fact, it can be scaled – the principle is the same if you adapt whole subsystems.

22.1 An Introductory Example

Let's generalize the plug example. You have two systems – the hairdryer and the plug socket – which have to work together. The "must" means that you have no other option in London than to dock with the UK socket. In IT, "must" can mean that you want to use a system or class that represents something unique or highly complex, such as a premium or deadline calculation in the insurance industry. A complex adapter is also JDBC, for example. The interaction of the systems that "must" work together is only disturbed by the fact that the client expects a different interface than the system to be used declares. The adapter has the task of mediating between the two systems. The GoF describes the adapter in two ways: object-based and class-based. Both designs are discussed in this chapter.

22.2 A Class-Based Design

What is the task to be solved in this chapter? Take a look at the Adapter_ClassBased sample project. You have purchased a third-party library that sorts numbers using a blazing fast algorithm.

Supplementary Information The online version contains supplementary material available at https://doi.org/10.1007/978-3-658-39829-3_22.

O. Musch, *Design Patterns with Java*, https://doi.org/10.1007/978-3-658-39829-3_22

```
public class SorterExternalProduct {
    List<Integer> sort(List<Integer> numberList) {
        // ... black box
    }
}
```

All you know about this library is that you need to pass an integer list as a parameter and get back a sorted integer list. However, your software is programmed to expect a sorter object with the following interface.

```
public interface Sorter {
    int[] sort(int... numbers);
}
```

The source code of the third-party library is not available to you, so you cannot make any changes to it. Your own application is an established tested procedure that has already been delivered to many customers – it must not be changed under any circumstances. So you have to design an adapter that mediates between the foreign library and your application. What does such an adapter look like? The class-based approach is to let the adapter inherit from the foreign library. At the same time, the adapter takes on the role of a sorter object, that is, it implements the expected interface.

```
public class SorterAdapter
        extends SorterFremdprodukt implements Sorter {

    @Override
    public int[] sort(int[] numbers) {
        // ... we'll deal with later
    }
}
```

The client can now send its message as it expects.

```
public class Client {

    public static void main(String[] args) {
        final int[] numbers = { 9, 4, 7, 3, 5 };
        var sorter = new SorterAdapter();
        final var sorted = sorter.sort(numbers);

        for (var number : sorted)
            System.out.println(number);
    }
}
```

   The adapter's sort method converts the array of numbers into a list and calls the correct method on the foreign library. So the adapter pretends to be a sorter, but is actually a subclass of the foreign library. Now here is the entire code of the adapter:

```
public class SorterAdapter
        extends SorterFremdprodukt implements Sorter {

    @Override
    public int[] sort(int[] numbers) {
        int z = new int[numbers.length];
        List<Integer> numberList = new ArrayList<>();
        for (var number : numbers)
            numberList.add(number);
        List<Integer> sortedList = sort(numberList);
        for (var i = 0; i < sortedList.size(); i++)
            z[i] = sortedList.get(i);
        return z;
    }
}
```

   The GoF describes the class-based approach using multiple inheritance (in C++). Since Java does not know multiple inheritance, you have to make the compromise that you declare the expected interface by an interface.

22.3   An Object-Based Design

If the class-based design has already solved the problem, we could actually close the chapter, right? There are two reasons against being satisfied too quickly. The first reason is that one design principle is to prefer composition to inheritance. The second reason is quite trivial – the provider of the third-party library has marked the class as final in an update.

```
public final class SorterExternalProduct {
    // ... abridged
}
```

   The adapter of the previous solution can now no longer be used. Your only option is to program an object-based adapter. How do you do this? You create an attribute that holds a reference to an object in the foreign library. The sort method calls the method sort() on this attribute. You can find this variant in the Adapter_ObjectBased sample project.

```
public class SorterAdapter implements Sorter {
    private final SorterExternalProduct externalProduct =
                    new SorterExternalProduct();
```

```
@Override
public int[] sort(int[] numbers) {
    List<Integer> numberList = new ArrayList<>();
    for (var number : numbers)
        numberList.add(number);
    var sortedList =
                    externalProduct.sort(numberList);
    for (var i = 0; i < sortedList.size(); i++)
        numbers[i] = sortedList.get(i);
    return pay;
}
}
```

You are now familiar with both approaches – object-based and class-based. In the following section, you will look at the advantages and disadvantages of both approaches.

22.4   Criticism of the Adapter Pattern

Please look again at the clients of the two approaches. You can see that the client knows the target interface and the adapter. Everything beyond the adapter is not visible to the client. Therefore, there may be another class or an entire system behind the client. Since the client does not know the system behind the adapter, this can be replaced without any problems. The only important thing is that the adapter is implemented correctly. In Sect. 21.4, you looked at the Law of Demeter. The adapter pattern also helps you to develop systems where classes communicate only with close friends.

In this context, let me distinguish the adapter from the facade. In both cases, you have a system that a client wants to access. It does not access this system directly, but via another abstraction. The main difference is the target direction. In the case of the facade, the goal was to facilitate access to a complex or complicated system. The adapter has the task of enabling two systems to communicate with each other in the first place. This brings up another obvious difference: who creates the abstraction? In the case of the facade, it was clear that the provider of the system must create a facade; it provides simplified handling. With the adapter, things are usually different. The vendor of a system invests a lot of time and effort in creating his software. He develops an interface to which the client can direct its requests. With that, his job is done. If the client needs another interface, he has to create it and define an adapter.

An adapter is usually a class that has been written and optimized for a single use case. The adapter I developed in the example above is difficult to reuse, which is sometimes described as a disadvantage in the literature. You will undoubtedly have to consider whether it is better to refactor one of the interfaces in such cases. However, you cannot rework the interface if the adapter allows you to access the Internet or a database (JDBC).

If you choose the class-based approach, the adapter can easily override methods of the classes to be adapted. However, it is then bound to a class because it has itself become a subclass of the class to be adapted. A new adapter must be developed for each subclass of the classes to be adapted. What about the object-based approach? In Sect. 2.4, I touched on Liskov's substitution principle, which states that a subclass should behave exactly like its base class; in other words, a subclass must be able to represent its base class. If an inheritance hierarchy takes this principle into account, it is possible for an object-based adapter to be used not only for a class but also for its subclasses.

> **Background Information**
>
> Did you know that the adapter pattern can already be traced back to the Brothers Grimm? Surely you know the fairy tale Little Red Riding Hood. The wolf disguises himself as grandmother; Little Red Riding Hood sees an object lying in bed that corresponds to the interface grandmother, and at first does not suspect anything. Later, however, it realizes that a class-based WolfAdapter is hidden behind the interface – otherwise it would never have come to the legendary quote: "Grandmother, why do you have such a horribly big mouth?" So the adapter is obviously poorly implemented and throws a WolfException.
>
> The fairy tale can teach us that it's always a bad idea for people to concoct their own solutions without checking with IT first.

22.5   A Labeling Fraud

You will find a large number of classes in the class library that have "adapter" in their name. In Swing, for example, there are MouseAdapter, FocusAdapter, etc. The MouseAdapter class implements the MouseListener, MouseMotionListener, and MouseWheelListener interfaces. All methods are overridden empty, so you can define a MouseListener without having to override all methods yourself. If you want to override a method from the MouseMotionListener interface, expand the MouseAdapter and specifically override only that one method.

Is this an adapter in the sense of the Adapter Pattern? No – the MouseAdapter class does not bring you any added value, nor does it mediate between two systems. It does, however, make it easier for you to deal with the interfaces mentioned. Simplified access to a subsystem was the hallmark of the facade. So the MouseAdapter class should be called MouseFacade. So not everywhere that says adapter on it is adapter in it.

22.6   Adapter – The UML Diagram

Figures 22.1 and 22.2 show a comparison of the UML diagrams from the two sample projects Adapter_Class-Based and Adapter_Object-Based.

22.7   Summary

Go through the chapter again in key words:

- There are two systems whose interfaces are incompatible.
- An adapter mediates between the two systems.
- It converts the interface of the system to be adapted into the one expected by the client.
- The original classes are not changed.
- An adapter is written for exactly one use case.
- Client and adapted system are loosely coupled.
- Both systems can be interchanged independently as long as the adapter fits.
- The adapter exists in two forms: Object-based and class-based.

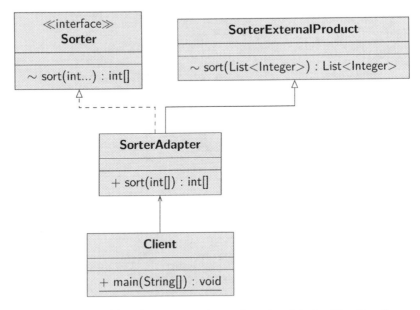

Fig. 22.1   UML diagram of the adapter pattern (example project Adapter_ClassBased)

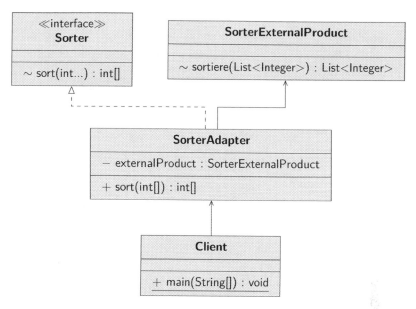

Fig. 22.2   UML diagram of the adapter pattern (example project Adapter_Object-based)

22.8   Description of Purpose

The Gang of Four describes the purpose of the "Adapter" pattern as follows:

Adapt the interface of a class to another interface expected by its clients. The adapter pattern lets classes work together that would otherwise be unable to do so because of incompatible interfaces.

Proxy

The proxy pattern I'll show you in this chapter is a structure pattern and has similarities to the facade and adapter. In all three patterns, you don't access an object directly, but through a third. Remember – the facade allowed you to deal with a complicated interface. With the adapter, the third object made it possible for two others to interact in the first place. And what will that be like with the proxy? With the proxy, you're also encapsulating access to an object. But why would you want to do that? Four reasons might be:

1. Virtual Proxy: You need a placeholder for a certain duration to create a large object.
2. Security Proxy: You want to block or at least control access to the object.
3. Smart Reference: You want to add functionality to the object; for example, you want to check whether the object is locked before actually accessing it.
4. Remote Proxy: The desired object is not in the same address space.

These four application areas are the most common; they are discussed by the GoF. However, you will find other proxies in the literature: the firewall proxy, the synchronization proxy, and many more. This chapter is one of the longer ones in the book. So, get comfortable, and let's get started.

23.1 Virtual Proxy

The Virtual Proxy should only be addressed here theoretically for the sake of completeness. Imagine you create a software with which photos can be displayed. For example, there should be 100 pictures in a certain folder. With the chosen setting 25 pictures fit on one screen page. When you open the folder, the first thing to do is to register all the images,

---

Supplementary Information The online version contains supplementary material available at https://doi.org/10.1007/978-3-658-39829-3_23.

O. Musch, *Design Patterns with Java*, https://doi.org/10.1007/978-3-658-39829-3_23

determine their size, create the previews and draw them. If the photos are quite large, this process may well take a while. Now it would be very unsatisfactory for the user if your program freezes. It is much more comfortable if the preview is generated only from the pictures that are currently displayed on the screen. At first the screen shows 25 frames as placeholders for the later previews. Gradually, these placeholders, the proxies, are replaced by the actual preview images. You proceed accordingly with the following screens. You create frames as placeholders and when the user scrolls the frames into the visible area of the screen, the previews are created.

23.2   Security Proxy

It can be useful to prevent write access to an object. As an example, consider the unmod-ifiableList() method of the Collections class in the Java class library. You pass a List object to the method and get back a read-only list. The method wraps your list in an object of the UnmodifiableList inner class. The UnmodifiableList extends the UnmodifiableCollection class, which is also an inner class. Now, when you want to access the actual database, you don't access the original list, you access the UnmodifiableList that surrounds it. The UnmodifiableList forwards requests to the original database – write accesses excluded. Take a look at the Unmodifiable sample project; there I extracted the relevant code portions of the Collections class from the class library into the file unmodifi-able.java. This file is by no means complete in this excerpt and will therefore not compile. But that's not what it's intended for, it's just a reference for you. You can of course alter-natively look directly in the source code of the class library, if you have also downloaded or linked it.

```
class UnmodifiableList<E>
                        extends UnmodifiableCollection<E>
    implements List<E> {
        final List<? extends E> list;
        UnmodifiableList(List<? extends E> list) {
            super(list);
            this.list = list;
        }

        @Override
        public E get(int index) {
            return list.get(index);
        }

        @Override
```

```
                public E set(int index, E element) {
                    throw new UnsupportedOperationException();
                }
        // … abridged
    }
```

For the test, a client creates an ArrayList with various strings. Then he lets the
Collections class return a read-only list. This list is then no longer an instance of the
ArrayList class. Rather, it is an object of the UnmodifiableRandomAccessList
class. As expected, an UnsupportedOperationException is thrown when trying
to add another string.

```
List<String> text = new ArrayList<>();
System.out.println(text.getClass().getName());
text.add("alpha");
text.add("bravo");
text.add("charly");
text.add("delta");
text.add("echo");
text = Collections.unmodifiableList(text);
System.out.println(text.getClass().getName());
Thread.sleep(2);
text.add("foxtrot");
```

The console outputs:

```
java.util.ArrayList
java.util.Collections$UnmodifiableRandomAccessList
Exception in thread "main"
                java.lang.UnsupportedOperationException
at java.base/java.util.Collections$
        UnmodifiableCollection.add(Collections.java:1060)
at Test.main(Test.java:43)
    C:\...\run.xml:111: The following error occurred while executing
this line:
    C:\...\run.xml:68: Java returned: 1
```

The UnmodifiableRandomAccessList is a subclass of the UnmodifiableList that is used
to improve performance. The documentation in the Collections library says: "Many of the
List algorithms have two implementations, one of which is appropriate for RandomAccess
lists, the other for "sequential". Often, the random-access variant yields better performance on small sequential access lists." However, the principle does not change: The client only accesses the actual target object via the proxy.

23.3   Smart Reference

The Smart Reference adds more functionality to the represented class, for example to control it. In the first step, I'll show you a version that has nothing to do with the proxy (yet). It should only introduce the project to you.

23.3.1 The Basic Version

The example in this section goes back to the Adapter Pattern example. You can find it in the sample project Proxy_1: There is a third-party library that provides an algorithm that is quite unique. The super-strict-secret algorithm sorts a list in a highly efficient way.

```
public final class SorterExternalProduct {
    List<Integer> sort(List<Integer> numberList) {
        // … abridged
    }
}
```

However, your client internally works with an int array. To allow the client to work with the foreign library, an intermediate object provides a method to convert an int array to an integer list. The modified database can be passed to the foreign library for sorting. Finally, the foreign library provides a method to convert the sorted list back to an array. The interface Sorter declares these methods.

```
public interface Sorter {
    List<Integer> convertToList(int[] numbers);
    int[] convertToArray(List<Integer> numberList);
    List<Integer> sort(List<Integer> numberList);
}
```

A helper class implements these three methods.

```
public class SorterHelper implements Sorter {
    private final SorterOtherProduct otherProduct =
                        new SorterForeignProduct();

    @Override
    public List<Integer> convertToList(int... numbers) {
        // … abridged
    }

    @Override
```

```
public int[] convertToArray(List<Integer> numberList) {
    // ... abridged
}

@Override
public List<Integer> sort(List<Integer> numberList) {
    // ... abridged
}
}
```

The client defines a certain number of unsorted random numbers with the method `createArray()`. Then it creates an instance of the class `SorterHelper`, lets it convert the array with the database into a list, sorts this list, converts it back into an array and processes the array further.

```
public static void main(String[] args) {
    var number = 100;
    var numbers = new int[number];
    numbers = createArray(numbers);
    var sorter = new SorterHelper();
    var convertedList = sorter.convertToList(numbers);
    var sortedList = sorter.sort(convertedList);
    var sortedArray = sorter.convertToArray(sortedList);

    for (var i : sortedArray)
        System.out.println(i);
}
```

The user asks whether it is worthwhile to convert the client software so that it works internally with a list. This would eliminate the need for conversion. You want to find out if the time it takes to convert the data is significant enough to make refactoring worthwhile. To do this, you measure time for conversions.

23.3.2 Introduction of a Proxy

To perform timing, develop a class that implements the same methods as the original `SorterHelper` class. The proxy can reference an object of type Sorter. The sort() method is used as an example to describe the procedure. The method first stores the current timestamp, executes the actual method on the sorter instance, and then measures the time again. The difference between the two timestamps is determined and output formatted on the console. You can find this code in the sample project Proxy_2.

```
public class SorterTimeProxy implements Sorter {
    private final sorter sorter;
    private final SimpleDateFormat dateFormat =
                    new SimpleDateFormat("HH:mm:ss:SSS");

    SorterTimeProxy(Sorter sorter) {
        this.sorter = sorter;
    }

    @Override
    public List<Integer> convertToList(int... numbers) {
        // ... abridged
    }

    @Override
    public int[] convertToArray(List<Integer> numberList){
        // ... abridged
    }

    @Override
    public List<Integer> sort(List<Integer> numberList) {
        var start = Instant.now();
        numberList = sorter.sort(numberList);
        var end = Instant.now();
        var duration = Duration.between(start, end);
        var time = duration.toMillis();
        System.out.println("sort: " +
                                dateFormat.format(time));
        return numberList;
    }
}
```

The sort method can be divided into four steps:

1. Code before the call – Pre-Invoke
2. Calling the actual method – Invoke
3. Code after the call – Post-Invoke
4. Return of the result

As in the previous project, the client creates an array of unsorted random numbers. It then creates an instance of the classes SorterHelper and SorterTimeProxy. You pass the instance of the SorterHelper class to the constructor of the SorterProxy class. You pass the commands for converting and sorting the database to the proxy.

```
public static void main(String[] args) {
    var number = 5000000;
    var numbers = new int[number];
    numbers = createArray(numbers);
    var sorter = new SorterHelper();
    var sorterTimeProxy = new SorterTimeProxy(sorter);
    var convertedList =
                sorterTimeProxy.convertToList(numbers);
    var sortedList = sorterTimeProxy.sort(convertedList);
    var sortedArray =
            sorterTimeProxy.convertToArray(sortedList);
}
```

Each method that is called executes its own behavior on the one hand, but also triggers the desired behavior of the target object on the other hand. Through the upstream proxy you measure the time and get the sorted database. The following text is output on the console.

```
convertToList: 01:00:00:137
sort: 01:00:01:979
convertToArray: 01:00:00:087
```

In the next section, we extend this approach even further.

23.3.3 Introducing a Second Proxy

Your client now wishes to be able to log the algorithm. So, you need to write a second proxy. And now it becomes clear why it makes sense to have the proxy implement the same interface as the SorterHelper?

You already sense that the new proxy, which you find in the sample project Proxy_3, also has to take the role Sorter. And just like the old proxy, it also holds a reference to another sorter object. Using the sort() method as an example, we will show that the proxy first performs its own task – logging – and then calls the desired method of the target object.

```
public class SorterLogProxy implements Sorter {
    private final sorter sorter;

    SorterLogProxy(Sorter sorter) {
        this.sorter = sorter;
    }

    @Override
```

```
    public List<Integer> convertToList(int... numbers) {
        // … abridged
    }


    @Override
    public int[] convertToArray(List<Integer> numberList){
        // … abridged
    }


    @Override
    public List<Integer> sort(List<Integer> numberList) {
        // Pre-Invoke
        var strNumber = Long.toString(numberList.size());
        print("Sorts a list of " + strNumber +
                                        " numbers");
        // Invoke and return
        return sorter.sort(numberList);
    }

    private void print(String message) {
        System.out.println("\tLog-Level INFO: " +
                                        message);

    }
}
```

The client determines which class is passed to the constructor – this can either be an instance of the class SorterHelper or an instance of the class SorterTimeProxy. So, the client determines whether it needs one, none or multiple proxies.

```
public static void main(String[] args) {
    var number = 1000000;
    var numbers = new int[number];
    numbers = createArray(numbers);
    var sorter = new SorterHelper();
    var sorterLogProxy = new SorterLogProxy(sorter);
    var sorterTimeProxy =
                new SorterTimeProxy(sorterLogProxy);
    var convertedList =
            sorterTimeProxy.convertToList(numbers);
    var sortedList = sorterTimeProxy.sort(convertedList);
    var sortedArray =
            sorterTimeProxy.convertToArray(sortedList);
}
```

When you run the code, the following text is output to the console:

```
    Log-Level INFO: Convert an array with 1000000 numbers.
convertToList: 00:00:00:033
    Log-Level INFO: Sort a list with 1000000 numbers.
sort: 00:00:00:368
    Log-Level INFO: Convert a list with 1000000 numbers.
convertToArray: 00:00:00:024
```

The client can switch the proxy before the actual call of the target object and thus control or direct the access.

23.3.4 Dynamic Proxy

When you analyze the code of the proxy classes, you notice that the pre-invoke and post-invoke in each method are the same or very similar. Code duplicates are usually a sign of poor design. There is another drawback to this: The proxy classes fully implement the interfaces of the target classes. If you insert a new method in the interface Sorter, all proxy classes must be adapted and implement this new method.

The goal of this section is to use Reflection to isolate common pieces of code and have the proxy classes automatically get generated. In other words, extract the behavior and let it generate the proxy classes at runtime. Sounds crazy? It is! Let's take it one step at a time.

23.3.4.1 The Reflection API

I can't give a comprehensive introduction to the Reflection API here. My notes on this are limited to what is needed for Dynamic Proxy.

As a programmer, one often has an interest in examining objects and classes at runtime. The Java language includes the `instanceof` operator, which checks whether an object is (also) of the type of the designated class. The call `new Student() instanceof human` returns `true` if the class Student inherits from human.

The other tools of the Reflection API are found in the `java.lang` and `java.lang.reflect` packages, primarily in the `Class`, `Method`, and `Field` classes. With the call `Class.forName()`, you load the class at runtime whose fully qualified class name you pass to the method as a parameter. You get a Class object when you call the `getClass()` method on an object. The Class object describes the class to which it refers from a meta view. For example, you can use it to query the declared methods. In the main method of the client in the sample project ProxyDynamic, I have excerpted the following code:

```
var sorter = new SorterHelper();
var sorterClass = sorter.getClass();
var methods = sorterClass.getMethods();
for (var tempMethod : methods)
    System.out.println(tempMethod.getName());
```

All methods are queried from the Class object and their names are output to the console:

```
sort
convertToArray
convertToList
wait
wait
wait
equals
toString
hashCode
getClass
notify
notifyAll
```

The class `SorterHelper` has no superclass, so it inherits automatically from the class `Object`, in which the last new methods are declared public, each with different parameters. The first three methods are prescribed in the interface `Sorter` and implemented by `SorterHelper`. The call `sorterClass.getClassLoader()` returns an object of type `ClassLoader`. The class loader is responsible for loading a class into memory.

23.3.4.2 The InvocationHandler

For the Dynamic Proxy you need two components: the InvocationHandler and the Proxy. The InvocationHandler describes the behavior of all methods; the Proxy class is created dynamically and has the same task as the Proxy from the previous project. This section discusses the InvocationHandler; it describes in general terms how the methods should behave. To generate the InvocationHandler, a class must implement the `InvocationHandler` interface and define the `invoke()` method. The proxy object, the method to invoke, and an array of parameters to the method to invoke are passed to this method. In addition to `invoke()`, the InvocationHandler can define its own behavior and data fields. For example, the InvocationHandler in the sample ProxyDynamic project holds a reference to the Sorter object whose methods are invoked. In addition, the InvocationHandler stores how many times the foreign library has been called. Probably the most important call within the method is the `invoke()` method on the `Method method` parameter. You pass this method the target object on which you want the method to run. You also pass the parameters to the method. In the example, you can simply pass the parameters. You also simply pass on the return value of the method of the target object.

```
public class TimeHandler implements InvocationHandler {
    // … abridged

    private final Object object;
```

```
    private static int calls = 0;

    // ... abridged

    public static int getCalls() {
        return calls;
    }

    @Override
    public Object invoke(Object proxy, Method method,
                              Object[] args) throws Throwable {
        var start = Instant.now();
        var result = method.invoke(object, args);
        var end = Instant.now();
        var duration = Duration.between(start, end);
        var millis = duration.toMillis();
        var methodName = method.getName();
        System.out.println(methodName + ": " +
                              dateFormat.format(millis));
        if (methodName.equals("sort"))
            calls++;

        return result;
    }
}
```

What's missing now is the actual proxy class – and that's generated at runtime, which I'll show in the following section.

23.3.4.3 The Proxy Class

It is important to note that with Dynamic Proxy, the proxy class is not only **loaded** dynamically at runtime, but it is actually **defined** at runtime. In the previous section, you described the behavior of the methods. Now the actual proxy class is to be created. The code for the proxy class is defined dynamically at runtime. To do this, call the static method `new-ProxyInstance()` of the class Proxy. Pass it the class loader object of the target interface, an array of target interfaces, and the InvocationHandler. Cast the return value of this method to the `Sorter` interface and pass it to a variable of type `Sorter`. This variable now references an instance of the proxy class created at runtime.

```
var sorter = new SorterHelper();
var timeHandler = new TimeHandler(sorter);

var targetClasses = new Class[] {Sorter.class};
```

```
var sorterProxy = (Sorter) Proxy.newProxyInstance(
        Sorter.class.getClassLoader(), targetClasses,
                                        timeHandler);
```

That's it! When you run the client's main method, your program behaves exactly as if you had generated the proxy yourself.

> If you've never worked with the Reflection API before, you may find the Dynamic Proxy a bit confusing. Perhaps the best way to understand the principle is to realize that the InvocationHandler in the `invoke()` method describes the behavior of all methods in the target interface. The proxy, which is the instance of the class that is first created at runtime, determines all methods from the interface. Each method is equipped with the same behavior, namely a forwarding of the request to the InvocationHandler: `handler.invoke()`; Analyze the sample project. Be sure to also read the API documentation for the Proxy class and the InvocationHandler interface. There you will find important information about working with Dynamic Proxy.

You can also find the sample project ProxyDynamicTable. In this project the result array is displayed in a table. For this purpose, I have inserted the lines printed here, among others, in the main method of the Client class:

```
var tblModel = new TableModel() {
    @Override
    public int getRowCount() {
        // Methods of the TableModel Interface
    }
};

var handler = new TimeHandler(tblModel);
var gateway = new Class[] {
    TableModel.class
};

var tableModelProxy = (TableModel)
        Proxy.newProxyInstance(
            TableModel.class.getClassLoader(),
            gateway, handler);
tblNumbers.setModel(tableModelProxy);
```

On the console, all accesses to the methods of the `TableModel` interface are now logged and evaluated. To produce measurable results, each method call is randomly slowed down. What I want to show you with this is that the InvocationHandler can be reused. It is only bound to an interface by the dynamically created proxy class.

23.4   Remote Proxy

Each Java program is executed in its own virtual machine. In this VM, instances of all required classes are created. These objects swim around in the VM like fish in an aquarium. When an object needs information from another object or wants to use its services, it sends a message to that object. Just like a fish in an aquarium can only communicate with a fish from the same aquarium, objects only know about other objects on the same VM. With RMI, you have a way to look beyond the edge of the aquarium.

23.4.1 Structure of RMI in Principle

In the project I will present in this section, you will program a client that wants to know what value Pi has. There is a server that knows this value and announces it on request. This project is a bit simplified and does not cover all aspects of the technology behind it, RMI. But it shows the relation to the proxy pattern.

A client does not communicate directly with the server, but through a proxy, called a stub on the client side. To the client, it looks like the proxy is the server object. In fact, however, the proxy only pretends to be the server object; it packages the client's request into a data stream and sends it to the server. The server unpacks the request and sends it to the actual object. The way it works in reverse is the same. The server object sends its response to a proxy, called a skeleton on the server side. The skeleton packages the response into a data stream and sends it back to the client over the network. The data stream relies on serialization; therefore, all parameters and return values must be serializable or a primitive data type.

The following project recreates this proxy access on a small level. You can find the code in the subdirectory RMI_Test, and this time for once not as a NetBeans project. How to get the whole thing working, I explain below.

23.4.2 The RMI Server

Let us first program an RMI server. The server is to consist of two classes and one interface. The `PiImpl` class provides three methods. The `getState()` method returns that the instance is alive. The return value of the other method – method `getPi()` - is the number Pi. Finally, the `getCounter()` method tells us how many times the `getPi()`

method has been called. The PiIF interface declares the getPi() and getCounter() methods, which are implemented by PiImpl. The class ServerStart creates an object of the class PiImpl, announces it as RMIServer and queries the state of the server in an endless loop.

23.4.2.1 The PilF Interface
It is best to start by looking at the PiIF interface. The interface specifies which methods can be called by an RMI client; it extends the Remote interface. Remote does not prescribe any methods by itself, but signals that all interfaces derived from it can be invoked remotely; thus, Remote is purely a marker interface. If the communication between client and server does not work, a RemoteException is thrown. Since this can happen in any method, each method must declare a RemoteException.

```
import java.rmi.Remote;
import java.rmi.RemoteException;

public interface PiIF extends Remote {
    public int getZaehler() throws RemoteException;
    public double getPi() throws RemoteException;
}
```

The class PiImpl implements the interface PiIF.

23.4.2.2 The PiImpl Server Class
The server class PiImpl implements PiIF and defines the mandatory methods getZaehler() and getPi(). In addition, the method getState() is defined.

```
public class PiImpl implements PiIF {
    private int counter =0;

    @Override
    public int getCounter() {
        return counter;
    }

    @Override
    public double getPi() {
        counter++;
        return 3.1415…;
    }

    public String getState() {
        return "Server is alive";
    }
}
```

Please note that only objects within the same VM can call the `getState()` method. The methods `getCounter()` and `getPi()` can also be called by objects outside their own VM – the interface Remote ensures this.

23.4.2.3 The Class ServerStart Starts the Server

The main method of the ServerStart class first creates an instance of the PiImpl class. The static methodUnicastRemoteObject.exportObject(pi) is then called so that the object can be accessed remotely at all. This instance is then registered with the RMI registry – also: "bound". The registry is the register of the server VM where the client can request the stub. In the example, the instance is registered under the name "PiCalculator". Instead of rebind() you could have coded bind() – the instance could then have been entered only once.

```
public static void main(String[] args) {
    var pi = new PiImpl();
    try {
        var remote = UnicastRemoteObject.exportObject(pi,
                                                 8077);
        Naming.rebind("PiCalculator", remote);
    } catch (RemoteException | MalformedURLException ex){
        ex.printStackTrace();
    }

    // … abridged
}
```

Finally, the main method enters an infinite loop that queries every 5 s to see if the server is still active.

```
public static void main(String[] args) {
    // … abridged
    while (true) {
        try {
            Thread.sleep(5000);
        } catch (InterruptedException ex) {
            // … abridged
        }
        var state = pi.getState();
        System.out.println(state);
    }
}
```

This already describes the server classes. Let's take a look at what the client looks like.

23.4.3 The RMI Client

The start class creates an instance of the Calculator class and queries the number Pi there; the returned value is output to the console. Afterwards, the calculator is instructed to output to the console how often Pi has already been queried.

```
public class ClientStart {
    public static void main(String[] args) {
        var calculator = new CalculationEngine();
        System.out.println("Pi is: " +
                                    calculator.tellMePi());
        calculator.printCounter();
    }
}
```

From the RMI point of view, the constructor of the calculator is interesting. It calls the `lookup()` method, which returns a reference to the stub object from the registry. `Naming.lookup()` is something like looking into the server's registry. Returned is the stub of the service, which is cast to the correct interface.

```
public class CalculationEngine {
    private final PiIF pi;

    CalculationEngine() {
        pi = lookup();
    }

    private PiIF lookup() {
        PiIF result = null;
        var serverName = "localhost";
        var serviceName = "PiCalculator";
        try {
            result =
                    (PiIF) Naming.lookup("rmi://" +
                            serverName + "/" + serviceName);
        } catch (NotBoundException |
                MalformedURLException |
                RemoteException ex) {
            ex.printStackTrace();
        } finally {
            return result;
        }
    }
    // ... abridged
}
```

On the stub, the client can now call the designated methods as if they were local.

```java
public class CalculationEngine {
    // ... abridged

    public double tellMePi() {
        double result = 0;
        try {
            result = pi.getPi();
        } catch (RemoteException ex) {
            ex.printStackTrace();
        } finally {
            return result;
        }
    }
}
```

You now know all the code – let's look at how to make the project work in the following paragraph.

23.4.4 Making the Project Work

You will find all java files in the subdirectory RMI_Test as mentioned before. Copy them locally to your computer. Open a console window and change to this directory. Translate the source files with `javac *.java`. Now call the RMI registry: `rmiregistry`. Please wait a few seconds and if necessary confirm a Windows share request dialog for network access. Now you can start the server in a new prompt with `java ServerStart`. Again, wait (and confirm another network share request if necessary) until you see the message "Server is alive" in the output, which is repeated every few seconds. If you now call the client from a third console with `java ClientStart`, the value of Pi and the number of answered requests for Pi since the last server start will be printed on the console.

If you start the server too soon after calling rmiregistry, you will most likely get an exception at first, but this will be followed by the "server is alive" messages after communication is established. On the other hand, if you start the client too early, it will abort with an exception and a value of 0.0 for Pi. You will then have to restart it and should get the correct information from the server.

Both the client and the server object communicate with their proxies – stub and skeleton – without knowing it. The proxy objects are responsible for transporting the data streams across the network to the other virtual machine.

The sequence of communication is shown in the sequence diagram in Fig. 23.1.

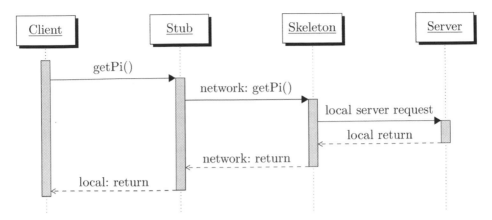

Fig. 23.1 RMI – Communication via upstream proxy

23.5 Proxy – The UML Diagram

Figure 23.2 shows the UML diagram from the sample project ProxyDynamicTable.

23.6 Summary

Go through the chapter again in key words:

- With a proxy, you do not access an object directly, but via its proxy.
- The main application areas are Remote Proxy, Security Proxy, Smart Reference and Virtual Proxy; however, there are other areas as well.
- Virtual Proxy: You do not load all images in an album, but only those that are currently to be displayed on the screen.
- Security Proxy: The actual target object is encapsulated in another object that – as in the UnmodifiableList example – prevents write access.
- Smart Reference: The function of an object is extended with the motivation to log or extend accesses.
  - The proxy implements the interface of the target object.
  - It is placed in front of the actual object.
  - The client calls the desired method.
  - The call is first processed by the proxy.
  - The call is then forwarded to the actual target object.
  - The procedure is inflexible when the interface is extended.
  - Dynamic Proxy is a relief for the programmer since Java 5:
  - The InvocationHandler defines the behavior of all methods of an interface in a general way.
  - The proxy class is created dynamically at runtime.

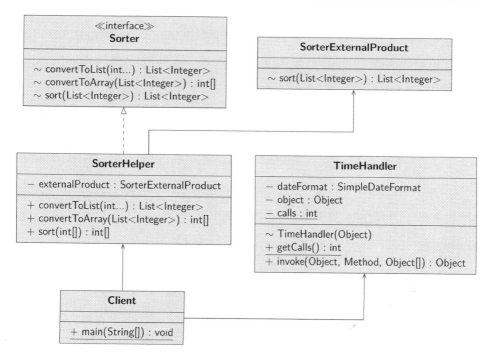

Fig. 23.2 UML diagram of the proxy pattern (example project ProxyDynamicTable)

- Remote Proxy: allows access to objects outside the own address space
  - A client wants to access a server object outside its own address space.
  - The client gets a stub from the server to which it sends its request.
  - The stub – the client proxy – forwards the request over the network to the server.
  - The server proxy – the skeleton – passes the request to the server object.
  - The server object sends the return value to the skeleton.
  - The skeleton sends the response to the stub, which sends the response to the request-ing local object.
  - Neither client nor server object knows that they are sending their messages to proxies.

23.7   Description of Purpose

The Gang of Four describes the purpose of the "Proxy" pattern as follows:

Control access to an object using an upstream proxy object.

24

The Decorator pattern – another structural pattern – adds responsibilities to objects. In the last chapter, you saw how the proxy extends objects by responsibilities. Remember – the actual object to be addressed and the proxies implemented the same interface; a proxy references another object without knowing whether it is another proxy or the desired object. You'll take a similar approach with the decorator. When I present you with an example in a moment, you may not find the difference between a proxy and a decorator clear at all – but I will discuss that below.

24.1   Build Cars

Take a look at what a car dealer has to offer. There are a few basic models with what feels like a thousand trim levels. Model A is the rolling shopping bag, Model B the down-to-earth mid-size car and Model C the upmarket variant. In addition, each model comes with an optional navigation system, air conditioning, leather upholstery, etc. Let's consider how you might code this situation.

24.1.1 One Attribute for Each Optional Extra

One could first come up with the idea of providing an attribute for each feature. If the attribute is zero, it is not desired; otherwise, it has been ordered for it.

Supplementary Information The online version contains supplementary material available at https://doi.org/10.1007/978-3-658-39829-3_24.

```
public class ModelA {
    private AC ac = null;
    private GPS gps = null;

    // … abridged

    public void setAC(AC ac) {
        System.out.println("The customer buys A/C ");
        this.ac = ac;
    }

    // … abridged
}
```

The disadvantage is obvious: Each object drags around a lot of unnecessary data that has nothing to do with its actual core business. There is too much duplicate code, which makes the project error-prone and not very maintenance-friendly. When changes are due, existing code has to be drilled up. The **OpenClosed Principle** has obviously been violated.

24.1.2 Extending with Inheritance

Another approach might be to specialize, because a car with air conditioning is a car. For example, ModelA_Climate could be defined as follows:

```
public class ModelA {
    // Properties of Model A
}
public class ModelA_AC extends ModelA {
    // additional features of an air conditioner
}
```

What would be the consequence? The number of subclasses would explode because you would need to cover every conceivable combination. For example, you would need the following classes: ModelA, ModelA_With_AC, ModelA_With_GPS, ModelA_With_AC_And_GPS, ModelB, ModelB_With_AC, etc. With three basic models with three optional extras, that's $3 * 2 ^ 3 = 24$ subclasses. Earlier, we talked about preferring composition to inheritance – and again, it shows that inheritance is not the means to an end. In this admittedly contrived example, the weakness of inheritance is obvious. However, I would like to assume that in practice there are cases where inheritance less evidently leads to a rigid inflexible system.

24.1.3 Decorating According to the Matryoshka Principle

Do you know the Matryoshka principle? You have a beautifully painted wooden doll that encloses another wooden doll, which in turn encloses another wooden doll, which itself encloses a wooden doll, and so on. That's kind of how the Decorator works. Each new feature encloses ("wraps") the previously assembled product. Sounds complicated? It isn't at all.

But please note that in contrast to the composite pattern from Chap. 12, we do not assemble branched structures here (this would then degenerate into a similar number of variants as in the approach with inheritance), but rather close the components "around" each other. This approach gives us the flexibility to add optional extras to the basic model in any order and frequency.

24.1.3.1 Defining the Basic Models

Basic models and optional extras implement the same interface: Component. This interface describes what each item must be able to do, namely name its price and describe itself. Open the sample project AutoCatalog. You will find the interface `Component` in the package `commons`.

```
public interface Component {
    public int getPrice();
    public String getDescription();
}
```

In the package `basicmodels` you will find different models, for example `ModelC`.

```
public class ModelC implements Component {
    @Override
    public int getPrice() {
       return 50000;
    }

    @Override
    public String getDescription() {
       return "A car of the upper middle class";
    }
}
```

In the following paragraph, you will define the optional extras.

24.1.3.2 Defining the Optional Extras

The optional extras are intended to inherit from the common upper-tier optional extra, which is itself also of type Component and holds a reference to another Component.

```java
public abstract class OptionalEquipment
                                    implements Component {
    protected final Component basicComponent;

    protected OptionalEquipment(Component component) {
        this.baseComponent = component;
    }
}
```

All special features define the methods of the interface Component. They access the data of the referenced component and add or concatenate their own value.

```java
public class AC extends OptionalEquipment {
    public AC(Component component) {
        super(Component);
    }

    @Override
    public int getPrice() {
        return basicComponent.getPrice() + 500;
    }

    @Override
    public String getDescription() {
        return basisComponent.getDescription() +
                                " and air conditioning";
    }
}
```

The following paragraph shows you how to put the individual components together.

24.1.3.3 The Client Plugs the Components Together
The main method of the ApplStart class first creates the base model and wraps it with a navigation system. Afterwards the navigation system is wrapped with an air conditioner. Since the client now has no further requests, you can call getDescription() and getPrice() on the air conditioner as the outermost wrapper.

```java
public class ApplStart {
    public static void main(String[] args) {
        Component basicModel = new ModelC();
        Component gps = new GPS(basicModel);
        Component ac = new AC(gps);
        System.out.println("CustomerRequest: \n\t" +
```

```
                              ac.getDescription() + "\nPrice: \n\t"
                              + ac.getPrice());
        }
    }
```

The console outputs:

```
Customer requirement:
       A car of the upper middle class and a satellite navigation and
air conditioning
    Price:
        51380
```

You can plug together the basic models and the equipment variants as you wish and, above all, flexibly. Even the number of components no longer plays a role. Theoretically, you could fit two air conditioners and three navigation units – if that's what the customer wants. The code is robust and maintainable because each class has a single function. High cohesion is an indication of proper design. If the price of the navigation system goes up, you only have to change the code in one place. And finally, let me introduce Decorator terminology: The interface component is a component. Each base model is a concrete component. The interface of the optional extras is a decorator; the optional extras themselves are the concrete decorators.

The realization of the pattern is similar to the realization of the proxy pattern. With the Proxy I offered you the example of the UnmodifiableList. In the internet and in the literature, you can find this example partly also with the Decorator. Is there something wrong? Where does this class belong? To come to an answer, I have to think about the task of the UnmodifiableList. I also need to keep in mind the goal of the Patterns. The UnmodifiableList controls access to a list. When I sort it in at the Proxy, I emphasize the controlling nature; a Proxy controls access to the actual system, perhaps even restricts it. The Decorator, on the other hand, adds functionality to a system without changing it itself. Therefore, the UnmodifiableList is clearly a proxy to me.

In the next paragraph you will learn where you have already encountered the Decorator in practice.

24.2 Practical Examples

Use the Decorator Pattern to add scroll bars to Swing components and send data via streams.

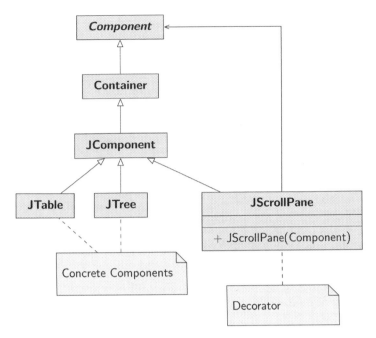

Fig. 24.1 Class hierarchy of the Swing components around JComponent (simplified)

24.2.1 The "JScrollPane" Class

You can add scroll bars to any component: a JTree, a JPanel, a JTable, and so on. In doing so, you plug the component together like the matryoshka and add it to a container.

```
JFrame frmDisplay = new JFrame();
JTable tblData = new JTable();
JScrollPane scrTable = new JScrollPane(tblData);
frmDisplay.add    (scrTable);
```

A table with scrollbars is displayed on the JFrame. You can plug the components into each other because they are all of type JComponent and the constructor of JScrollPane expects an object of supertype Component. The interaction can be found in Fig. 24.1.

24.2.2 Streams in Java

When you start looking at streams, you see the drawback of the Decorator Pattern. You have a multitude of classes that, at first glance, all do the same thing. Looking at the java.io package doesn't really make any programmer happy. With knowledge of the Decorator Pattern, you can bring order to the hodgepodge of classes.

24.2.2.1 Streams as Decorator

Streams connect data sources and destination. Data to be transmitted can be either bytes or characters. The inheritance hierarchies are different in each case: ByteStreams are processed by the abstract superclasses `InputStream` and `OutputStream`, CharacterStreams by `Reader` and `Writer`.

The `FilterInputStream` class is the superclass for the Decorator classes. An object of this instance references another InputStream and overrides all methods so that any request is forwarded to the referenced object. The API documentation for the FilterInputStream states:

> A FilterInputStream contains some other input stream, which it uses as its basic source of data, possibly transforming the data along the way or providing additional functionality. The class FilterInputStream itself simply overrides all methods of InputStream with versions that pass all requests to the contained input stream. Subclasses of FilterInputStream may further override some of these methods and may also provide additional methods and fields.

If you read through the quote, you will find exactly the purpose description of the Decorator Pattern.

The idea is to extend the functionality of objects without creating subclasses. For example, a subclass of FilterInputStream is BufferedInputStream, which writes the data to a buffer, which improves performance. The API documentation describes the task like this:

> A BufferedInputStream adds functionality to another input stream-namely, the ability to buffer the input …

The `FileInputStream` and `ByteArrayInputStream` classes are the components to be decorated; they both inherit from `InputStream`. The `FileInputStream` class connects to a file and `ByteArrayInputStream` expects an array of bytes as the data source. Both classes can read bytes from the data source and decorate it with a BufferedInputStream. You could decorate a zipped file with another decorator, the `ZipInputStream`. To do this, you plug the objects together like nesting dolls.

```
InputStream in =
    new ZipInputStream(
        new BufferedInputStream(
            new FileInputStream( /* filename */ )));
```

The inheritance hierarchy after the `OutputStream` class is set up accordingly. For example, you have a FileOutputStream there that connects to a file that you write data to. The Decorator interface is represented by the `FilterOutputStream` class. And from this class, BufferedOutputStream is derived:

> By setting up such an output stream, an application can write bytes to the underlying output stream without necessarily causing a call to the underlying system for each byte written.

With what you have read in this paragraph you can read and write a file byte by byte. The code of such a small copy program can be found in the sample project Streams_1.

```
public static void main(String[] args) {
    var chooser = new JFileChooser();
    var returnValue = chooser.showOpenDialog(null);
    if (returnValue == JFileChooser.APPROVE_OPTION) {
        var input = chooser.getSelectedFile();
        returnValue = chooser.showSaveDialog(null);
        if (returnValue == JFileChooser.APPROVE_OPTION) {
            var output = chooser.getSelectedFile();
            try ( var in = new FileInputStream(input);
                var out = new FileOutputStream(output)) {
                int i;
                while ((i = in.read()) != -1)
                    out.write(i);
            } catch (IOException ex) {
                ex.printStackTrace();
            }
        }
    }
}
```

So far all is well, you can verify the Decorator pattern in the API.

24.2.3 Streams as Non-Decorator

You could also go one step further and wrap the FileOutputStream in a DataOutputStream to be able to output primitive data types. In this way, you extend the functionality of the FileOutputStream – in the sense of the Decorator Pattern – without changing it. You can find a corresponding example in the sample project Streams_2.

```
private static void write() {
    final var file = new File("person.txt");

    try ( var fos = new FileOutputStream(file);
            var dos = new DataOutputStream(fos);) {
        var id = 4711;
        var salary = 2466.77;
        var isBoss = true;
        dos.writeInt(id);
        dos.writeDouble(salary);
        dos.writeBoolean(isBoss);
```

```
    } catch (IOException e) {
        e.printStackTrace();
    }
}
```

And accordingly read out the file again.

```
private static void read() {
    final var file = new File("person.txt");

    try ( var fis = new FileInputStream(file);
            var dis = new DataInputStream(fis);) {
        var id = dis.readInt();
        var salary = dis.readDouble();
        var isBoss = dis.readBoolean();
        System.out.println("The employee with the personnel number
" + id + " earns " + salary + " Euro");
        if (isChef)
            System.out.println("He's the boss");
    } catch (IOException e) {
        e.printStackTrace();
    }
}
```

Then when a method calls write() and read(), it prints to the console:

```
The employee with the personnel number 4711 earns 2466.77 Euro
He's the boss
```

Why is this construct not a decorator? The decorator pattern allows another object to extend the interface. However, the client code must not be affected by this; decoration must be transparent to the client. In this example, however, that would be exactly the case – the specialized methods cannot be called on an object of type InputStream, or OutputStream. If the programmer wants to make use of this, he must program against the interface of the DataInput/OutputStream.

Streams are mentioned in the Decorator Pattern context in almost every Patterns book – including the GoF. That's true as long as you don't need to change the interface. I have repeatedly read (quoting mutatis mutandis): "Everything that is IO is also Decorator." I don't think such an absolutely worded statement is tenable.

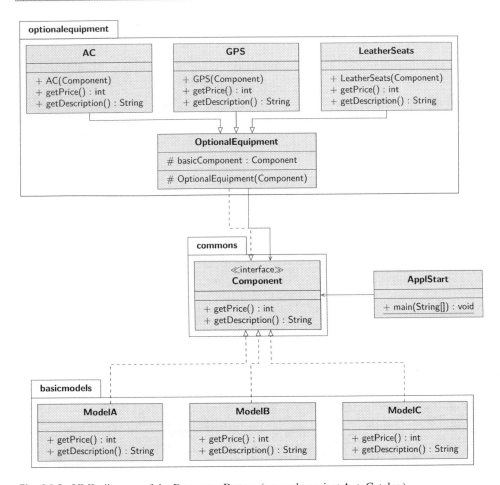

Fig. 24.2 UML diagram of the Decorator Pattern (example project AutoCatalog)

24.3   Decorator – The UML Diagram

This time you can see the UML diagram in Fig. 24.2 from the first example project
AutoCatalog.

24.4   Summary

Go through the chapter again in key words:

- You need to add responsibilities to objects.
- Inheritance leads you into a rigid, inflexible, and unmaintainable system.

- The extension should not change the object to be extended.
- The Decorator Pattern provides an alternative to subclassing.
- In the Decorator, there are components that are decorated.
- The Decorator classes implement the same interface as the components.
- The decorator references the object to be decorated.
- Decorators can have their own methods, but must adhere to the component interface.
- The advantage is a stable, flexible and cohesive system.
- The disadvantage is that many similar classes are formed.
- The difference with the proxy is that the proxy controls the object, but the decorator adds functionality to the object.
- Unlike the composite, the decorator does not specify a fixed dependency and frequency.
- In contrast to the adapter, the interface of the Decorator is identical in both directions – so that further Decorators can also be connected.

24.5   Description of Purpose

The Gang of Four describes the purpose of the "Decorator" pattern as follows:

> Dynamically extend an object with responsibilities. Decorators provide a flexible alternative to subclassing to extend the functionality of a class.

25

The Bridge Pattern literally bridges the gap between the implementation of a functionality and its application. It separates the abstraction from the implementation. This allows both sides to be developed independently of each other. At the same time, the implementation remains hidden from the client. Various examples of this can also be found in the Java class library.

25.1 Two Definitions

I want to define two terms before I get to the Bridge Pattern. If you are reading this section, you may find my execution trivial. However, a precise definition of the terms abstraction and implementation is important for understanding the Bridge Pattern.

25.1.1 What Is an Abstraction?

The first concept I want to address is abstraction. When you develop a class, you always have to decide what part of the real world you want to represent and with what accuracy. If you're writing software that a college uses to manage its students, you're going to pick out very specific relevant characteristics of a student and include those in your classes. For example, date of birth, address, and exams passed are relevant to the university. Irrelevant are likely to be hair color, weight, number of siblings, and many other characteristics. In your university software, you **reduce the** student to the relevant characteristics; you create a **model**, you **abstract**. For example, another abstraction is a calculator, which will be relevant to the sample project in a moment. When you look at the calculator on your desk,

---

Supplementary Information The online version contains supplementary material available at https://doi.org/10.1007/978-3-658-39829-3_25.

O. Musch, *Design Patterns with Java*, https://doi.org/10.1007/978-3-658-39829-3_25

it has certain features: a specific weight, a color, different arithmetic operations, and so on. When you develop the class Calculator, you ignore numerous features and capabilities; you reduce the real object to the features and capabilities that are relevant to the given context.

The next listing from the sample project Calculator shows such an abstraction. I only print the interface here, because it is important for the client. I leave out the implementation behind it to your own analysis.

```
public class Calculator {
    public double add(double summand_1,
                                     double summand_2) {
        // Implementation
    }

    public double subtract(double minuend,
                                     double subtrahend) {
        // Implementation
    }

    public double multiply(double factor_1,
                                     double factor_2) {
        // Implementation
    }

    public double divide(double dividend,
                                     double divisor) {
        // Implementation
    }
}
```

When a client creates an object of this class, it calls the methods that the interface provides. The abstraction specifies what the object can do.

25.1.2 What Is an Implementation?

If the client relies on the abstraction, it does not have to worry about the implementation behind it. The details of the implementation may even remain hidden from him. I've never been interested in how the candy machine in the office turns a euro piece into a candy bar. Nor do I care how the calculator adds two numbers. For me as a user, the implementation, the how of a method, is not important.

Let's look at the implementation in the following step. In the first approach, you could simply implement the school methods.

```
public class Calculator {
    public double add(double summand_1,
                                    double summand_2) {
        return summand_1 + summand_2;
    }

    public double subtract(double minuend,
                                    double subtrahend) {
        return minuend - subtrahend;
    }

    public double multiply(double factor_1,
                                    double factor_2) {
        return factor_1 * factor_2;
    }

    public double divide(double dividend,
                                        double divisor) {
        return dividend / divisor;
    }
}
```

You now want to change the implementation. There are alternative multiplication methods that – especially for long numbers – are much more performant than the multiplication algorithm taught in school. If you want to change the implementation, you can simply create a subclass that overrides the multiply() method. If you want to multiply two numbers using the Fast Fourier Transform (FFT), use the following class.

```
public class FFT extends calculator {
    @Override
    public double multiply(double factor_1,
                                    double factor_2) {
        // not printed - FFT multiplication
    }
}
```

A client can now choose whether to use the simple multiplication algorithm or the FFT. Accordingly, it can start an instance of the calculator either with.

```
Calculator calculator = new calculator();
```

or with.

```
Calculator calculator = new FFT();
```

By the way, I find the different multiplication methods quite exciting. If you want to deal with FFT multiplication, I recommend the following site: http://www.inf.fh-flensburg. de/lang/algorithmen/fft/fft.htm. You can also find the article by Prof. Dr. Lang deposited there as "Transformations.pdf" in the directory of sample projects for this chapter.

There are many other multiplication algorithms, such as the peasant multiplication (PM). A few of these algorithms are highly performant, others impress with elegance.

25.1.3 A Problem Begins to Mature

Right after you have published your calculator, extension requests come in. The calculator should also support quadrature. Since you want to distribute this feature separately, you develop the abstraction, the interface, further. Since squaring means multiplying a number by itself, you can use the existing methods.

```
public class CalculatorDeluxe extends Calculator {
    public double square(double number) {
        return multiply(number, number);
    }
}
```

As a result, you have the class diagram in Fig. 25.1.

This solution has a catch. They had further developed the implementation up front and implemented high performance multiplication algorithms. But when a customer buys the CalculatorDeluxe, he only gets the standard implementation of the multiplication method. He can't use FFT multiplication any more than he can use peasant multiplication. Maybe the cow is off the ice when the CalculatorDeluxe doesn't inherit from Calculator but from FFT.

```
public class CalculatorDeluxeFFT extends FFT {
    public double square(double number) {
        // Implementation
    }
}
```

Fig. 25.1 Incomplete class diagram of the project calculator

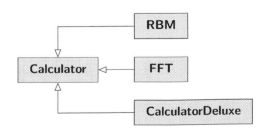

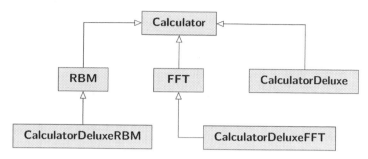

Fig. 25.2 "Advanced" class diagram of the project calculator

However, this solution leaves out the peasant multiplication and the school multiplication implemented by default. You cannot avoid extending the inheritance hierarchy according to these two algorithms accordingly (Fig. 25.2).

It becomes clear that the inheritance hierarchy is too broad and too inflexible. If either the abstraction is extended or an algorithm is added to the implementation, the number of classes grows rapidly. Assume that division is to be replaced. The algorithm you know from school asks how many times the divisor fits in the dividend. An alternative approach might be to multiply by the reciprocal of the divisor. You approach the reciprocal of a number iteratively using a formula from Newton. If you were to try to implement the division algorithm by inheritance, you would have to consider that you have two abstractions – the Calculator and the CalculatorDeluxe. Both abstractions would want to optionally multiply using FFT, the PM, or the school method, and optionally divide using the school method or Newton's method.

Conclusion: The problem is that abstraction and implementation depend too much on each other and influence each other. The Bridge Pattern will solve this problem.

25.2   The Bridge Pattern in Use

The Bridge Pattern separates the abstraction from the implementation. How does this work? You may remember the State Pattern and the Strategy Pattern! There you defined the behavior of an object in its own classes. You have specified an interface in your abstraction that the implementation of the classes that define the behavior must match.

25.2.1 First Step

The Bridge Pattern takes a similar approach. You define the abstraction with all the methods it should offer. The execution is delegated to an object of type Implementor. It is allowed that the methods of the abstraction and the implementor have different identifiers. Have a look at the sample project CalculatorBridge.

```
public class Calculator {
    private Implementor implementor;
    public Calculator(Implementor implementor) {
        this.implementor = implementor;
    }

    public void setImplementor(Implementor implementor) {
        this.implementor = implementor;
    }

    public double add(double summand_1,
                                    double summand_2) {
        return implementor.add(summand_1, summand_2);
    }

    public double subtract(double minuend,
                                    double subtrahend) {
        return implementor.subtract(minuend, subtrahend);
    }

    public double multiply(double factor_1,
                                    double factor_2) {
        return implementor.multiply(factor_1, factor_2);
    }

    public double divide(double dividend,
                                        double divisor) {
        return implementor.divide(dividend, divisor);
    }

}
```

The implementor can be either an interface or an (abstract) class. In the current project, I equipped the implementor with the computational methods I learned in school.

```
public class Implementor {
    double add(double summand_1, double summand_2) {
        return summand_1 + summand_2;
    }

    double subtract(double minuend, double subtrahend) {
        return minuend - subtrahend;
    }

    double multiply(double factor_1, double factor_2) {
        return factor_1 * factor_2;
    }
```

Fig. 25.3 Class diagram of
the project CalculatorBridge

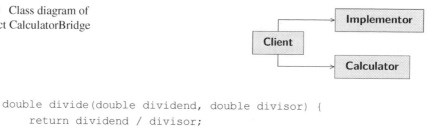

```
        double divide(double dividend, double divisor) {
            return dividend / divisor;
        }
    }
```

The client creates an instance of the implementation and parameterizes the abstraction
with it:

```
    Implementor implementor = new Implementor();
    Calculator calculator = new calculator(implementor);
    System.out.println("30 * 12 = " + calculator.multiply(30, 12));
```

The class diagram looks as follows at this stage of development (Fig. 25.3).

The implementor and the abstraction are connected via an aggregation – thus bridging
the gap between the two.

25.2.2 Second Step

Up to this point, it all looks harmless. But let us convince you that with this solution you
have an incredibly powerful tool in your hands.

25.2.2.1 Extending the Abstraction

First, let's expand the abstraction. As in the first example, the client wants to be able to
square a number. Since the square of a number is the number times itself, the implementation is completely unaffected.

```
    public class CalculatorDeluxe extends Calculator {
        public CalculatorDeluxe(Implementor implementor) {
            super(implementor);
        }

        public double square(double number) {
            return multiply(number, number);
        }
    }
```

Further abstractions would be conceivable. If you want to calculate the square root of a number, you can fall back on the implementation already defined. The square root of y is the multiplication of y by the reciprocal of the square root of y. To calculate the reciprocal of the square root of a number, there is an iterative procedure that goes back to Newton. Starting from an approximated value, the respective consequent value is calculated – the consequent value is calculated by addition, multiplication, difference and division alone.

```
public class CalculatorNewton extends CalculatorDeluxe {
    public CalculatorNewton(Implementor implementor) {
        super(implementor);
    }

    public double square(double number) {
        // iterative scheme according to Newton
    }
}
```

The client can now choose the abstraction it wants to have and parameterize it with the implementor. It is important that only the abstraction changes or is extended.

25.2.3 Extending the Implementation

Regardless of the abstraction, the inheritance hierarchy can be extended according to the Implementor class. The Implementor itself provides only the simple implementation of the basic arithmetic operations, which are then used in the calculator. As in the previous project, I defined the classes FFT and RBM, which override the multiplication algorithm – i.e. do not add any fundamentally new functionality. I did not implement the respective methods. But you are welcome to try that yourself.

```
public class RBM extends Implementor {
    @Override
    double multiply(double factor_1, double factor_2) {
        System.out.println("\tPeasant multiplication");
        return factor_1 * factor_2;
    }
}
```

The client can now choose its abstraction and a suitable implementation at will.

```
implementor = new PM();
calculator = new calculator(implementor);
System.out.println("30 * 12 = " + calculator.multiply(30, 12));
```

The Implementor can be extended at runtime.

```
calculator.setImplementor(new FFT());
System.out.println("30 * 12 = " + calculator.multiply(30, 12));
```

When you run the code, it prints to the console:

```
Peasant multiplication
30 * 12 = 360.0
FFT multiplication
30 * 12 = 360.0
```

It is important – and the class diagram in Fig. 25.4 should make this clear once again – that the implementation can now evolve independently of the abstraction.

However, some tasks can no longer be accomplished with the basic arithmetic already defined. For example, if the client needs a random number generator, you need to extend both the abstraction interface and the implementor.

25.3   Discussion of the Bridge Pattern

In this section, I will conclude by showing where you can find the Bridge in the class library. I will also distinguish the Bridge from other patterns.

25.3.1 Bridge in the Wild

When you deal with AWT and peer classes, you dig deep into the primordial slime of Java's evolution. An AWT component is not drawn by Java itself, but by the operating system. For example, the developer has a `Button` class that inherits from `Component`. `Component` is the top of the inheritance hierarchy of abstraction. On the other side of the bridge is the interface `ComponentPeer`, from which the implementation, for example, the class `ButtonPeer`, is derived. As a programmer, you have no access to this implementation (at least in theory).

You can also find the Bridge Pattern in a completely different context – database programming. Take a look at how you work with JDBC. You load a database driver with `Class.forName(<driver name>)`. Then you let it give you the connection to the database:

```
Connection connection =
    DriverManager.getConnection(<url>, <user>, <password>)
```

From this connection, get an object of type `Statement`:

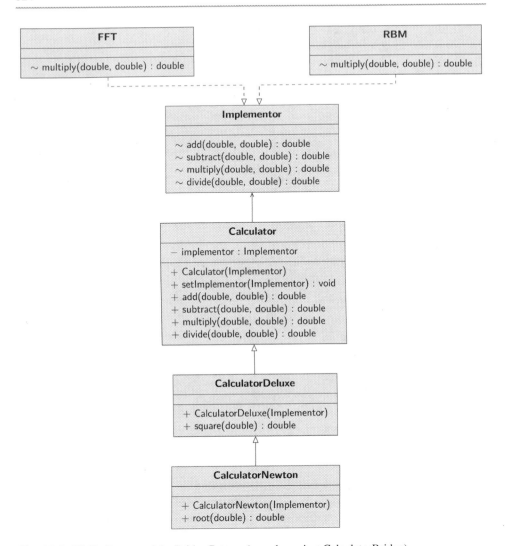

Fig. 25.4 UML diagram of the Bridge Pattern (sample project CalculatorBridge)

```
Statement state = connection.createStatement();
```

You place your SQL command on this statement object:

```
ResultSet result = state.executeQuery( ... command ... );
```

You iterate over the returned ResultSet to get the data you want. If you initialize the abstraction – your application – with a given driver, you can choose to access an Access database or an Oracle database or any other database. You always work with the given

Connection, Statement, and ResultSet components. The question of how your query is processed is not relevant to you, i.e.: you have no access to the implementation running in the background.

Abstraction and implementation evolve independently of each other. Both can evolve and be reused independently.

25.3.2 Distinction from Other Patterns

Facade, Adapter, Proxy, Decorator and Bridge are very similar. They use composition to wrap another object. A method call is delegated to the wrapped object.

The task of the adapter is to relate two interfaces of different types in such a way that they can work together. Since multiple objects can be adapted, this compensates for the lack of multiple inheritance in Java. Adapters are typically very lean because their only task is to relate two systems; own intelligence might provide, for example, that data is converted.

Decorators bring intelligence of their own – they are of the same type as the wrapped object and extend its behavior. A typical textbook example is the FileInputStream, which is wrapped into a BufferedInputStream. Both classes are of type `InputStream`.

The proxy is primarily a proxy for another object. The implementation of a proxy can be very similar to the decorator. The goal of a proxy can be to control access to the represented object.

The facade is most likely to be confused with the adapter. Its task is to simplify access to a (sub)system. Think of booking a holiday trip, which consists of many individual steps.

You can vary an implementation with many patterns: The Strategy Pattern lets you vary an algorithm. The State Pattern defines different behavior depending on the context. With the Adapter pattern, you access a different library. The Bridge Pattern differs from these patterns in that, in addition to the implementation, the abstraction can also be developed further. While you can implement an adapter or a facade at any time, the decision for a bridge must be made as early as possible.

After all, the task of the bridge is to separate an implementation – i.e. the arithmetic operations – from the abstraction – the calculator on which the user types in his calculation. The goal is to be able to develop behavior and abstraction independently of each other.

25.4 Bridge – The UML Diagram

The UML diagram from the sample project CalculatorBridge can be found in Fig. 25.4.

25.5   Summary

Go through the chapter again in key words:

- You model a section of the real world in a class.
- The class is an abstraction of reality.
- The abstraction represents the interface for the client.
- The interface is the contract between client and class.
- The client may rely on the provided methods to perform the defined behavior.
- The behavior is defined by the implementation behind it.
- Abstractions and implementation can change.
- One possible way to define new behavior or abstractions is inheritance.
- When abstraction and implementation both change, inheritance leads to a rapidly unmanageable system.
- The Bridge Pattern separates the abstraction from the implementation.
- The implementation is not defined in the class of the abstraction, but in its own.
- Abstraction and implementation are connected via aggregation.
- Abstraction and implementation form independent inheritance hierarchies.
- Implementation details remain hidden from the client.

25.6   Description of Purpose

The Gang of Four describes the purpose of the pattern "Bridge" as follows:

Decouple an abstraction from its implementation so that the two can be varied independently.

Combine Patterns

26

In the last 23 chapters I have explained the individual patterns. Now we will deal with an example for which we want to use several patterns at the same time. Using a concrete example, we will combine five different design patterns in one application. Among other things, this is done by combining several interfaces or composing classes. What to pay attention to will be the topic of this chapter. And I will also give you a few approaches for your own extensions and improvements.

26.1 The Example

First, a warning: I pointed out in the introductory chapter that I think it is critical for programmers to make excessive use of patterns, see Sect. 1.1.2.4. This example is not meant to motivate you to implement patterns "at any cost". It is merely meant to show how patterns can be combined, and what you should keep in mind when doing so.

We want to combine several design patterns using the example of an alarm system of a rudimentary "smart home". The basic requirements for our system are:

There should be both smoke detectors and motion sensors, but they can come from different manufacturers. For the test, all sensors are to be connected to a "control center" from which they can also be triggered. When triggered, the sensors will send SMS messages with possibly different contents. In the case of smoke detection, a sprinkler system should also be activated, and in the case of motion detection, a rotating warning light should be switched on. Both the sprinkler system and the warning light should be able to be switched off again by remote control. And of course, all events are logged at a central location.

Supplementary Information The online version contains supplementary material available at https://doi.org/10.1007/978-3-658-39829-3_26.

In the following subchapters, we will take a look at these things in detail. You can find the corresponding example project under the name SmartHome.

I found the inspiration for this example on the Internet (https://ruysal.com/post/2019-01-23-Combining-Multiple-Design-Patterns-in-Java/) and kindly got permission from the author Ramazan Uysal to use his idea. I have revised the code and adapted it for this book.

Let me tell you in advance that you will find a class diagram under Fig. 26.1, which you can use as a guide when working through this chapter.

26.2 Singleton: Logging

The "simplest" pattern for our example is the singleton we use to provide a centralized protocol service.

Each using object first fetches the instance and then places its message there. The log output could then be as complicated as desired, but here we only output supplemented text to the console.

```java
public class LogOutput {
    private static final LogOutput INSTANCE =
                                new LogOutput();

        private LogOutput() {
        System.out.println("Protocol service ready");
    }

    public static LogOutput getInstance() {
        return INSTANCE;
    }

    public void showMessage(String s) {
        System.out.println("logFile: " + s + " detected");
    }
}
```

You can see that there is already an output in the (private) constructor that the protocol service is now available. The method getInstance provides this service centrally and the service itself consists only of the method showMessage, which outputs a framed text.

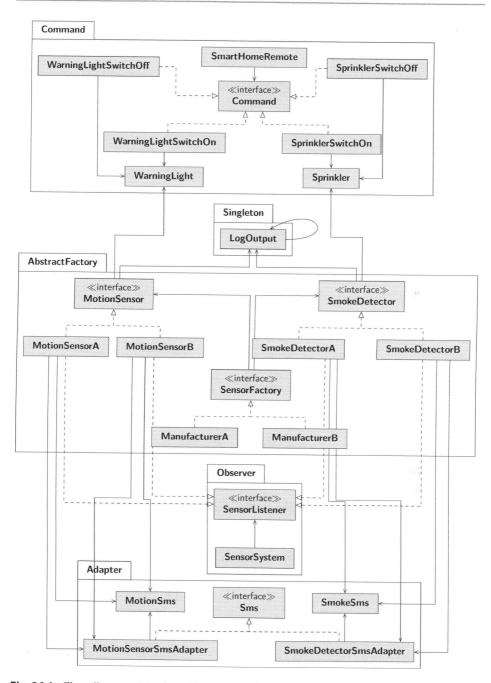

Fig. 26.1 Class diagram of the SmartHome example project

26.3   Abstract Factory: Building the Sensors

Two different types of sensors that can come from different producers. This sounds suspiciously like an abstract factory, which we already discussed in Chap. 15. And the approach fits pretty well here, too: First, we define the interface of a sensor factory with the methods to build a motion sensor or a smoke detector.

```
public interface SensorFactory {
    MotionSensor buildMotionSensor();
    SmokeDetector buildSmokeDetector();
}
```

We also need interfaces for the sensors. I print the version for the motion sensor here, but it looks very similar for the smoke detector.

```
public interface MotionSensor {
    String getDescription();
    void setLog(LogOutput l);
    void setWarningLight(WarningLight w);
}
```

A class for a sensor then looks – here using the example of the motion sensor from manufacturer A – something like this:

```
public class MotionSensorA
                implements MotionSensor, SensorListener {
    static final String DESCRIPTION =
                        "… Motion Sensor … A";
    LogOutput logFile;
    WarningLight warningLight;

    @Override
    public String getDescription() {
        return DESCRIPTION;
    }

    @Override
    public void setLog(LogOutput l) {
        this.logFile = l;
    }

    @Override
    public void setWarningLight(WarningLight w) {
        this.warningLight = w;
```

```
        }

        @Override
        public void detected() {
            // ... abridged
        }
    }
```

For the motion sensor of manufacturer B and the smoke detectors of both manufacturers you will find very similar codes. This should not hold any surprises. The methods setLog and setWarningLight enable the "installation" of a sensor in a concrete system. Since this information is not available at the time of manufacture, it must be accessible via subsequent setter methods and, of course, called by the customer. In addition to the MotionSensor interface already shown, we also implement another SensorListener interface here. We'll get to its details in the next section on triggering, but ultimately this is where the integration of the abstract factory with an Observer pattern takes place, which we can use to trigger the sensors in this test case.

For now, let's continue with the abstract factory. The only thing missing now is the comparatively simple code for a manufacturer. Let's look at manufacturer B this time:

```
public class ManufacturerB implements SensorFactory {
    @Override
    public motion sensor buildMotionSensor() {
        return new MotionSensorB();
    }

    @Override
    public smoke detector baueRauchsensor() {
        return new SmokeDetectorB();
    }
}
```

I will spare myself a class diagram at this point. If you look at the package smart-home.AbstractFactoy in the example project, you will find three interfaces and six classes. The diagram looks practically the same as in Sect. 15.4, you just have to change the names.

With this, we have implemented our first design pattern and created the approach to connect to a second pattern, which we will look at in the next section.

26.4   Observer: The Trigger

In our example, we want to be able to trigger all connected sensors with a single command. Of course, this is only useful for testing purposes. In real life, each sensor would of course react to a corresponding event within its range. Here, however, we use the Observer pattern from Chap. 5 for the test. We thus register each installed sensor with a central instance, which in turn sends a uniform message to each sensor, which the latter must of course be able to process.

So first we need the rather simple interface of the SensorListener:

```
public interface SensorListener {
    void detected();
}
```

As you can see, only the trigger method to be addressed externally is specified here.

However, the client, which we will see later, when a sensor is installed in the house, must also register it with the central location, the sensor system:

```
public class SensorSystem {
    private final List<SensorListener> listeners =
                                    new ArrayList<>();

    public void register(SensorListener sensorListener) {
        listeners.add(sensorListener);
    }

    public void trigger() {
        listeners.forEach(SensorListener::detected);
    }
}
```

In the ArrayList, all sensors are recorded by means of the register method and then addressed in the trigger method. There I use the so-called method reference this time, to call for each sensor in the list its detected method. This way of writing is possible since Java 8, and together with the forEach method on the ArrayList its use results in a very short but well understandable form.

So if you look at the class model from the Observer chapter, you will now find the interface (instead of ApartmentObserver now SensorListener) and the "Exchange" (instead of ApartmentBoerse now SensorSystem). The equivalent of the Workers class are the sensors, which are registered through the SensorListener interface common to all. They are the recipients of a "broadcast" from the client. We don't need an equivalent to the class Apartment in this case, because we don't exchange additional information about concrete objects in another list.

By the way, you will notice that I have not implemented a "deregister" of a sensor. So once a sensor is installed and registered, it would not be possible to remove it. But this should not be a problem for you if you want to extend this example now.

We will deal with the method `detected` in detail a little later, because there are still a few building blocks missing to understand it, which we have to look at first.

26.5   Adapter: Send Notifications

There is still the question of what a sensor actually does when it is triggered. According to the requirements, it should send messages. But if you have different manufacturers and different sensors in the game, you have to agree on some format for messages. But there is another way.

Let's assume that the manufacturers had agreed on a "minimum" format for SMS messages from motion sensors and one from smoke detectors. First of all, there would be those corresponding classes. Here is the SMS of a smoke detector. That of the motion sensor is similarly simple.

```java
public class SmokeSms {
    public void sendMessage(String s) {
        System.out.println("SMS from smoke detector: "
                                                    + s);
    }
}
```

Now, when triggered, a sensor could directly create a corresponding object and call its sendMessage method. However, the clients would then be completely dependent on the performance of this method and would have no possibility to introduce independent additions.

The manufacturers circumvent this with an adapter – which we already know from Chap. 22 – whose code they make accessible to the customer. At this point, the customer can make any adjustments (e.g. also call the original sendMessage method). First of all, everything is based on a simple SMS interface:

```java
public interface Sms {
    void sendMessage(String s);
}
```

Now the adapters have to implement this. For the smoke detector, let's take a closer look:

```java
public class SmokeDetectorSmsAdapter implements Sms {
    private final SmokeSms fromSensor;
```

```
public SmokeDetectorSmsAdapter(SmokeSms smokeSms) {
    this.fromSensor = smokeSms;
}


@Override
public void sendMessage(String s) {
    fromSensor.sendMessage(s);
    var log = LogOutput.getInstance();
    log.showMessage("SMS dispatch of the smoke detector adapter");
}
}
```

You can see here that the method `sendMessage` first calls the "supplied" method. Before the call, any adjustments to the text or other measures that may be technically necessary for the SMS dispatch would now be possible. Also other notification systems could be connected here, which can pass the message text from the sensor to other recipients. Afterwards, a log entry is generated to indicate that something has happened via the adapter. For the motion sensor, the adapter looks basically the same, but I created a separate version (instead of a single "message adapter") for greater flexibility. So the response to a motion sensor message can be different than a smoke detector trigger.

So we use the adapter pattern here a little bit differently than explained in the chapter about the adapter. Here the manufacturer provides both the interface Sms and a basic version of the adapter, but thereby allows the user of the sensor to "intervene" in the notification function without intervention in the code of the sensor.

I will show you the exact integration of this adapter from a sensor when we have all the components together. One is still missing.

26.6   Command: Actuators and Remote Control

A sensor that can pass on messages is already half the battle in an alarm system, but now devices are still missing to react directly to the respective alarm. For smoke detectors, a sprinkler system is a good choice to extinguish any burgeoning flames. For motion detectors, we use warning lights in our example, which should scare away the "intruder" or alert "guards".

In our example, these devices must be switched on once by the respective sensors, but must also be able to be switched off again by a remote control. For this we use the command pattern from Chap. 9.

Again, the two variants for smoke detectors and motion sensors are almost identical. So I print here one variant, the other you will find of course also in the sample code.

So let's take a look at the warning light as an example:

```
public class Warning Light {
    public void switchOn() {
        System.out.println("Warning light is on");
    }

    public void switchOff() {
        System.out.println("Warning light is off");
    }
}
```

The command interface looks like this with us now:

```
public interface Command {
    public void execute();
}
```

And an encapsulated command for the warning light then has this appearance:

```
public class WarningLightSwitchOff implements Command {
    WarningLight warningLight;

    public WarningLightSwitchOff(WarningLight warningLight) {
        super();
        this.warninglight = warninglight;
    }

    @Override
    public void execute() {
        var logFile = LogOutput.getInstance();
        warninglight.off();
        logFile.showMessage("Warning light off");
    }
}
```

I'm not printing the code for turning it on here.
These commands can now also be controlled from a remote control:

```
public class SmartHomeRemote {
    Command command;

    public void setCommand(Command command) {
        this.command = command;
    }
```

```
        public void pressButton() {
            command.execute();
        }

    }
```

This is a very simple version, but of course you can extend it as you wish. In the version presented, a command can be associated with the button at some time. If the button is pressed, the command is executed.

26.7   A Sensor Triggers

Now we have all the pieces together to look at the method detected of a sensor in its entirety. Here is an example:

```
public class MotionSensorA
                implements MotionSensor, SensorListener {
    // … abridged

    @Override
    public void detected() {
        var s = """
                Motion sensor - Manufacturer A
                    Movement detected
                """;

        if (logFile == null)
            s =
            s.concat("No protocol service configured!\n");
        else
            logFile.showMessage("MOVEMENT!");

        if (warningLight == null)
        s = s.concat("No alarm annunciator configured!\n");
        else {
            var turnOn =
                new WarningLightSwitchOn(warningLight);
            turnOn.execute();
        }
        Sms sms =
            new MotionSensorSmsAdapter(new MotionSms());
        System.out.println("Motion Sensor - Manufacturer A");
            sms.sendMessage(s);
    }

}
```

I have designed the method of the motion sensor of manufacturer A bit more extensive than the others. Here we build up a text which, depending on the configuration of a protocol service and a warning light, contains appropriate information or carries out the respective actions. Finally, the message with the final text is sent via the adapter. Here we connect the products of the abstract factory with the adapter and also with the command pattern.

Please note the multi-line string at the beginning of the method. This possibility of text representation called Text Block has become available in production with Java 15 (JEP 378). It is also already available as a preview in Java 13 (JEP 355) and Java 14 (JEP 369).

In essence, we can now use multi-line text starting and ending with three quotes even without control characters for the line break in the source code. However, we are still dealing with the `String` data type. The most important thing is the indentation depth of the starting quotation marks, because whitespaces to the left of them (spaces, tabs) do not become part of the captured text. More precisely, all whitespaces in all lines of a text block that are to the left of the leftmost character of any line are not included.

In the example above, this means that the line "Motion sensor – Manufacturer A" is left-justified, although it is indented by 16 characters in the source code. However, the line below "Motion detected" is then output indented by four characters.

Handling whitespaces in text blocks also takes up a large portion in the above JEPs. Please be sure to check them out if you want to work with text blocks.

NetBeans marks the characters that actually belong to the string with a colored background, so that you can easily see which spaces or tabs belong and which do not. If you try moving the line with "Motion sensor ..." one or two characters to the left by deleting preceding spaces, you will see from the changed background marking what this will do to the other lines.

The `detected` methods of the other sensors do not use text blocks in this example and are also simpler in design. Therefore I do not show them here.

26.8   Class Diagram

Now we have a total of five patterns "plugged together". Let's have a look at the class diagram, which you can find in Fig. 26.1.

If you compare this diagram with the UML diagrams of the individual patterns from the previous chapters, you should be able to recognize the individual parts, but also identify the new connections.

26.9   The Client

All that's missing now is the client, which assembles the sensors from the various manufacturers into one system, triggers all of them on a test basis, and then also switches off the sprinkler system and the warning light.

The `main method` and the constructor of the `SmartHome` class are simple at first:

```
public final class SmartHome {
    // ... abridged

    SmartHome() {
        init();
        test();
    }

    public static void main(String[] args) {
        var smartHome = new SmartHome();
    }
}
```

The `init method` now connects four products of the abstract factory – one motion sensor and one smoke detector from each manufacturer – with the singleton for the log output, the warning light or the sprinkler system, which will later receive the commands to switch on, and the control center, where the sensors act as observers. Finally, a remote control is created, which can take care of switching off the systems.

```
public final class SmartHome {
    // ... abridged

    void init() {
        log = LogOutput.getInstance();

        sprinkler = new Sprinkler();
        warningLight = new warningLight();

        SensorFactory factory;


        factory = new ManufacturerA();
        smokeDetector1 = factory.buildSmokeDetector();
        motionSensor1 = factory.buildMotionSensor();

        factory = new ManufacturerB();
        smokeDetector2 = factory.buildSmokeDetector();
        motionSensor2 = factory.buildMotionSensor();

        smokeDetetector1.setLog(log);
        smokeDetector2.setLog(log);
        motionSensor1.setLog(log);
        motionSensor2.setLog(log);
```

```
            smokeDetector1.setSprinkler(sprinkler);
            smokeDetector2.setSprinkler(sprinkler);

            motionSensor1.setWarningLight(warningLight);
            motionSensor2.setWarningLight(warningLight);

            sensorSystem = new SensorSystem();
            sensorSystem.register((SensorListener)
                                          smokeDetector1);
            sensorSystem.register((SensorListener)
                                          smokeDetector2);
            sensorSystem.register((SensorListener)
                                          motionSensor1);
            sensorSystem.register((SensorListener)
                                          motionSensor2);
            remote control = new SmartHomeRemote();
        }

        // … abridged
    }
```

In the end, these are all comprehensible steps that are actually involved in assembling an alarm system.

And then in the test method we try out everything. First, all sensors get the command to trigger their alarm. Then, via the remote control, first the warning light and then the sprinkler system are switched off again.

```
public final class SmartHome {
        // … abridged

    void test() {
        System.out.println("Starting tests:");
        sensorSystem.trigger();
        remote.setCommand(
                new warningLightSwitchOff(warningLight));
        remote.pressButton();
        remote.setCommand(
                new SprinklerSwitchOff(sprinkler));
        remote.pressButton();
    }

    // … abridged
}
```

When you run the program, you should get the following output:

```
Protocol service ready
Starting Tests:
SMS from smoke detector: SMOKE detected!
logFile: SMS-dispatch of the smoke detector adapter detected
Smoke detector - Manufacturer A
logFile: SMOKE! detected
Sprinkler is on
logFile: Sprinkler system switched on detected
SMS from smoke detector: SMOKE detected!
logFile: SMS-dispatch of the smoke detector adapter detected
Smoke detector - Manufacturer B
logFile: SMOKE! detected
Sprinkler is on
logFile: Sprinkler system switched on detected
logFile: MOVEMENT! detected
Warning light is on
logFile: Warning light switched on detected
Motion sensor - Manufacturer A
SMS from motion sensor:
Motion sensor - Manufacturer A
     Movement detected

logFile: SMS-dispatch of the motion sensor adapter detected
SMS from motion sensor: MOVEMENT detected!
logFile: SMS-dispatch of the motion sensor adapter detected
Motion Sensor - Hersteller B
logFile: BEWEGUNG! detected
Warning light is on
logFile: Warning light switched on detected
Warning light is off
logFile: Warning light switched off detected
Sprinkler is off
logFile: Sprinkler system switched off detected
```

The first line comes from the singleton and is output during its initialization. After that, the test method reports and then all sensors one after the other, first the smoke detectors, then the motion sensors. For the motion sensor of manufacturer A you can also see two error messages in the sample output. For this run, I commented out the LogOutput and WarningLight assignments to motion sensor 1 in the init method to demonstrate its fault tolerance. If you try this with the other sensors, NullPointerExceptions are thrown in this version.

26.10 Considerations

The example is intended to show you a way to combine different patterns in a meaningful way. There are two fairly obvious approaches to extending and modifying this example: First, the `detect` methods should all be extended to also respond to missing log outputs or actuators. Alternatively, you can make the detect methods very rudimentary and even move the log entry and triggering of the warning light or sprinkler system to the respective adapter. Feel free to experiment with this a bit.

Or you can go the other way, and remove one of the patterns (according to my introductory warning in this chapter). Do you really need the adapter, or can't you do without it? What alternatives would you have then? Not everything that is technically possible necessarily makes sense at this point. For your respective tasks, always think carefully about what is necessary, what makes sense, and what might even be annoying.

You should be able to find the connections between the patterns in the source code:

- The singleton is used in various places by requesting the instance and then calling its `showMessage` method.
- In the sensors that are created in the abstract factory, the interface `SensorListener` is also implemented, which identifies each sensor as an observer.
- Also in the sensors you will find the call of the respective adapter in the `detected` methods.
- And in the `detected` methods as well as in the remote control there's also the use of the Command Pattern.
- The `init` method of the client contains the registration of the observers as well as the creation of the actuators warning light and sprinkler, which act as command receivers.
- In the client's `test` method, the Observer pattern and the Command pattern are then actively used.

Please try to create a detailed UML diagram for this by yourself.

26.11 Summary

Go through the chapter again in key words:

- A singleton is comparatively easy to integrate into programs, the connection of other patterns with each other requires a little more effort.
- Implementing multiple interfaces can make a class part of multiple patterns.

- The composition of pattern components in classes of other patterns also enables the connection of multiple patterns.
- The more patterns are connected in a program, the more complex the structure can become.
- Caution is required in order not to lose the overview and the respective functionalities offered. The structuring in packages can support this.

Correction to: Design Patterns with Java

Correction to:

O. Musch, *Design Patterns with Java*, https://doi.org/10.1007/978-3-658-39829-3

"Electronic supplement material was added in this book."

The updated version of this chapter can be found at
https://doi.org/10.1007/978-3-658-39829-3

Concluding Remarks

I hope you enjoyed reading the book, and that you may have learned something along the way. As mentioned at the beginning, you should use it as a reference book if you don't quite remind any individual issues. Now would also be a good time to take another look at the chapter on design principles (Chap. 2) and then discover them again in the patterns mentioned.

If you have discovered any inconsistencies or errors from your point of view, I would be very grateful for your feedback. You can best reach me at designpatternsjava16@gmail.com.

You are free to use and manipulate the source code of this book for your private purposes – that's what I'm providing it for.

Thank you so much for sticking it out this far.

Olaf Musch

Printed in the United States
by Baker & Taylor Publisher Services